D1556510

POPULATION THEORIES
AND THE ECONOMIC INTERPRETATION

INTERNATIONAL LIBRARY OF SOCIOLOGY

Founded by Karl Mannheim
Editor: John Rex, University of Warwick

A catalogue of books available in the INTERNATIONAL LIBRARY OF SOCIOLOGY and other series of Social Science books published by Routledge & Kegan Paul

POPULATION THEORIES AND THE ECONOMIC INTERPRETATION

by

SYDNEY H. COONTZ

ROUTLEDGE & KEGAN PAUL
LONDON AND HENLEY

First published 1957
by Routledge & Kegan Paul Ltd,
39 Store Street,
London WC1E 7DD and
Broadway House, Newtown Road,
Henley-on-Thames,
Oxon RG9 1EN
Printed in Great Britain
by Redwood Burn Ltd
Trowbridge & Esher

© Routledge & Kegan Paul Ltd 1957, 1961
Second impression 1961
Third impression 1968
Fourth impression 1979

No part of this book may be reproduced in any form
without permission from the publisher, except for
the quotation of brief passages in criticism

ISBN 0 7100 3361 3

CONTENTS

PREFACE

SINCE the time of Malthus, few indeed remain indifferent to the so-called 'population problem'. Outside the academic sphere there are those who, on the one hand, still see in population phenomena the explanation of the existing world distribution of material goods; and, on the other, those who continue to believe that essentially the population 'problem' is a red herring invoked, as in the past, to justify the *status quo*.

Within academic circles, the situation is much different. Here a dispassionate attempt is made to understand population phenomena. Tools of greater precision are devised for the measurement and ordering of the diversity of demographic patterns and developments, explanatory hypotheses are tested, etc. Nevertheless, there is evidence that even in academic circles, political preconceptions, as well as pure reason, determine a population 'attitude': e.g. upon the publication of the anti-Malthusian *Geography of Hunger* by Josué de Castro, an important population study centre in the United States published in a special issue, which was widely and gratuitously circulated, an ill-conceived and over-anxious critique of Castro's work. It seems clear, then, that there are population attitudes as well as purely theoretical interests in demography.

A further difficulty encountered in pursuing the study of demography is the great interest the subject arouses in students engaged in different lines of academic endeavour. Frequently biologists, physiologists, sociologists, economists, mathematicians, physicists and philosophers advance a population theory.

Thus it is that in view of the diversity of thought and the variety of contributions to population theory, the author is not entitled to assume that his audience is familiar with the various hypotheses adduced to explain population dynamics. Hence in Part I of the book, 'Population Theories Since Malthus', the exposition is burdened, perhaps, by too much detail and documentation. However, since Part I is not only expository but polemic, it seemed best to quote extensively.

In Part II, 'The Economic Interpretation', the approach deviates from current thought on labour problems. To me, labour-power is a commodity and demand for labour governs supply. Since completing the book it has occurred to me that this analysis leads to an important qualification of Marx's theory of the declining rate of profit: The economic interpretation stresses that the commodity, labour-power, increased in value during the second phase of the industrial revolution, i.e. that the historic rise in labour's standard of living reflects the costs of a more highly skilled, educated and more intensively utilized labour force. The significance of this development for population theory is stressed in Part II of the book. However, concerning Marx's theory of the falling rate of profit, the historic rise in the average value of labour-power introduces another counter-tendency to the rise in the organic composition of capital.

That is to say, assume with Marx that the rate of exploitation, S/V, is constant. (This is a reasonable first approximation which is discussed in more detail in Chapter V.) Assume further, as Marx did, that the *technical* composition of capital, $C/C + V$, rises. It follows that if the value of labour-power is rising, there exists an important counter-tendency, not emphasized by Marx, to the rise in the organic composition of capital. For C, the congealed or dead labour, is of lower value than the living labour with which it is combined; or stated otherwise, living labour's value is rising relative to C, dead labour. But this means, *ceteris paribus*, that the tendency for the organic composition of capital to rise is countered by the rise in the value of V.

I am deeply indebted to Professor D. V. Glass and Mr. H. L. Beales of the London School of Economics. The interest, advice, and generous disposal of their time facilitated and made pleasurable a project which might otherwise have proved onerous. Further, it was largely through the sustained interest of Professor Glass that the work now appears in print.

My friend, William Blake, also gave unstintingly of his time. His encyclopaedic knowledge, excellent judgment, and enthusiastic interest contributed greatly to improving the content and form of the work.

Finally, my wife, Patricia Coontz, made a number of valuable suggestions for improvements as well as carrying on with the burdensome detail preparatory to publication.

SYDNEY H. COONTZ

December 1956
State University College of Forestry
at Syracuse University
Syracuse 10, New York

INTRODUCTION

THE preliminary stage of any scientific inquiry is the collection and classification of data. Through classification differing phenomena are separately examined and their peculiarities observed. Further investigation often reveals unsuspected similarities and significant relations between phenomena originally considered quite dissimilar and autonomous. Again, differences emerge which were not apparent at first.

But, as Thorstein Veblen long ago emphasized, the aim of science is to pass beyond the taxonomic level.[1] Questions arise as to the origin, evolution and future development of the phenomena under investigation. Explanatory hypotheses are formulated and their validity tested. The criteria of validity are correspondence with observed fact, coherence, and successful prediction. Further, on the principle of Occam's Razor, that hypothesis is preferable which makes the least number of assumptions, other things being equal.

The practical accomplishments of investigators in the natural sciences such as astronomy, chemistry, and physics account for their prestige. To predict an eclipse, or construct an atomic bomb, is dramatic evidence of the success of the pursuit. Unfortunately, however, social scientists do not command the same prestige. Difficulty of prediction is encountered not only from the extreme heterogeneity of the data but, also, because the phenomena under investigation are more dynamic. Observed uniformities are relatively less frequent, and where they appear there is no guarantee that they will continue. Thus it is

---

[1] *Cf.* e.g. 'Why is Economics not an Evolutionary Science', *The Quarterly Journal of Economics*, July 1898; 'Professor Clark's Economics', *ibid.*, February 1908, and other essays reprinted in *The Place of Science in Modern Civilisation* New York, 1932.

possible to discover a pattern or trend in social phenomena, the extrapolation of which yields fruitful results, but at other times, however, extrapolation leads to disaster. The trend is reversed and continuity of development is apparently destroyed.

A strictly empirical approach, then, is especially vulnerable. Actually, it may be objected, such an approach is impossible since, as Immanuel Kant long ago pointed out, we do seem compelled to devise theoretical explanations. Nevertheless, the distinction between a purely empirical approach and an approach within an adequately conceived theoretical framework is of value. It sounds a warning bell, viz. that the mere continuation of a trend should afford small ground for complacency if we have failed to provide an adequate theory to explain the phenomenon. Rather, we should increase our efforts to understand its nature and function. Otherwise there is always the possibility that 'we'll awake one morning to find it gone'.

Such, indeed, has been the case for demography in regard to the anticipated fertility decline. The shock administered to the science of demography by the recent reversal of the downward trend of the birth rate is evident from the following quotations: as late as 1946, it was stated that 'With improved data, new techniques, and the precise measurement of the demographic transition that was occurring, demography tended to become science rather than literature'.[1] However, by 1949 we are told:

Population study has developed no conceptual framework for investigating short-run variations in marital and childbearing patterns. In addition, theoretical consideration of the long-run, as distinguished from the short-run, aspects of population change is likely to be an increasingly important prerequisite to the refinement of future empirical research.[2]

The inadequacy of the 'conceptual framework' is strikingly evident when we consider the European and American population projections of the past two decades. However, prior

[1] Irene Taeuber, 'Population Studies in the United States', *Population Index*, October 1946, p. 254.
[2] George J. Stolnitz and Norman B. Ryder, 'Recent Discussion of the Net Reproduction Rate', *Population Index*, April 1949, p. 124.

to a discussion of these projections, it should be noted that the criterion of the accuracy of a population prediction is *not* the degree of correspondence between estimated *total* population and the actual census of *total* population at the end of the period. This is obvious from a consideration of the following.

Suppose a country now has a population of 200 million people, and it is estimated that its population ten years from now will be 210 million. But ten years later the census shows that there has been a population increase of 20 million. How accurate was the prediction? It might be argued that the estimate was fairly accurate since the amount of error was only 10 million on a population of 220 million, i.e. less than 5 per cent. Actually, however, the estimate understated the population increase by 50 per cent. A planning authority, constructing houses on the basis of the estimate, would suffer keen embarrassment.

There is a further difficulty. Suppose the future population of a country is estimated to decrease by two million but, instead, the country experiences a population growth of one million. A test of the accuracy of the prediction based merely on the degree of correspondence between the estimated total population and the actual population at the end of the period would completely obscure the magnitude of the error.

Table I, page 4, presents a summary of population projections for the United States. In estimating the future population of the United States, Thompson and Whelpton made three projections based on different assumptions, viz. 'high', 'reasonable', and 'low'. The greatest estimates of the future population assumed a high fertility and a low mortality (with or without immigration). The 'reasonable' and the 'low' estimates assumed medium birth and mortality rates, and low birth and high mortality rates, respectively.

It should be noted that only the high fertility-low mortality projections are included in Table I. No advantage is gained by including the forecasts based on the probable and low fertility assumptions, since the census data indicate that the projections based on the least probable assumptions (high fertility-low mortality) greatly understated the actual population growth.

The fertility estimates of the high projections are all based on the assumption of a cessation of the historically observed downward fertility trend.[1] Thus, the 1937 high fertility estimate was obtained by assuming the maintenance of the fertility rates prevailing during 1930–4. The high fertility assumption for the 1943 projection was obtained by averaging the gross reproduction rates for 1940–2. But by 1947 the increasing discrepancy between the judgment of what constituted a high fertility assumption and the observed rise in the fertility rate led Thompson and Whelpton to modify their procedure. Instead of calculating one high fertility projection, two were computed. What might be termed a 'low-high' projection was made on the assumption of 14 million births for the 1945–50 period, and a 'high-high' projection of 15 million births for the 1945–50 period. After 1950 the gross reproduction rate for both high projections was assumed to fall to 112, the average for the 1936–45 period.

Two conclusions can be drawn from Table I. First, even the high fertility-low mortality forecasts, considered least probable

TABLE I

Summary of Population Projections for the United States
High Fertility, Low Mortality (No Immigration)
Census Data Included

(in thousands)

Year	1937*	1943†	1947‡ 'low-high' projection	1947‡ 'high-high' projection	Census
1940	133,282	—	—	—	131,669
1945	138,916	137,738	—	—	139,621
1950	144,627	144,004	146,087	146,987	150,697
...	...	...	...	...	...
1975	170,575	172,680	175,750	177,304	—

* U.S. National Resources Committee, *Population Statistics*, I. National Data, Washington, 1937, Table 6, p. 22.
† U.S. National Resources Planning Board, *Estimates of Future Population of the U.S. 1940–2000*, Washington, 1943, Table 5, p. 57.
‡ U.S. Department of Commerce, Bureau of Census, *Forecasts of the Population of the U.S. 1945–1975*, Washington, 1947, Table 28, p. 41.

[1] We confine ourselves to a discussion of the fertility assumptions since errors in mortality projections are of secondary importance, considered from the point of view of the discrepancy between population forecasts and the census data.

by Thompson and Whelpton, consistently understated the future population of the United States. Second, there is a surprising amount of variance in the estimates in different years. For example, the 1937 projection placed the population for 1975 at 170,575,000. The 1943 projection placed it at 172,680,000, and the 1947 projections placed the population for 1975 at 175,750,000, and 177,304,000. A method which purports to anticipate with some degree of accuracy the future population thirty to fifty years from now, and yet changes the values of these estimates in a relatively short period of time, dramatizes the bankruptcy of the purely empirical approach.

In the decade of the 'thirties, Dr. Enid Charles projected the future population of England and Wales on the basis of two estimates.[1] As shown in Table II, the first estimate (*a*) assumed that fertility and mortality per age group would remain at the 1933 level, whereas the second estimate (*b*) was computed

TABLE II

Total Population for England and Wales
January 1935–2035
(in thousands)

Year	Estimate (a)*	Estimate (b)*	Registrar General's Estimate of Population
1935	40,563	40,563	40,645†
1940	40,828	40,655	41,862†
1945	40,876	40,392	42,636†
1950	40,678	39,766	43,745‡
...	...	...	...
2035	19,969	4,426	—

* Enid Charles, *op. cit.*, Tables II and III, p. 82.
† Mid-year estimates, U.N. *Demographic Yearbook*, 1953.
‡ Preliminary Estimate, *Statesman's Yearbook*, 1954, p. 62.

on the assumption of a continuation of the downward trend in mortality and fertility that characterized the 1923–33 period. Dr. Charles pointed out 'that (*a*) is a conservative estimate of

[1] 'The Effect of Present Trends in Fertility and Mortality Upon the Future Population of Great Britain and Upon Its Age Composition', *Political Arithmetic: A Symposium of Population Studies*, London, 1938, Chapter II.

the immediate prospect of a declining population, and that (*b*) represents a more reasonable forecast of the trend of population, if no new social agencies intervene to check declining fertility'.[1]

According to estimate (*a*) population reaches its maximum in 1945 and then declines. According to estimate (*b*), the 'more reasonable forecast', population begins to decline after 1940.

There is nothing to be gained in multiplying examples of unsuccessful population projections. In passing we may note, however, that the failures are by no means confined to the above examples: 'The reversal of the birth trend was in itself sufficient to invalidate most of the pre-war population projections. Superimposed on the effects of the first world war, it rendered the immediate situation still more diversified and fluid.'[2] Regarding those population forecasts which were apparently successful, Frumkin further remarks:

It is a matter of some astonishment to note the naïve satisfaction occasionally displayed by reputed scholars when they find that, despite the war, certain pre-war forecasts happen to show a surprising degree of accuracy. They seem to forget that, since there *has been* a war, forecasts made on the assumption of a peace trend are, as a rule, no longer valid. A computation in which errors offset one another and which has to rely on war upheaval as a salvation from discredit is not correct, even if its results happen to coincide with the facts.[3]

Another writer, after reviewing the population forecasts for the United States, indignantly states:

If any speculative investor had been led so far astray by forecasters on whom he relied, he would be bankrupt. If any businessman had been so misled by forecasts of business conditions, he would put no further trust in them. Surely the time has come for us to admit that our best population specialists cannot make dependable forecasts of our population for five or ten years ahead.[4]

---

[1] *Political Arithmetic: A Symposium of Population Studies*, p. 103.

[2] Gregory Frumkin, *Population Changes in Europe Since 1939*, London, 1951, p. 17. Frumkin was editor of the *Statistical Yearbook* of the League of Nations throughout its existence.

[3] *Ibid.*, p. 17, footnote 2.

[4] Joseph S. Davis, *The Population Upsurge in the United States*, Stanford, 1949, p. 37.

Davis further notes that in population forecasting 'the fundamental errors have clearly been those of misjudgments in choosing assumptions that time has proved unreasonable'.[1]

Although not attempting to suggest what would constitute reasonable assumptions, Davis does 'challenge the view—held by almost all demographers of all schools—that our population must, later if not sooner, reach a peak of any size, at any time, from which a decline is probable, if not inevitable'.[2]

British and American demographers are further indicted for having led astray such notable economists as J. M. Keynes, Alan Sweezy, Alvin Hansen, George Terborg, etc.:

> Paul Samuelson will surely not say in his second edition, as he said in the first (*Economics*, McGraw-Hill, 1948, p. 29): 'The population crisis of our age may be summarized in the statement that the net reproduction rate is beginning to drop below unity in . . . many . . . countries. The United States is balanced just around unity.'[3]

Davis concludes that although demographers are not to be censured for their errors since 'To err is human'; nevertheless, he reproves them for their tardy recognition of the unsatisfactory state of the science: 'I wish that at least some of them had been more alert to warn the rest of us that apparently well-settled ideas were becoming unsettled and in danger of being upset.'[4]

What, then, is the explanation of the failure of population forecasts? In my opinion, this failure of demography stems from its divorce from economics. The older economists treated population as the dependent variable and regarded its growth as an index of increased prosperity. For example, Arthur Young wrote:

> Can anything be more simple than this principle? Can anything prove clearer that the idea of a village population beyond the

---

[1] *Ibid.*, p. 39. [2] *Ibid.*, p. 69.

[3] *Ibid.*, p. 85. Examples of economists who accepted the thesis of a declining population and evinced concern over its implications include J. M. Keynes, 'Some Economic Consequences of a Declining Population', *Eugenics Review*, April 1937; Alvin Hansen, 'Economic Progress and Declining Population Growth', *American Economic Review*, March 1939; W. B. Reddaway, *The Economics of a Declining Population*, London, 1939; S. G. Tsiang, 'The Effect of Population Growth on the General Level of Employment', *Economica*, November 1942.

[4] *The Population Upsurge in the United States*, p. 92.

demand for its surplus is chimerical? Is it not evident that demand for hands, that is employment, must regulate the number of people? And that if employment is greater in this age than in the former, the total of people must be greater.[1]

Adam Smith, too, thought that population growth was a result of improved economic conditions. But, as Hansen pointed out, Smith also considered population increase a cause of economic progress since it widened the market, thus creating the possibility for a further division of labour.[2] And the subsistence theory of Malthus, which Ricardo accepted, assumes that population growth is dependent upon economic development.

But modern economists, impressed by the fertility decline in the last quarter of the nineteenth century and finding no economic explanation for the phenomenon, now treat population as an independent variable. Since it is believed that fertility decline is a function of custom, social habit, civilization, etc., it would follow that the economist can contribute little to an understanding of the dynamics of population growth. True, the economist remains interested in population but he must now reconcile himself to regarding population as a datum, something given for the analysis; an analysis which may be concerned with the optimum population or with the implications of a declining population on the marginal efficiency of capital.

What was written of economists more than twenty years ago still holds true, viz. 'For a quarter of a century before the World War the declining birth rate was the main theme of population literature. Economists had practically ceased to contribute to population theory, and sociologists and biologists took it up, not always with scientific caution.'[3]

To return population theory to its natural habitat, the field of economics is the object of this work. So it will be contended that population is a dependent variable, a function of 'civilization'—not however of civilization considered in the abstract

[1] Arthur Young, *Political Arithmetic*, p. 86.

[2] Alvin Hansen, 'Economic Progress and Declining Population Growth', *American Economic Review*, March 1939.

[3] A. B. Wolfe, 'Population Theory', *Encyclopaedia of Social Sciences*, Vol. XII, p. 250.

but rather of specific civilizations, each with its own peculiar economic characteristics.

To assert that population is the dependent variable is not to deny, of course, that population can and does influence economic development. Obviously, the age composition of a society, considered merely from the point of view of production, is of extreme importance to an economy. Again, while remaining intensely sceptical toward Cassandras who, noting the fall in fertility among the upper socio-economic groups, conclude that the average 'I.Q.' of the nation is bound to decline; we can agree with Spengler that 'significance attaches to the fact that seventy-five or more per cent of our population growth is being contributed by about three-fifths of the nation's families who as a group receive only about one-fourth of the national income'.[1]

It is obvious that a dynamic theory of population must account for changes in the fertility patterns of the so-called 'lower classes' since the numerical size of these groups determines the general fertility pattern of a country. However, as will be seen in Part I, it is here that the majority of population theories are open to criticism.

The work is divided into two parts: Part I contains a review and appraisal of population theories since Malthus. Part II presents a theoretical framework for the economic analysis of demography. Here the problem is to provide a conceptual framework for the analysis of secular changes in population which is also applicable to short-run variations. In brief, it will be contended that it is possible to develop a *general theory* of population dynamics which explains both long- and short-run demographic phenomena.

[1] Joseph J. Spengler, 'Population Movements and Economic Equilibrium in the United States', *Journal of Political Economy*, April 1940, p. 159.

PART I

Population Theories Since Malthus

CHAPTER ONE

Methodology

BY a 'theory of population' is understood an attempt to eluci-
date the major factor or factors determining population growth.
This excludes from consideration literature on the optimum
population and concomitant discussion of under and overpopulation.[1] Such theories, regardless of their merit, lie outside
an inquiry which is concerned with the hypotheses adduced to
explain the dynamics of population growth.

Moreover, although recognizing the importance of mortality
and migration in influencing the magnitude and rate of population growth, the theories to be considered are united in
emphasizing the central importance of fertility which, as was
seen in the introductory chapter, is the significant variable
which has so far eluded analysis. Essentially, population theories
are oriented towards an explanation of changes in fertility
patterns and existing class differences in fertility.

Ideally considered, a theory of population should be able to
explain not only historically observed changes in fertility patterns as well as class differences in fertility but, also, should
provide the basis for predicting with some accuracy the future
fertility pattern of a country or group of countries, given the
stage of economic development and type of social organization.

In the following hypothetical case the ideal requirements
would be satisfied: assume a society composed entirely of
producers, all receiving the same amount of income and, assume further, that it has been ascertained that every increment

[1] Our definition, therefore, excludes from analysis just those theories
which E. F. Penrose considers in detail in his *Population Theories and Their
Application*, Stanford University, 1934: On the other hand, Penrose does not
discuss the type of population theory we will be considering.

13

in income leads to a corresponding reduction in fertility, and, *vice versa*, every decrement in income results in a corresponding increment in fertility. It follows that, if we knew the future economic development of a country, we could predict its fertility pattern and accurately gauge the future population.

It is obvious, of course, that we do not have a homogeneous society as was assumed in the above case. This, however, is a relatively minor point in that allowances could be made, an average computed and, with the assumption of no drastic change in distribution, prediction would be fairly accurate. The real difficulty is the lack of certainty as to the effect of an increase in material prosperity on fertility. Whereas some studies suggest that increasing prosperity lowers fertility, other investigations seem to demonstrate the opposite.[1] Again, even if we knew the relation between income or wealth and fertility, economists are not agreed in their prognosis of the economic future.

Nevertheless, the recognition of what would constitute an ideal theory of population provides the criteria for discriminating between the various demographic theories. To the extent that one theory more closely approaches the ideal requirements than another, it is preferable. So it is that a theory which is loosely formulated and includes an ensemble of determining factors in which the magnitude and order of their contribution is left unspecified, fails to meet the ideal requirements. Again, suppose that in the above hypothetical case the relation between fertility and income had been discovered more or less accidentally, and that no attempt had been made to determine how a change in income resulted in a changed fertility pattern. In such a case, an extrapolation might be unsuccessful since the observed empirical relation between income and fertility might only hold within certain limits, beyond which a different correlation is observed. If then, along with the observed relation, we had a rational explanation, i.e. one which revealed the causal nexus and the conditions necessary for the realization of this relationship, our chances for a successful prediction would be greatly improved.

Such are some of the general considerations to be borne in mind in our subsequent review of the different population theories. It is important to realize that a population theory

[1] See below, Chapter III.

which can reveal the causal relation between economic status and fertility, even if the same analysis is as yet incapable of determining the future course of economic development, will have made an important contribution.

For purposes of providing a theoretical framework, existing population theories are divided into three general categories, viz. biological, cultural, and economic. The difficulties which attend such a classification are the same as are inherent in any attempt to categorize complex phenomena. Anomalies and peculiar combinations frequently obtrude and embarrass the formal simplicity. Such difficulties are inevitable and require no special comment. On the one hand, they may be over-emphasized to the point of frustration so that no generalization is possible; or, on the other hand such difficulties may be ignored or insufficiently appreciated so that oversimplification results.

Under biological theories are included those which contend that the law regulating human population growth is fundamentally the same as that which regulates the growth of plants and animals. The tendency here is to stress that which is common to all living matter and to minimize that which is peculiar to man. Philosophically, the outlook approaches reductive materialism; but incompletely, since, as yet, the biologists have not considered abandoning their field to the physicists.

Yet a number of these expositors, although emphasizing the importance of biology, are led to a consideration of economic and social conditions. To some extent this is unavoidable. Thus if one believes with Doubleday and Castro that human fertility is essentially a function of protein intake, the question immediately becomes an economic one, i.e. why do some people get more proteins than others? Since, however, their explanation of differential fertility is based on diet and only indirectly considers socio-economic factors as determinants of fertility differences, these theories have been classified as biological.

Under the heading of cultural theories are subsumed those of writers who endeavour to relate demographic changes to changing mental characteristics of humanity. While such theories agree in stressing the importance of man's psyche, they differ among themselves in the emphasis they place on the volitional, intellectual, hedonistic, and previsional aspect of man's character in determining his fertility pattern. As such, the theories are purely psychological in their approach; however, the general tendency among these theorists is to relate the psychological phenomena to the prevailing culture. In other words, a particular culture or civilization is instrumental in creating a particular type of mentality. These theories, therefore, are classified as cultural.

Per se the concept 'culture' or 'civilization' is difficult since it refers to an ensemble of economic, technical, social, political, legal, religious, and moral factors operative in a physical environment. As such, culture is the ALL which embraces everything materialist and non-materialist and, in the absence of additional information, it is impossible to order the members of the ensemble according to their influence on demography. So it is that a writer advancing a cultural theory of population states: 'Such a theory will not imply a single or uniform factor as the cause for varying rates of growth. It will search for distinctive types of causal factors in different social groups, and will assume that varied combinations of *material and non-material* culture elements may account for observed statistical trends.'[1]

However, these theorists do attempt to isolate one or more cultural factors of special importance influencing the psychological attitude toward reproduction. For example, one writer, interpreting man's behaviour hedonistically, explains the fertility decline by the relative decrease in the pleasure of parenthood consequent upon the growth in the variety of other pleasures available outside the home in the present culture. Again, another writer attributes the fertility decline to the rational mentality engendered by the present culture which leads men to weigh carefully all their actions and, like accountants, balance the gains and losses of parenthood.

Philosophically, the cultural school is eclectic. In its emphasis on mental phenomena it approaches idealism but may at any time, when convenient, have recourse to one of the materialistic factors in the cultural ensemble.

The economic classification presents no difficulty. The theory is avowedly materialist but is not, as sometimes alleged, a reductive or mechanical materialism. The theory recognizes 'that the chief considerations in human progress are social con-

[1] E. T. Hiller, 'A Culture Theory of Population Trends', *Journal of Political Economy*, October 1930, p. 550. My italics.

siderations, and that the important factor in social change is the economic factor. Economic interpretation of history means, not that economic relations exert an exclusive influence, but that they exert the preponderant influence in shaping the progress of society.'[1]

Historical priority for the explicit recognition of the importance of the economic factor in sociological analysis belongs to Karl Marx.[2] But from this it does not follow that one is logically bound to accept other tenets of the Marxian system. On the contrary, adherents of the economic interpretation of history, although in accord on a basic philosophical postulate, differ widely and may even reach diametrically opposite conclusions in their analyses of the economic evolution of capitalism. So it is that Seligman emphasizes that 'There is really nothing in common between the economic interpretation of history and the doctrine of socialism except the accidental fact that the originators of both doctrines happened to be the same man. Socialism is a theory of what ought to be, historical materialism is the theory of what has been.'[3]

The view that economic relations do not exert an exclusive but a 'preponderant influence in shaping the progress of society' means that the content of the political, legal, artistic—in short, the ideological factors—is largely, but not exclusively, a reflection of the economic content of society. It is a generalization about the *general content* and, as such, obviously must not be understood to mean that the work of a specific artist can be described *exhaustively* by a knowledge of the economic relations of the period, and, more particularly, the class position of this artist. Nevertheless, to the extent that an artist is typical of his period, it will be found that what is typical and significant is related to the general evolution of society in which economic relations exert the preponderant influence.

The economic interpretation also recognizes that these ideological factors, once established, have their own independent

---

[1] Edwin R. A. Seligman, *The Economic Interpretation of History*, New York (second edition, revised), 1924, p. 67.

[2] See, in particular, the Preface to *A Contribution to a Critique of Political Economy*, New York, 1904.

[3] 'History and Economics' in *The Social Sciences* (edited by William Fielding Ogburn and Alexander Goldenweiser), London, 1927, p. 183.

existence—their own laws of motion.[1] However, their independence is limited in that, should these cultural phenomena come
into contradiction with the economic necessities of the times,
the economic and not the ideological emerges victorious. Seen
thus, ideology is not a mirror of economic development—as it
was thought to be by the syndicalists, particularly the American
movement known as the 'Industrial Workers of the World'—
but can and does, in certain historical periods, come into contradiction with the economic relations. Hence it follows that an
ideology that is in conflict with the economic needs of the times
operates as a brake on economic development, and, *vice versa*,
an ideology appropriate to the economic stage of development
operates as a stimulus to economic development.

That the economic interpretation does not exclude the significance of ideas, even if at a certain level of abstraction they are
relegated to secondary importance, is evident in the following:

> To the economic historian the ideas are as important as the
> events. For though conceptions of social expediency are largely the
> product of economic conditions, they acquire a momentum which
> persists long after the circumstances which gave them birth have
> disappeared, and act as over-ruling forces to which in the interval
> *between one great change and another*, events themselves tend to
> conform.[2]

To put the matter concretely and in reference to population
theory, it will be recalled that the Bradlaugh-Besant trial in
the 1870's had the effect of greatly publicizing family limitation.
Morally considered, birth control became more acceptable
and, concomitantly, the necessary knowledge for its practice
was made increasingly available to larger sections of the population. But, as Field rightly stresses, propaganda for family
limitation did not have its origin in this period. On the contrary, the Neo-Malthusian movement of the 'seventies was in
fact a renewal of the extensive propaganda for family limita-

---

[1] *Cf. The Correspondence of Marx and Engels*, London, 1934, particularly
Engels' letters to Conrad Schmidt and J. Bloch (pp. 472–84); also Engels'
letter to Mehring (pp. 510–12).
[2] R. H. Tawney, *The Agrarian Problem in the Sixteenth Century*, London,
1912, p. 4. My italics.

tion that had existed in England during the period of the 1820's.[1]

The question then arises: 'Why was the propaganda successful in the 1870's and not in the 1820's?' Here the economic interpretation would stress the changed social conditions that led to the success of the Neo-Malthusian movement in the 1870's. In other words, the analysis does not deny the effect of the Bradlaugh-Besant trial, and, in general, the activities of the Neo-Malthusian League in promoting family limitation. It recognizes their contribution, but emphasizes that success was dependent upon certain essential social conditions; and, by contrast, notes that similar propaganda fifty years earlier had no such observable result.

Again, the economic interpretation, recognizing within limits the independent existence of cultural factors, does not attempt to reduce all presently existing fertility differences to immediate economic necessity. On the contrary, it recognizes that a certain fertility pattern, itself a product of past economic development or, at least, consistent with past economic necessities, may continue long after its economic motivation has ceased, i.e. provided its present existence is not in fundamental contradiction to present basic economic needs. The point is this: given an historically observed change in fertility patterns, is the explanation for this change to be sought in the economic evolution of society, in the changed material needs; or, is the change in fertility habits an expression of man's intellectual progress, a product of his greater enlightenment? Frequently, since the two occur together, the question appears almost meaningless and unanswerable. But the difference is of the following nature: Does one believe with Keynes that in the long-run it will be found that ideas are decisive in determining man's behaviour;[2] or, on the contrary, that ideas change in accord with the

[1] James Alfred Field, 'The Malthusian Controversy', *Essays in Population*, Illinois, 1931, pp. 45–53.

[2] J. M. Keynes, *General Theory of Employment, Interest and Money*, London, 1936, pp. 383–4. It should be noted that not only Keynes' economic theory but also his philosophy underwent a great change. In contrast to the above position, Keynes once held that 'The great events of history are often due to secular changes in the growth of population and other fundamental economic causes which escaping by their gradual character the notice of contemporary observers, are attributed to the follies of statesmen or the fanaticism of atheists.' *Economic Consequences of the Peace*, London, 1919, p. 12.

material requirements and that economic evolution, not progress in pure reason, is the fundamental factor determining human conduct?

In the economic interpretation, population is the dependent variable, a function of economic development. It follows that there is no general law of population holding good for all times and places, i.e. there are not absolute but relative laws of population. Yet to say that something is relative tells us nothing. The question arises: 'What is it relative to?' and dialectically we arrive at an absolute. The answer given by the economic interpretation is that population laws are relative in the sense that they come and go, but absolute in the sense that they are always determined by the stage of economic evolution. Thus, a shift from a pastoral to an agricultural economy gives rise to a change in the tempo of population growth. Similarly, a certain stage of industrialization leads to a rapid growth in population. Again, according to Russian demographers, a new law of population comes into operation in the period of imperialism.[1]

The economic interpretation furnishes valuable suggestions for a general theory of population growth. However, as yet, it has not been thoroughly exploited. In particular, although classical economic theory stressed the effect of economic development on population growth, specifically the importance of demand for labour on its supply, Neo-Classical economists have not pursued this line of inquiry. Rather, their attention has been directed toward qualifications of the Malthusian analysis with respect to modern industrial communities; its applicability to non-industrialized communities; and, more generally, the theory of the optimum population. On the other hand, Russian demographers have attempted an economic explanation of population dynamics. But although their approach is consistent with the Classical school in that stress is laid on the importance of the demand for labour in regulating its supply, the economic interpretation as applied here suffers a loss of prestige. True, the emphasis on the demand for labour is correct but the *modus operandi* is left obscure; the argument resting entirely on the statistical correlation between the 'final phase of capitalism, imperialism', and the decline in fertility.

[1] See below, Chapter V.

Further, the failure to consider other material factors, in particular the evolution in the economic function of the family and qualitative changes in the demand for labour, results in oversimplification—a one-sided mechanical approach which glosses over certain difficulties.

CHAPTER TWO

Biological Theories

THE DENSITY PRINCIPLE

IN 1830 Michael Thomas Sadler published a two-volume work entitled *The Law of Population*. The work, consisting of many tables and over 1,300 pages, was largely polemic, more than two-thirds of it being devoted to a refutation of the Malthusian system. Therefore, in justice to the author, we are obliged to consider Sadler's objections to the principle of population; objections which, he believes, are so powerful that even if Sadler's own theory be found inadequate it would still be impossible to assent to the Malthusian theory of population.[1]

For Sadler, Malthus is not 'the simple-minded virtuous man' of Miss Martineau. Rather, he is the advocate of a theory 'that could we but trace its effects, it would be found that it has already been the means of inflicting greater mischiefs than any error ever received, and that it threatens still deeper evils; in a word, that it is equally injurious to man and derogatory to his maker'.[2]

Moreover, Malthus is a plagiarist. Thus when Townsend lays

it down as a maxim, that 'the human race everywhere makes strong efforts to increase', Mr. Malthus, in like manner speaks of its 'constant effort to increase'. The former says their numbers will go on increasing, and be limited only by their food; the latter reasserts the idea in the very words. The means by which population is kept down to the level of food are enumerated, and are precisely of the same nature in both, and clearly resolvable into vice, misery, or, as it is called, moral restraint. The principal proofs by which the reverend Travellers demonstrate their point are identical. Does Mr. Townsend

---

[1] Vol. II, p. 308.   [2] Vol. I, p. x.

bring forward China as an example of a country 'where population is advanced to the utmost ability of the soil to nourish', and in which infanticide is resorted to in order to keep down the number? So does Mr. Malthus. On the other hand, Mr. Townsend proves his principle of increase by shewing it, as he supposes, in full operation in North America; so, therefore, does Mr. Malthus.

Not only did Malthus borrow the concept of superfecundity from Townsend but, continues Sadler:

The only attempt to substantiate it, is that first made by Mr. Townsend, who says, 'the population in North America doubles every twenty-five years, but in some provinces in fifteen years'. Transferring this ratio of increase, which he takes to be true, to the old world, he says: the reason it did not take place here is 'obvious— want of food'. This demonstration, if it must be so denominated, is made not an atom stronger by the verbal repetitions of Mr. Malthus; who tells us, in like manner, that 'in the northern states of America, the population has been found to double itself in twenty-five years; in the back settlements, in fifteen years'. 'Why', the latter asks, 'does not an equal number produce an equal increase, in the same time, in Great Britain?' He answers, in the words of the former—'the obvious reason to be assigned, is want of food'. . . . Thus, not only the principle of population, to use Mr. Townsend's phrase, which Mr. Malthus has likewise adopted, but the proofs by which it professes to be demonstrated, the nature of the checks which restrain its increase, and even the precise periods of its natural duplication, are repeated by the latter, with something more like the servility of the copyist, than the accidental coincidence of an original writer.[1]

Convinced of Malthus's dishonesty, Sadler will accept no evidence adduced by him until Sadler, himself, has had the opportunity to verify it. So if Malthus uses a biblical illustration, appeals to historians, ancient philosophers, or contemporary statistics, Sadler follows in hot pursuit. A few illustrations will suffice.

Where Malthus finds the strife between the herdsmen of Abram and Lot evidence of population pressure on the means of subsistence, Sadler shows that in fact the struggle arose from superfluous wealth, which as a heathen writer observed long ago, had been 'the cause of war through all ages and countries of the world'; . . . To call this a struggle for 'room and food' is as gross a

---

[1] Vol. I, pp. 43-5.

perversion of the meaning of words as can be conceived; it was the rivalry of exorbitant wealth.[1]

Again, when Malthus argues that in ancient Greece

population followed the products of the earth with more than equal pace; and when the overflowing numbers were not taken off by the drains of war or disease, they found vent in frequent and repeated colonization,

and that the tendency for population to increase beyond the means of subsistence was noted by Greek legislators and philosophers of that period, Sadler shows that 'immense tracts still remained unappropriated and uncultivated'. Further, the low esteem in which husbandry was held by both Plato and Aristotle does not suggest a society on the brink of starvation. Again, both Thucydides and Polybius trace the wars of Greece, 'those internal, as well as external conflicts, which ended in their ruin—to wealth of soil and territory; to those effects which superior riches always produce'. And Greek colonizing was not directed toward a search for subsistence but, rather, to the plunder of both men and cattle; else how could one explain why the fertile territories of the interior parts were ignored by the Greek colonists and, instead, they concentrated their settlements in maritime locations?[2]

Further, the attitude of Plato and Aristotle toward population did not, as Malthus asserts, spring from a fear of a dearth of subsistence. Actually, both Plato and Aristotle were more concerned over the possibility of too small rather than too large a population. But to the extent that they were worried over an excessive population, the fear originated not from population pressure on subsistence but, rather, from the peculiar social conditions of the country where a form of primitive communism in land was still practised by the upper classes:

Had the citizens multiplied beyond the number of their allotments, the excess would have been unprovided for; had they fallen short of the latter, the state would have become weakened and endangered. . . . But, although both alternatives were anticipated by them . . . their great anxiety was about a ruinous diminution, rather

---

[1] Vol. I, pp. 154-5. [2] Vol. I, Book I, Chapter X.

than a pernicious increase, of their citizens; and tenfold more pre-
cautions were dictated with reference to the former, than to the
latter case.[1]

In reference to the arithmetic progression, Sadler denies first
that population is regulated by the quantity of subsistence
already on hand. Rather, additions to population create
additions to subsistence not, however, according to the law
of diminishing returns. On the contrary, increasing returns is
the law of progress:

> Geometry says, indeed, and truly enough, as applied to matter
> within its own province, that the whole is only equal to the sum of all
> its parts; but . . . applied to the subject before us, this axiom would
> be false. Regarding labour, the great pillar of human existence, it
> may be said that the entire product of combined exertion almost in-
> finitely exceeds all which individual and disconnected efforts could
> possibly accomplish.[2]

Regarding the geometric progression, illustrations of population doubling every fifteen or twenty-five years are sharply
criticized. Among other objections, the age-composition is
overlooked, i.e. unless all members of society are in the reproductive age group, a generation doubling itself will not
double population. Again, the mortality and fertility assumptions of the 'antipopulationists' are unrealistic or absurd.
Further, the statistics used by Malthus to demonstrate that
population in North America tends to double itself every
twenty-five years are of little value. For Malthus has treated
immigration as of no significance; whereas the evidence of
contemporary writers, bills of mortality, custom-house books,
percentage of foreigners serving in state legislatures, the lengthening of the residence requirements for naturalization by the
United States Government, etc., all demonstrate that immigration was an important source of population growth both
before and after the revolution.

Statistics on the proportion of sexes in the United States show
that, as compared to Europe, America had a higher proportion
of males in its population which, also, can only be explained
by immigration. Further, the fact that in the United States
the sex ratio for the age group 15 to 45 was almost equal

[1] Vol. I, pp. 253-4.   [2] *Ibid.*, p. 84.

increased the opportunities for population growth, i.e. women had a greater opportunity to obtain husbands. Again, the contribution of immigrants to population growth is relatively great since, arriving in the prime of life, they naturally marry and beget children.[1]

Malthus had said that the preventive check is loosened or relaxed by high mortality, i.e. deaths make room for marriages. This Sadler denies, but prior to examining the argument in detail, he maliciously suggests the source of Malthus's error:

> There may, indeed, be some exempt cases . . . in which, it is true, the death of present possessors can alone 'make room' for waiting aspirants; and it is not unlikely that the early professional habits and feelings of one of the most strenuous assertors of the theory I am opposing, may have forced the idea upon his mind, as well as given it entrance to that of many others, similarly circumstanced, where it is known to be espoused, and may have suggested its application to the general condition of society.[2]

For proof of his thesis that deaths make room for marriages, Malthus states that in Prussia and Lithuania 'the number of marriages in the year 1711 was nearly double the six years preceding the plague'. Authority for this statement is supposed to come from data found in the first volume of Susmilch's *Göttliche Ordnung*, 'a work which', comments Sadler,

> with some little difficulty, I obtained; being convinced, from its title, that it was not very likely to furnish arguments in favour of such a theory as that I am opposing; and having, moreover, an increasing disinclination to trust implicitly, and without personal examination, to quotations, however formally given: an impression which, I think, the reader will have been already convinced I am fully justified in retaining.[3]

---

[1] Vol. I, Book II, Chapters V to XV.

[2] Vol. II, p. 189. Compare Petty's advice to the protestant clergy (*A Treatise on Taxes and Contributions*, London 1667) 'not to breed more churchmen than the Benefices' since the unemployed churchmen 'will seek ways how to get themselves a livelihood, which they cannot do more easily than by persuading the people that the . . . incumbents do poison or starve their souls, and misguide them in their way to Heaven'. Quoted by Marx, *Capital*, Vol. I (Kerr edition), pp. 675–6, footnote 3.

[3] Vol. II, p. 189.

So the table which 'Mr. Malthus has very unaccountably omitted' is reproduced by Sadler.[1]

Jahre	Getraute Paare (Married Couples)	Getaufte (Baptisms)	Gestorbene (Deaths)
1709	5,477	23,977	59,196 } Pest.
1710	,,	,,	188,537 }
			Sum. 247,733
1711	12,028	32,522	10,131
S. 3 J.	17,028	56,499	,,

Comments Sadler:

Nothing, one would imagine, can be plainer than this part of the table. Indeed, it is so expressed as to render any mistake, more especially the one under consideration, almost impossible. The brackets which connect 1710 and 1711, as far as the births and marriages are concerned, shew just as plainly as the bracket which connects the deaths of 1709 and 1710, that two years are unquestionably included in both instances; but to end all doubt upon the matter, in the total line of the marriages and births are placed these characters, S. 3 J. or *Summe drey Jahren*, not S. 2 J. If, therefore, one year only of marriages and births is included in the bracketed total of 1710 and 1711, amounting to 12,028 of the former, and 32,522 of the latter, as Mr. Malthus reads, or rather misreads, the table; then he holds that Susmilch reckons one and one, THREE. Without implicating Mr. Malthus's intentions upon the occasion, justice to my subject compels me to assert that so gross a misrepresentation of any author has been rarely attempted; nor, moreover one more obviously absurd.[2]

Nor will Sadler accept the qualification appended in a note to a subsequent edition where Malthus admits that 'It is possible that there may be some mistake in the table, and that the births and marriages of the plague years are included in the year 1711. . . . It is, however, an error of no great importance. The other years will illustrate the general principle.' For the other years which Malthus 'continues to omit inserting'

[1] Vol. II, pp. 190–1.   [2] *Ibid.*, pp. 191–2.

are reproduced by Sadler and shown to prove the very opposite of what Malthus has asserted.[1]

Having reached the point where the Malthusian hypothesis has been shown to be 'not only irreconcilable with every received notion of the wisdom and benevolence of the Deity, and the whole course of human experience, but is totally refuted even by the facts brought forward in its support',[2] Sadler is now in position to advance a law of population 'perfectly confirmatory of the principles of divine benevolence, as manifested in the government of the world, and agreeable to the analogies of nature throughout; and which, in fine, reconciles the true theory of human increase with the affections, duties, and interests of mankind'.[3]

The true law of population is that fertility varies inversely with the density of population, i.e. 'the prolificness of a given number of marriages will, all other circumstances being the same, vary in proportion to the condensation of the population'.[4] Thus stated the thesis merely refers to space considered purely extensively. But space must also be considered qualitatively. For by space Sadler understands the capacity to sustain life; from which it follows that a mountainous area or a region under ice and snow is not comparable to a fertile area of equal extension located in a temperate zone.

This qualification or extension of the definition of space does not, Sadler argues, destroy the operational or practical value of the concept. For with the exception of a small number of cases where there are marked differences in the subsistence capacity of the land,

the great mass of civilized society . . . from which . . . our proofs will have to be chiefly derived, inhabits the temperate and fertile regions of the earth, the variation in the productiveness of which is, on the main, but little and that little rendered still less by the continuous efforts of an industry which can overcome all but physical obstacles, and, indeed, partly remove even them.[5]

Yet there is still another principle regulating fertility which Sadler requires to complete his theory of population, viz.:

[1] Vol. II, Table XXXIII, p. 202. [2] *Ibid.*, p. 307.
[3] *Ibid.*, p. 316. [4] *Ibid.*, p. 352.
[5] *Ibid.*, p. 354.

the prolificness of an equal number of individuals, other circumstances being similar, is greater. where the mortality is greater, and, on the contrary, smaller where the mortality is less.[1]

Apparently, Sadler believed that this second principle qualifies but does not contradict the general principle that fertility is regulated by density.

However, it is difficult to see how the principle that fertility varies inversely with density is in any way related to the second principle that fertility varies directly with mortality. Actually, we are given *two distinct laws* regulating fertility and, although Sadler stresses the density principle and treats it as fundamental, there is no explanation of how the mortality principle is limited or subordinate to the density principle.

So it is that after showing fertility to vary inversely with density within a number of European countries, Sadler invokes the other principle that fertility varies directly with mortality to explain the higher fertility of the more densely populated regions within the Netherlands.[2] Moreover, in the course of resolving this apparent contradiction of the density principle, the argument is shifted from fertility to net population increase:

It is, therefore, quite clear that the increase is not regulated by the relative proportion of the births merely.

Nothing, then, remains as an adequate cause of these variations (and Nature never acts without one), but that which has been found operative in every country hitherto examined; namely, Space, or the comparative condensation of the population. If we apply this principle to the facts of a single year, the severest test that can well be imagined, we shall find the proportion of the births and deaths so regulated as clearly to indicate its truth.[3]

Sadler's proof consists in showing that the higher fertility of the more densely populated regions of the Netherlands is

[1] Vol. II, p. 354. Sadler argues that the British and European statistics clearly demonstrate that marital fertility rises during periods of great mortality (Vol. II, Book IV, Chapters XIX and XX). Incidentally, Sadler never recognizes that whenever high mortality and high fertility are associated together, it does not follow that high mortality is the cause of high fertility. In other words, Sadler never considers that a high mortality may itself be a function of high fertility.

[2] *Ibid.*, Book IV, Chapter XIII.

[3] *Ibid.*, p. 450.

more than compensated for by a high mortality so that these regions actually experience a smaller population increase.[1]

Sadler appears unaware that the shift from fertility to population increase, with the emphasis now on the importance of increasing density for increasing mortality, has exposed a basic difficulty in his law of population. For according to the first principle, fertility varies inversely with population density; whereas, according to the second principle, fertility varies directly with mortality. But increasing mortality itself is now asserted to be a function of increasing density. In other words, we are told that increasing density *decreases fertility* but *increases mortality* which, in turn, *increases fertility*. Moreover, in his discussion of the fertility of the Netherlands he is led to conclude that increasing density operating *indirectly* by increasing mortality raises fertility more than increasing density, operating directly on fertility lowers it!

To preserve the theory and make the system determinate, Sadler could, of course, reformulate the density principle to include the indirect, modifying effect or counter-tendency produced by increasing mortality, itself a function of increasing density. But if the density principle operating directly on fertility is held to be *fundamental* and is *only qualified and not negated* by the indirect effect of increasing mortality, Sadler is unable to explain the fertility phenomena of the Netherlands. Such is the dilemma which, apparently, Sadler never realizes.

Sadler believed that the density principle not only explained differences in rural-urban fertility but, also, the low fertility of the upper classes. He begins his discussion by noting that man 'is comparatively sterile when he is wealthy, and that he breeds in proportion to his poverty' not, however, to the point of actual starvation as the Malthusians assert. So the situation most favourable to fertility is that of a 'considerable degree of labour and even privation' such as is characteristic of thinly populated regions where a primitive society maintains itself by hunting and fishing. But as social evolution continues, mankind passes to the pastoral stage, then to the agricultural stage and finally attains to a high level of civilization. Now this progress in social evolution is progress in wealth which, for Sadler, is synonymous with increasing density of population.

[1] Vol. II, pp. 450-2.

The basis on which wealth is identified with increasing density of population has been indicated. For Sadler, it follows simply from his theory of increasing returns from labour.

Now the state of wealth or abundance has been recognized by the keenest minds of all ages as not conductive to fertility. To mention only two: the ancient Greek physician, Hippocrates, noted that a sedentary life was the cause of the low fertility of the rich; Adam Smith also realized that 'Luxury while it inflames, perhaps, the passion for enjoyment, seems always to weaken, and frequently to destroy altogether the powers of generation'. In short, Sadler identifies increasing density of population with wealth and finds that wealth adversely affects the physiological capacity to reproduce.[1]

Thus Sadler finds no evidence to support the Malthusian theory. Rather, the universal history of the human species shows that the downfall of countries cannot be traced to

superfecundity, and its concomitants. . . . It was the excess of wealth; it was ease and luxury and refinement, that prepared the catastrophe of every country destined to destruction: a state which so diminished the prolificness of all such communities, that no examples, however elevated, no laws, however severe, no efforts, however strenuous, could replenish their decreasing numbers.[2]

In summary, many of Sadler's objections to the Malthusian theory were well-founded and credit rightly belongs to him for taking pains to demonstrate the unscrupulous manner in which Malthus attempted to utilize Susmilch's data to support the thesis that deaths make room for marriages. Unfortunately, however, regarding his own theory of population, Sadler did not meet with equal success. Thus Sadler claimed that although space must be interpreted qualitatively and not purely extensively, this did not rob the concept of precision; nevertheless, to explain the high fertility of the inhabitants of maritime provinces, Sadler included under space at their disposal the vast resources of the sea and, therefore, concluded that density here was low. On such an argument, wherever trade is well developed, city density might be proved to be lower than country. Further, the procedure by which Sadler attempted to establish the inverse relation between fertility and density was not

[1] Vol. II, Book IV, Chapter XXI.   [2] *Ibid.*, p. 583.

convincing. The proof was based on a comparison of average densities with average fertilities; but the data, grouped differently, could be made to yield opposite results.[1] Again, as was pointed out above, the relation between density, mortality, and fertility was never clarified. Moreover, if the above analysis is correct, Sadler could have resolved the difficulty only by abandoning his explanation of the high fertility-density ratio found in the Netherlands.

Almost a century after the publication of Sadler's work, the biologist Raymond Pearl, in collaboration with Lowell J. Reed, reintroduced the density principle as an explanation of population growth. However, prior to a consideration of the argument that population is regulated by density, some of Pearl's observations on the significance of both the Malthusian theory and the results of biological investigations for an understanding of the population problem should be noted.

Although Pearl denies that war is an effective check to population growth, he agrees with Malthus in tracing its origin largely to population pressure:

Malthus, whom everyone discusses but few take the trouble to read, pointed out many years ago that the problem of population transcends, in its direct importance to the welfare of human beings and forms of social organization, all other problems. . . . For, in the last analysis, it can not be doubted that one important underlying cause of the great war, through which we have just passed, was the ever-growing pressure of population upon subsistence.[2]

But given population pressure as 'one important underlying cause of the great war', biology provides an explanation of the direct mechanism by which men are led to the actual state of hostilities:

In general, why men deliberately plan wars is because they are different biologically, in structure, habits, mental outlook, thought, or other ways. The more truly conscious they become of these group differences, the more likely they are to fight as groups. . . . But some will ask: *Why* does fighting follow? . . . The biological answer

---

[1] See T. B. Macaulay's criticism in the *Edinburgh Review*, July 1830 and January 1831.
[2] Raymond Pearl, *The Biology of Death*, Philadelphia, 1922, p. 243.

is again clear. The human animal, in common with other higher vertebrates, has come to be endowed with emotions, of which rage is a very important one. . . . The significant biological fact is that, however induced, the emotion of rage automatically and inevitably causes certain definite bodily changes and activities . . . which make the organism ready for fight. It is clear that we have here a first-class reason why men fight. It is, in short, because they get mad at each other.[1]

The major contribution of Malthus was to demonstrate that population could not realize its tendency to increase geometrically. For the operation of the Malthusian checks means that population in a spatially limited universe can only increase arithmetically. Recognizing, then, the validity of this thesis, a further study of population requires a biological investigation of the general laws of growth as exhibited throughout nature: 'While the increase in size of a population cannot on *a priori* grounds be regarded, except by rather loose analogy, as the same thing as the growth of an organism in size; nevertheless it is essentially a growth phenomenon.'[2]

Pearl and Reed's objective is to obtain a mathematical representation of the general pattern found throughout nature. But the mathematical representation must be a rational and not merely an empirical equation. The criteria are as follows:

1. The equation must be in accord with the known facts of population growth;
2. It must recognize the Malthusian proposition that a geometric increase in population is impossible; and
3. It must be consistent with the observed form or rhythm of growth characteristic of all living matter considered either individually or collectively.

Pearl and Reed then proceed to construct a mathematical representation of human population growth based on the following assumptions:

1. Population growth occurs in a finite area;
2. Population growth must have an upper limit, otherwise

---

[1] Raymond Pearl, *Studies in Human Biology*, Baltimore, 1924, pp. 542–3. It would be supererogatory to comment on such fatuity.
[2] *Ibid.*, p. 562.

the absurd conclusion follows that population can expand infinitely within a finite area;

3. The lower limit to population must be zero, i.e. it is impossible to conceive of a negative population;

4. There are cycles of population growth which reflect changes in the economic organization of society. Thus the transition from an agricultural to an industrial society creates the possibility of additional population growth. When such a transition is made the lower limit of the new population cycle is not zero but, rather, the level of population attained in the preceding cycle;

5. 'Within each cultural epoch or cycle of population the rate of growth of population has not been constant in time. . . . At first the population grows slowly, but the rate constantly increases up to a certain point where it, the rate of growth, reaches a maximum. . . . This point of maximum rate of growth is the point of inflection of the population growth curve. After that point is passed the rate of growth becomes progressively slower, till finally the curve stretches along nearly horizontal, in close approach to the upper asymptote which belongs to the particular cultural epoch and area involved.'[1]

In mathematical terminology this growth equation is known as the logistic curve. It should be noted that although the equation expresses rising and then falling rates of absolute population growth, the proportional rate of total population increase falls continuously from the point of origin.[2] Hence the logistic curve is consistent with the Malthusian theory of the impossibility of population increasing geometrically.

Pearl and Reed contend that the value of the logistic curve

[1] *Studies in Human Biology*, pp. 568–9.

[2] The application of the logistic curve was first suggested by Verhulst in 1838. Verhulst argued that 'If population is expanding freely over unoccupied country, the percentage rate of increase is constant. If it is growing in a limited area, the percentage rate of increase must tend to get less and less as the population grows, so that the percentage rate of increase is some function of the population itself, which falls continuously as the numbers of the population rise' (G. Udny Yule, 'The Growth of Population and the Factors which Control it', *Journal of the Royal Statistical Society*, January 1925, p. 4). But the work of Verhulst passed unnoticed until 1920 when Pearl and Reed were in the process of publishing their first mathematical statement of a general biological law of population growth.

is not only that it is founded upon rational assumptions, but also, when applied to the various populations of the world such as (to mention but a few) Austria, Denmark, England and Wales, Scotland, Philippine Islands, and Baltimore City, the curve describes the known facts of population growth. Thus by taking the census data of a country for a short period of the population cycle, it is possible with the logistic curve to deduce population values for the whole cycle. Now when these calculated values are compared with all the available census data for the country, it is found that the population estimates coincide remarkably well with the actual census count. Assuming no interruption of the population cycle, it is then possible with some confidence to predict a country's future population.

Actually the fitting of the curve to the known facts of population growth (censuses) is not the simple procedure that might be imagined. Basically it rests on the investigator's determination of the cycle of population growth, i.e. its point of origin and period of duration. This is evident when we contrast the difference in procedure followed by Pearl and Reed in fitting the curve to the population data of two countries.

For the United States, population is assumed to start from a zero value around 1700 and complete its cycle in 2100 when population reaches a maximum value of 197·274 million. For Germany, however, the period from 1700 to 2000 is divided into two cycles. The first cycle, beginning in 1700, ends approximately at the time of the Franco-Prussian War. For, it is argued, following the successful conclusion of the war, Germany completed its transition from an agricultural to an industrial state and thus embarked on a new cycle of population growth. But, presumably, since no such transition is considered for the United States we may conclude either that this country remained agricultural throughout the whole period from 1700 on; or, that it was always industrial. The point is that by adjusting the population cycles the logistic curve can be made to fit the data. In other words, no specific criteria are established by which we can determine when a country moves from one cycle to another. To determine the cycles by changes in the growth of population is obviously circular.

Again, if (as in the above case of Germany) nations increase in population by the superposition of cycles, then it follows that the growth of *human* populations does not conform to the general pattern of growth exhibited by infrahuman populations.[1]

As yet, Pearl has not discovered a biological principle governing the growth of all living matter. Thus in *Studies in Human Biology*, following application of the logistic curve to a number of individual countries and to the population of the world as a whole, it is concluded that 'this evidence makes it probable that the curve is at least a first approximation to a descriptive law of population growth'.[2]

However, a year later in the *Biology of Population Growth* we are informed that:

In the matter of population growth there not only 'ought to be a law' but six years of research has plainly shown that there is one. This is not the place for recondite statements in mathematical shorthand, but fortunately it is possible to state the law of population growth in plain language, without resort to mathematical symbols. It may be put this way:

Growth occurs in cycles. Within one and the same cycle, and in a spatially limited area or universe, growth in the first half of the cycle starts slowly but the absolute increment per unit of time *increases* steadily until the mid-point of the cycle is reached. After that point the increment per unit of time becomes steadily *smaller* until the end of the cycle. In a spatially limited universe the amount of increase which occurs in any particular unit of time, at any point of the single cycle of growth, is proportional to two things, viz.:

(a) the absolute size already attained at the beginning of the unit interval under consideration, and

(b) the amount of still unused or unexpended in the given universe (or area) of actual and potential resources for the support of growth.

There follows an explanation of (b). In the case of human populations, growth (b) will include the amount of agricultural land

still untilled or not cultivated to maximum productivity. New discoveries of improved agricultural methods, or of chemical methods of making food synthetically, will at once increase the importance of this factor in the case. The results will be either to move up some-

---

[1] This was noted by Sewall Wright in a 'Review of the Biology of Population Growth', *Journal of the American Statistical Society*, December 1926, pp. 494-5.   [2] p. 637.

what the upper limiting value of the population attainable in the current cycle of growth, or, if the potential addition is larger, to start the population off upon a new cycle of growth. . . . In the case of a simple experimental population like that of yeast cells the (*b*) element means practically the still unused amount of sugar and salts remaining in the given limited volume of solution in which the cells are growing. In the case of the growth in size of a single individual organism . . . the meaning of this factor is somewhat more difficult to define. It probably signifies the still remaining potentiality of the system of mutually inter-dependent cells and organs to expand in space without losing effective biological touch with each other.[1]

Neither the argument nor the experimental evidence adduced by Pearl in the *Biology of Population Growth* substantiates his conclusion that the logistic curve is no longer to be considered 'a first approximation to a descriptive law of population growth' but, rather, is the form in which the density principle operates in regulating the growth of all living matter throughout nature.

In the argument the term 'density' is ambiguous. For human populations, density is the relation of numbers to both *actual and potential food resources*; for yeast populations, density is the relation between numbers of cells and *actual food supply*; and for an individual organism, density 'probably signifies the still remaining potentiality of the system of mutually inter-dependent cells and organs to expand in space without losing effective biological touch with each other'.

Again, no criteria are provided by which to determine the stages of economic development. True, passing recognition is given to the differences between a pastoral, an agricultural, and an industrial society. But, as was pointed out in reference to the United States, the stages of economic development are not determined by a rigorous application of these criteria. On the contrary, we are told that if the increase in food resources is small, the result is 'to move up somewhat the upper limiting value of the population attainable in the current cycle of growth, or, if the potential addition is larger, to start the population off upon a new cycle of growth'. In short, in the abstract, Pearl recognizes stages of economic development which determine cycles of population growth; but, in practice, the stages

[1] New York, 1925, pp. 22-3.

of economic development are identified by observed cycles of population growth.

Concerning the experimental evidence, the results indicate that a population of yeast cells follows the growth pattern (logistic curve) required by the density principle. However, Pearl also experimented with fruit flies (*Drosophila melanogaster*) in order to demonstrate the applicability of the density principle to a population 'much higher than yeast in the biological scale, but still a great deal lower than man'.[1]

With painstaking care Pearl arranged the experiment. The spatially limited universe of the flies was a half-pint milk bottle into which an ingeniously constructed apparatus, a counting tube operated by suction, could be inserted in order to take periodic censuses. There was placed inside the spatially limited universe of the flies a carefully measured food supply of 'gelatinized banana pudding of standardized composition'.

However, in dealing with fruit flies a problem arose which was not encountered in the experiment with the simple yeast population. 'If (to the initial supply) no food is added from outside a point is fairly soon reached where the adult flies will literally have eaten up all the food in their universe. There remains but one thing left for them to do, which is to starve to death. This they rather promptly do.'[2] In such a case the flies only complete one-half of the growth cycle and then disappear.

Pearl finds a way out of this difficulty by the simple expedient of adding at regular intervals to the flies' universe a *constant* quantity of food. Pearl points out that now the experiment is analogous to the environmental conditions of human populations in which the situation never arises where the whole food supply has been completely exhausted. On the contrary, farmers are constantly producing and adding to the total stock of subsistence. Now with the addition of constant quantities of food the experiment is successful; the fruit fly population being observed to grow according to the logistic curve.

What this experiment proves the writer is unable to fathom. So far as the growth of an infrahuman population is concerned, all that is demonstrated is that fruit flies in a spatially limited universe do *not* grow according to the density principle manifested in the logistic curve. If it is contended that the experiment

[1] *Biology of Population Growth*, p. 26.   [2] *Ibid.*, p. 31.

is illuminating in reference to human population growth inasmuch as the additions to the food supply correspond to the actual conditions of human society, again the experiment proves nothing. For what the logistic curve posits is that the rate of population growth per unit of time increases up to the midpoint of the cycle, following which additional increments per unit of time decrease. But the experiment is designed to prove just this. For, obviously, a small number of flies will, given an initial supply of food, increase at first at an increasing rate of absolute growth; and, obviously, if to the initial supply additional food is provided in constant quantities (an arithmetic increase in the means of subsistence) the absolute rate of growth of the fly population will in time gradually decrease until a point is reached where further additions to size are negligible. To assume the validity of the logistic curve and then proceed to 'doctor' the experiment so that the assumption will be fulfilled does not constitute independent confirmation of the density principle.[1]

So far Pearl's experiments have only been concerned with the influence of density on total population growth, i.e. the mechanism by which density operates to limit population growth has not been considered. According to Pearl, increasing density does not increase mortality but, rather, decreases fertility. Evidence for this comes from another experiment with fruit flies where Pearl found that 'the rate of reproduction per mated female per day declines as density of population increases, at first extremely rapidly and then more and more slowly at higher densities'.[2]

Experiments on poultry reveal that fertility as measured by number of eggs per hen decreases with increasing density, where density means the number of hens per square feet of floor space. But the experiments also showed that when *density is held constant*, fertility per hen decreases with increasing size of

---

[1] Actually, of course, if one wished to test the Malthusian theory and did not assume the thesis to be proved, there is sufficient material in the census data of various countries. However, these data do not support the thesis that population cannot increase geometrically, as required by the logistic curve; on the contrary, the data prove the opposite. *Cf.* George H. Knibbs, 'The Laws of Growth of a Population', *Journal of American Statistical Society*, Parts I and II, December 1926 and March 1927.

[2] *Biology of Population Growth*, p. 136.

flock: 'The larger the crowd the smaller the egg production, even though the number of birds per unit area, or the unit area per bird, is the same in both crowds.'[1]

Turning to human populations, Pearl also attempted an investigation of the influence of density on fertility. Here the study cannot be conducted by experiments and so recourse is had to the statistical method which 'is rarely ever as satisfactory as the experimental'. There is a further difficulty or limitation arising from the 'considerable uncertainty as to what is a biologically *significant* measure of density in the case of human populations. . . . Higher density . . . may in a human population well bespeak greater ease, not difficulty, in getting an adequate food supply, by virtue of the operation of certain simple and fundamental economic factors in distribution.'[2] Nevertheless, the measure of density adopted by Pearl is the number of persons per acre.

The method followed by Pearl is one of partial correlation. Passing over certain questions which arise in connection with his choice of the significant variables which must be held constant, we find that Pearl obtains a correlation between density and the birth rate of minus 0·131 plus or minus 0·058, 'the net correlation between birth rate and density as measured by persons per acre is negative in direction (i.e. the greater the density the lower the birth rate) and in magnitude is now more than twice its probable error'.[3] It may be noted that Pearl would have obtained a much higher correlation had he defined density as the number of persons per cubic feet of dwelling space. However, here fertility would have been found to vary directly with increasing density!

It will be recalled that Sadler, having identified density with increasing wealth and finding that high and luxurious living adversely affect the physiological capacity to reproduce, was able (formally) to relate his density principle to differential fertility. For Pearl, however, this is impossible since his definition of density as the number of persons per acre is not related to wealth. That is to say, the number of rich urban dwellers is numerically small in comparison to the proletariat.

Pearl, however, does suggest another explanation of the high

[1] *Biology of Population Growth*, p. 144.   [2] *Ibid.*, p. 146.
[3] *Ibid.*, p. 154.

fertility of the 'lower' classes. From a questionnaire survey he finds that poverty increases sexual activity which, of course, tends to raise fertility. Furthermore (and here Pearl quotes with approval Doubleday's thesis which shall be considered next), this human behaviour may be in accord with a general biological principle. For he notes that although at present there is not sufficient evidence to demonstrate 'a direct correlation between harshness of environment and rate of reproduction among animals and plants living in a state of nature, it seems probable that within limitations it does exist . . .'[1]

Such is the evidence which Pearl adduced in the *Biology of Population Growth* to substantiate his contention that population is regulated by density and that the logistic curve is no longer to be considered as merely 'a first approximation to a descriptive law of population growth' as had been stated one year previously in his *Studies in Human Biology*. Fifteen years later in *The Natural History of Population* the density principle is again advanced; however, no new experiments are cited in confirmation of the thesis.[2]

In summary, Pearl's own investigation demonstrates that a fruit fly population in a spatially limited universe does *not* grow according to the logistic curve. The other experiment on flies showing that increasing density lowers fertility proves nothing regarding human behaviour.[3] Furthermore, regarding the statistical inquiry into human fertility and density, even if Pearl had succeeded in obtaining a high correlation, there would still remain a question as to the value of the definition of density adopted by him. Again, in dealing with cultural cycles (stages of economic development) the application to different countries is not consistent. Finally, one cannot but remark on the curious contradiction in Pearl's thinking on population. Along with mathematical precision we are presented with a theoretical construction in which the thesis is so formulated and

---

[1] *Biology of Population Growth*, p. 166.
[2] London, 1939.
[3] 'Finally, so far as the habits of *Drosophilia* are concerned, I must confess that I sympathize with Dickens' Eugene Wraybrun, who, when taunted with the example of the ant and the bee, "protested, on principle, as a biped".' Sir Athelstane Baines' comment in a discussion of G. Udny Yule's 'The Growth of Population and the Factors which Control it', *Journal of the Royal Statistical Society*, January 1925.

the terminology so broad and elusive as to almost preclude investigation into its truth or falsity.[1]

Indeed, so exasperating is the argument that one appreciates how Wolfe, following a review of Pearl's theory, was led to conclude:

> The biologists themselves, by their persistent refusal or inability to recognize the profound bearing of the psychology of the learning process and the significance of differential opportunity, have done much to retard the progress of eugenics as a science, and to turn many against it as an art. If now they are to turn their attention to the problem of population and propose 'scientific' solutions on lines of analogy, and mathematical statistics which take no account of the significant factors peculiar to human culture, we may perhaps well wish that the slight debt which biology owes to economics through Darwin's chance reading of Malthus, may be allowed to run. Population theory is not likely to be benefited by such repayment.[2]

THE DIET PRINCIPLE

In 1841, eleven years after the publication of Sadler's theory, Thomas A. Doubleday offered to the English public a work entitled *THE TRUE LAW OF POPULATION shewn to be Connected with the Food of the People.*

According to Doubleday, the discovery of the true law of population was the product of accidental causes which 'were the result of another inquiry, so far collaterally bearing upon the subject now under discussion as to throw light upon its

---

[1] It is also difficult to understand why Pearl holds that the population problem transcends all others in human importance, and why he emphasizes E. M. East's estimate that the maximum population that the earth can support is somewhat more than 5,000 million (*Studies in Human Biology*, pp. 532–3). Assuming the validity of his density principle and, particularly since in the *Studies in Human Biology* (pp. 632–3) the upper limit of the world population was set at 2,026 million, there would seem to be no grounds for alarm. Incidentally, in 1936 Pearl and Gould brought out a new world logistic curve 'because by 1930 the population of the world had already exceeded the upper asymptotic limit set by the curve. . . the asymptotic limit of the current cycle of growth is raised by 31 per cent of the former figure, to a new value of 2,645·5 millions' (*The Natural History of Population*, pp. 257–8).

[2] A. B. Wolfe, 'Is There a Biological Law of Human Population Growth?', *The Quarterly Journal of Economics*, August 1927, pp. 593–4.

fundamental principles, including as it did, a portion of the proofs of the reality of those principles . . .'[1]

The experiments which led Doubleday to embark on an inquiry into the law of population were concerned with an attempt 'to ascertain, if possible, the substance or substances which constitute the basis or stimulating principle of manures'. In the course of these experiments, Doubleday learned that an excessive application of manure 'invariably induced sterility in the plant, and, if the dose were increased, disease and death'. Trees, flowering shrubs, annuals and other flowers all ceased to seed under the influence of superabundant nutrition or, the plethoric state. However, it was possible to regenerate these plants by a process of 'depletion' which for trees included 'ringing the bark, extreme lopping, and trenching the roots'. Similarly, other plants and flowers could be rejuvenated by various expedients calculated to increase the harshness of the environment, e.g. exposure to cold of a greenhouse plant. When so treated the tree 'began to bear' and 'debilitated plants flowered plenteously'.

Thus was Doubleday 'naturally induced to ask if the same regulation extended through animated nature, and pursuing the inquiry, he found that it did so; that it pervaded the animal creation; and finally, was applied by his Creator to man himself'.[2]

The GREAT GENERAL LAW then, which as it seems, really regulates the increase or decrease both of vegetable and of animal life, is this, that whenever a *species* or *genus* is *endangered*, a corresponding effort is invariably made by nature for its preservation and continuance, by an increase of fecundity or fertility; and that this especially takes place whenever such danger arises from a diminution of proper nourishment or food, so that consequently the state of depletion, or the deplethoric state, is favourable to fertility, and that on the other hand, the plethoric state, or state of repletion, is unfavourable to fertility, in the ratio of the intensity of each state, and this probably throughout nature universally, in the vegetable as well as the animal world; further, that as applied to mankind this law produces the following consequences, and acts thus:

There is in all societies a constant increase going on amongst that

---

[1] London, 1843 (second edition), p. 4.
[2] *The True Law of Population* (second edition), pp. 265-7.

portion of it which is the worst supplied with food; in short, amongst the poorest.

Amongst those in the state of affluence, and well supplied with food and luxuries, a constant decrease goes on. Amongst those who form the mean or medium between these two opposite states . . . population is stationary.[1]

In the animal world it is a well-known fact that the rabbit and swine, remarkable for their fecundity, 'will *not* conceive if fed to a certain height of fatness'; similarly, horses, cattle, sheep, and fowl all confirm the principle that the 'number of the progeny is generally in the *ratio* of the leanness of the animal'.[2]

Equipped with this general law, Doubleday is able to explain both intra- and international differences in fertility. Within a country, differences in diet explain why the wealthy classes, the nobility and the bourgeoisie, fail to reproduce themselves; while the poor constantly increase and those midway between the two extremes merely maintain themselves.

International differences are similarly accounted for since countries with a high fertility consume little meat or wine, subsisting mainly on fish and vegetables. Thus a fish diet, recognized in tradition and specifically by Aristotle as inducing unusual prolificness, is the cause of the high fertility of the inhabitants of the Highlands and Western Islands of Scotland 'where even the eggs of sea-fowls are not eaten, but made an article of traffic; and where the only animal food tasted by the poorer natives is an occasional "braxie", or sheep which has died of the rot'. Other countries of high fertility are those whose diet is chiefly vegetable, such as Ireland, India, and China where potato and rice respectively constitute the main source of nourishment.

In fact, a study of the different countries reveals a universal pattern, viz. population is '*thin* in pastoral countries, where the food is animal food chiefly; *denser*, where it is mixed partly with vegetable aliment; *denser* still, where it is vegetable only, but with plenty; *densest of all*, where it is vegetable, but scarcity superadded'.[3]

Doubleday believed that Sadler had made an important contribution in disposing of the Malthusian theory, but 'the

[1] *The True Law of Population* (second edition), pp. 5–6.
[2] *Ibid.*, p. 14.   [3] *Ibid.*, pp. 25–7.

wonder is how the acute mind of Mr. Sadler' failed 'to discover what is really the law by which population is regulated'. For in combating the Malthusian argument Sadler brought forth evidence which clearly demonstrated that although marriages do not increase during plague years, as Malthus had asserted, conceptions do. But this observed rise in fertility during periods of famine, while of no value to Sadler's theory, clearly demonstrates 'that a diminution of the means of living comfortably, immediately *stimulates* population'.[1]

The argument that poverty stimulates population is also employed by Doubleday to explain England's population increase. The fact is that 'the condition of the majority of the English people has, for a series of years, been *deteriorating* and still continues to *deteriorate*'. Evidence for this Doubleday found in the great increase in the amount of the poor rate, especially in the last quarter of the eighteenth century; the decrease in malt duties by more than a half in the last three-quarters of a century at a time when domestic brewing had almost ceased in England; more recent statistics on crime which showed that in 1834 the number of commitments quintupled those of 1806; the sharp decline in meat consumption from 1815 to 1829; the increase in the consumption of the potato which 'had quadrupled in the last hundred years'.[2]

Nor does the growth of population in America present any difficulty for his theory. Such statistics as were available proved that the wealthier cities had a lower fertility than the poorer ones. But, like Sadler before him, Doubleday attributed population growth in the United States chiefly to immigration. Further, in reply to Dr. Loudon's objection that the western states of Ohio, Illinois, and Wisconsin had a higher fertility and consumed more animal products than the older states, Doubleday argued that the extremely arduous life of these pioneers neutralizes 'the tendency to repletion which the articles of diet, if obtained as in a more civilized society, would induce'.[3]

The argument that 'the life of the new settler is really one

---

[1] *The True Law of Population* (second edition), pp. 136–8.
[2] *Ibid.*, pp. 98–104 and 187–97.
[3] *Ibid.*, postscript, p. xiv. Dr. Charles Loudon's criticism in *Solution du Problème de la Population et de la Subsistance* was directed to the first outline of Doubleday's theory published in *Blackwood's Magazine*, March 1837.

of *toil*, because his *all* is the produce of the direct and constant exertions of himself and his family; and, in the effects of this constant exertion and exposure, is to be found the real cause of the greater fecundity which these states are said to exhibit',[1] suggests special pleading. Be that as it may, the fact remains that with this admission Doubleday has not advanced far beyond his predecessors who all stressed ease of life and luxurious living as the cause of the low fertility of the upper classes.

Before leaving Doubleday we may note what he considers the 'grand and salutary axiom' which can be deduced from the law of population, viz. 'that a long-continued depression, down to destitution, of a whole people, will, in the long run, be revenged on itself and those who caused it, by the superfluous and unmanageable pauper population which it is sure to generate'.[2]

Finally, Doubleday's theory of population exhibits 'the moral government of God in the world in a new and original light'. For the inequality of social position which is necessary to stimulate mankind to a full exertion of its faculties and which, unfortunately, has the further consequence of accumulating vast possessions in the hands of the few, is by the law of population meliorated. For 'the most equitable distribution possible, under a system in which inequality at all is necessary, is found to prevail. . . . The holders of wealth cannot maintain a posterity long to which to transmit it. . . . The offspring of the poor inevitably, in process of time, become possessed of the accumulations of the rich; and then, in their turn, yield them, for want of heirs, to the children of those who have not yet become rich; a distribution so beautifully equitable, in the midst of apparent inequality, as to be calculated to excite the deepest admiration of all reflective minds.'[3]

More than a century after Doubleday's work, the thesis that fertility is regulated by diet has been advanced again by Josué de Castro in the *Geography of Hunger* where it is contended that fecundity is regulated by the quantity and quality of protein consumption.[4] Evidence for this Castro finds in laboratory

---

[1] *The True Law of Population*, postscript, p. xv.
[2] *Ibid.*, p. 254.
[3] *Ibid.*, pp. 256–9.   [4] London, 1952. (Foreword by Lord Boyd Orr.)

experiments on the fertility of rats when diet is controlled for protein intake; and, also, from world statistics which demonstrate a relationship between fertility and protein consumption.

According to Castro, there has been a world conspiracy against the discussion of hunger. Part of this silence is traceable to the prejudice of a 'rationalist culture' where reason, seeking to dominate human behaviour, deprecates primitive animal instincts such as sex and hunger. Freud's contribution which led to the recognition and frank discussion of the primacy of the sex instinct unfortunately has not, as yet, been duplicated in the field of hunger. But

there were reasons even stronger than prejudice . . . for suppressing discussion of hunger. Dominant and privileged minorities used their deftest sleight-of-hand to keep the question of hunger from the attention of the modern spirit. It was to the advantage of economic imperialism and international commerce, both controlled by profit-seeking minorities, that the production, distribution, and consumption of food products be regarded as purely business matters rather than as phenomena of the highest importance to society as a whole.

Scientists, too, are guilty, having

kept a pointed silence about the living conditions of the world's hungry masses; consciously or unconsciously, they became accomplices in the conspiracy. The social reality of hunger stayed outside their laboratory walls.[1]

But there are grounds for optimism. Civilization is steadily progressing from 'the era of the economic man' toward the 'era of social man'. In all societies there is an increased interest in human welfare so that

capitalist democracy and Russian democracy do not represent two worlds in irreconcilable struggle, but rather two poles of a single world. As two poles they have their differences and peculiarities, but the growing interest of man in man himself and the anxious search for means of collective betterment mark an area where the two systems must converge.

Again, while in the past narrow and uncultured specialists have failed to see 'the problem of hunger in its world-wide perspective', more recently such works as those 'of Lord Boyd

[1] *Geography of Hunger*, pp. 15–17.

Orr, Imre Ferenczi, Frank Boudreau and a few others can be considered to have a broad outlook and to be genuinely scientific'.[1]

There are two particularly dangerous ways of looking at the problem of world hunger, 'dangerous because they falsify the social reality of the problem'. First, there are those who believe that hunger is a natural and inevitable concomitant of human existence; and, second, those who believe that the only solution to hunger is a forcible reduction in the world's birth rate.

Neither theory has any basis in fact. On the contrary, with the application of present agricultural techniques, authorities calculate that one-half the land surface of the world, 16 billion acres, can be cultivated. Allowing 2 acres per person to supply the indispensable elements of a rational diet there remains yet room for an additional population of 6 billions. However, even this calculation is modest, since it excludes the recent progress that has been made in transforming tropical deserts into fertile regions.[2]

As was indicated, the above calculation makes no provision for future progress in agricultural science. But in Chapter VII it is pointed out that growth hormones; insecticides; better and increased use of fertilizers; the discovery by the Massachusetts Institute of Technology of numerous plants, hitherto unutilized, which constitute a 'vast untapped food reserve'; the ridiculously low utilization of the existing food resources of the sea; artificial irrigation projects, etc., all suggest an almost limitless expansion of food resources: 'Some synthetic foods are beyond the planning stage. Proteins are actually being produced today by means of ferment, torula yeast, which is fed on molasses. A factory, operating on the technical principles of the English scientist A. C. Thayson, has been set up in Jamaica. It currently turns out five tons of proteins a day, at economically competitive prices.' During the last war German factories were able to manufacture 10,000 tons of synthetic fats a year.

Castro quotes the food experts of the Nutrition Division, Food and Agricultural Organization of the United Nations, who state: 'For the first time in history it is now possible to synthesize from nonbiological and even from inorganic materials a food of calorific value. . . . At the present time the

[1] *Geography of Hunger*, pp. 18–21.   [2] *Ibid.*, pp. 21–5.

cost of synthetic fats is higher than that of natural fats, but this is not necessarily a deterrent. New processes are always expensive, and their cost is gradually reduced as industrial research progresses.'

Castro admonishes us to forget soil erosion, a remote possibility in the sense of becoming general, and concentrate our attention on human erosion. Human erosion springs from hunger, where hunger is interpreted not as the mere lack of a sufficient quantity of food but, rather, as the lack of any of the forty or so elements necessary for a balanced diet. Considered thus, on a conservative estimate, at least two-thirds of the world's population suffers from hunger.

So the *Geography of Hunger* is a world survey of dietary deficiencies. Of these, one of the most serious is the dearth of animal proteins containing the indispensable amino acids. Deficiency of animal proteins accounts for many characteristics once considered the result of racial inheritance, viz. small stature, increased susceptibility to tuberculosis, pneumonia, dysentery, and typhoid fever.

It is not necessary to follow Castro in his discussion of other specific hungers, e.g. calcium, iodine, vitamins, etc.; but it is essential to realize that Castro is arguing that Neo-Malthusians err in considering population and production separately as if they were independent variables. They fail to appreciate the extent to which production depends upon the quantity and quality of population:

> During a several-year period of heavy internal migration in Brazil, hundreds of thousands of people abandoned the north-eastern area of chronic malnutrition and came to the more prosperous coffee-raising and industrial areas of the south. When they went to work in the fields, the men from the north were incapable of keeping up with the Italian colonists, or even with the better-fed southerners. They seemed a race of good-for-nothings, unable to exert themselves, lacking both will and ambition. But a short period of good nutrition was all that was needed to transform them into magnificent workers.[1]

The poor diet which leads to low productivity also, paradoxically, creates a labour shortage in the very areas thought to be overpopulated. Thus in regard to India it is true, as the

[1] *Geography of Hunger*, pp. 73-4.

Neo-Malthusians assert, that if diet is improved, the country provided with decent sanitation, vaccines, etc., the population will surely increase. But this will mean a great increase in both the quantity and quality of the working population: to eliminate the high mortality in India is to remedy a situation in which 'it is as though half the individuals born were defective, having mouths to feed but no hands to work. Half the Indian children are born merely to consume a starvation diet and to die before they are old enough to produce.'[1]

Where Neo-Malthusians stress conditions of natural scarcity, Castro emphasizes socio-economic causes since 'the world's great areas of endemic hunger are exactly the colonial areas'.[2] The indictment of imperialism is severe. Through colonization the subsistence economy of the natives is ruined and the land, monopolized by the imperialists, is devoted to the production of a money-crop commodity for export. Whole areas are turned to the cultivation of sugar, tobacco, groundnuts, etc., with the result that natives earning pitifully low wages are forced to purchase imported food at high prices. Again, the development of mines and factories creates in the area of exploitation a proletarian population who, uprooted from the soil and cut off from tribal organization, eke out a miserable existence.

But the poverty which arises from an inadequate diet is aggravated by increased fertility, itself a function of poor nourishment. To substantiate this Castro presents a table purporting to demonstrate a relationship between the crude birth rate and protein consumption.[3] The inverse correlation is perfect. Too perfect. No explanation is provided why certain countries are omitted, e.g. France, Austria, England and Wales, etc. Further, the year (or years?) to which the data apply are not specified, although it is well known that in recent times fertility in capitalist countries has fluctuated greatly.

Castro does, however, present evidence that fertility is regulated by diet. After noting, as did Doubleday before him, that cattle-raisers have long known that animals which become too fat frequently become sterile and that reduced feeding will frequently re-establish fertility, Castro cites R. J. Slonaker's experiments during the 1920's on changes in the fertility of rats when diet is controlled for protein consumption:

[1] *Geography of Hunger*, p. 151.   [2] *Ibid.*, p. 253.   [3] *Ibid.*, p. 68.

Slonaker subjected groups of rats to diets which varied in protein content, and studied their reproductive indices for six generations ... when male rats received a diet with only 10 per cent of its total calories in proteins, 5 per cent of them were sterile; when the protein content of the ration was increased to 18 per cent and 22 per cent, the sterility increased to 22 and 40 per cent respectively. With females, the same increase of protein in the diet lifted the sterility rate from 6 per cent to 23 per cent and 38 per cent respectively. There were impressive differences in the average numbers of offspring of the various groups of rats. Eating 10 per cent protein, each rat produced an average of 23·3 offspring; with 18 per cent protein, 17·4; and with 22 per cent, only 13·8.[1]

Further, experiments on human subjects which indicate a sharp decrease in sexual interest under conditions approaching starvation do not, Castro asserts, contradict Slonaker's findings. For it is necessary to distinguish between acute and chronic hunger. Now it is true that with acute hunger (which is the exception and not the rule) sexual activity declines; such, however, is not the case under conditions of chronic hunger. On the contrary,

the chronic starveling, whose appetite for food is dulled and easily satisfied, turns his attention away from his weakening nutritional instincts. The biologically important and psychologically satisfactory activity which presents itself is sexual. Thus one primary need is emphasized to compensate for the diminution of the other.[2]

In a later chapter Castro considers the process by which diet regulates human fertility:

Enough is known about protein metabolism so that we can trace the actual mechanism by which protein deficiency leads to increased fertility, while an abundance of protein has the opposite effect. ... Fecundation in women is closely related to the functioning of the ovaries, to the production of their hormones, particularly the oestrogens, and to the quantity of these present in the blood and internal organs.

It is known that there is a direct connection between the functioning of the liver and the ovaries, the role of the liver being to inactivate the excess oestrogens which the ovaries throw into the blood stream. Fatty degeneration of the liver and the tendency to cirrhosis are, as we have previously seen, some of the characteristic results

[1] *Geography of Hunger*, p. 67.   [2] *Ibid.*, p. 66.

of protein deficiency. . . . When degeneration of the liver occurs it begins to operate less efficiently, and is less effective at its job of inactivating excess oestrogens. The result is a marked increase in the women's reproductive capacity.[1]

It is, of course, a problem for the biologists and physiologists to determine whether and to what degree human fertility is regulated by diet. But even if we were to suppose that it could be demonstrated conclusively that a *high* protein diet limits *human* fertility, additional information would still be required. Specifically, we would want to know to what extent a human diet would have to be modified before there were observable effects on fertility. In other words, it is conceivable that within sufficiently broad limits fertility *might* be shown to be related to diet. But the question would still remain as to what determined the *intra-limit* variations. For example, during the last world depression the birth rate in a number of capitalist countries fell significantly. Surely it would not be contended that during the same period *per capita* protein consumption rose? Again, during recent relatively prosperous years the United States has experienced a great upsurge in births. Are we to conclude that protein consumption in this country has been lower in this period than in the worst years of the depression?

In summary, it is possible to accept Castro's thesis that poverty is mainly traceable to socio-economic conditions and should not be attributed to the niggardliness of nature while, at the same time, withholding assent to the proposition that human fertility is closely related to diet. Even if the reproductive capacity is determined by diet, it does not follow that capacity implies utilization. Again, as was noted above, fertility variations associated with the business cycle are obviously not a function of diet. Castro's emphasis on the gains in production arising from an improvement in the standard of living is positive; especially with reference to a country like India where a mere prolongation of life expectancy from 30 to 40 years will greatly expand the labour force.[2] Castro's optimism, more in accord with the historical evidence on the past progress of pro-

[1] *Geography of Hunger*, p. 140.
[2] Castro had previously argued that countries like India and China are not overpopulated but, rather, suffer from a maldistribution of population. *Geography of Hunger*, Chapter IV.

duction than the dreary prophecies of the Malthusian school, is evident in the following:

When deserts of ice and impenetrable tropical jungles are being turned to gardens and orchards, when the lands·we farm and the plants we grow are being made to multiply their yield, and while we are barely learning how to tap the great food reservoirs of the waters, the wild flora, and of artificial synthesis, the Malthusians go on setting up their sinister scarecrows. It is nothing to us, since we have no reason to fear them.[1]

SPENCER'S BIOLOGICAL THEORY [2]

According to Herbert Spencer, preservation of the species is the general biological law governing the growth of all populations, both human and infra-human. The means for the preservation of the species are two, individuation and genesis. Individuation is defined as the power of a species to maintain and conserve the life of its individual members; whereas, genesis refers to the capacity of the species to generate new individuals.

A priori, says Spencer, it is evident that these two processes are necessarily antagonistic and must vary inversely in strength. For, on the one hand, it is obvious that a species would soon become extinct if its members had both a very low survival capacity and a feeble capacity to reproduce; and, on the other hand, it is impossible to conceive of a species whose individuals possessed both great powers of self-preservation and multiplication. For,

the excess of fertility, if extreme, will cause extinction of the species by starvation. If less extreme, it must produce a permanent increase in the number of the species; and this, followed by intenser competition for food and augmented number of enemies, will involve such an increase of the dangers to individual life, that the great self-preserving powers of the individuals will not be more than sufficient to cope with them. That is to say, if the fertility is relatively too great, then the ability to maintain individual life inevitably becomes smaller, *relatively* to the requirements; and the inverse proportion is thus established.[3]

---

[1] *Geography of Hunger*, p. 250.
[2] *The Principles of Biology*, London, 1880, Vol. II, Part IV, 'The Laws of Multiplication'.   [3] *Ibid.*, p. 402.

Spencer finds empirical confirmation of the *a priori* argument in different patterns of multiplication found throughout nature. The most highly developed organisms, those which have progressed furthest on the evolutionary scale, are characterized by increased bulk, complexity, and activity, or any combination of the three. Such organisms exhibit a completely different fertility pattern:

> Whilst the minutest organisms multiply asexually in their millions; while the small compound types next above them thus multiply in their thousands; while larger and more compound types thus multiply in their hundreds and their tens; the largest types do not thus multiply at all.[1]

However, empirical observation does suggest a qualification to the *a priori* formulation of the relationship between individuation and genesis. While it is true that they remain antagonistic and must vary inversely, nevertheless 'Genesis decreases not quite so fast as individuation increases' so that whatever form individuation takes, whether of larger bulk, greater speed or agility, or a more economical utilization of sustenance,

the result is a greater surplus of vital capital; part of which goes to the aggrandisement of the individual, and part to the formation of new individuals. While the higher tide of nutritive matters, everywhere filling the parent-organism, adds to its power of self-maintenance, it also causes a reproductive overflow larger than before.[2]

Since the fertility of man is governed by the same law that regulates the fertility of all species, it follows that Doubleday is wrong in arguing that increase in nutriment decreases fertility. The cases Doubleday cites of infertility accompanied by fatness 'are not cases of high nutrition properly so-called; but cases of such defective absorption or assimilation as constitutes low nutrition'.

Spencer further objects that Doubleday's theory would not guarantee the preservation of the species. For the increase in fertility consequent upon the deplethoric state would increase population which, in turn, would lead to a greater competition for food: 'Thus, there will go on an ever-increasing rate of

---

[1] *The Principles of Biology*, pp. 426-7.   [2] *Ibid.*, pp. 477-8.

multiplication, and an ever-decreasing supply of food, until the species disappears.' On the other hand, an increase in food, 'the plethoric state, will also lead to extinction of the species since more food for each generation (since there are fewer) would lead to final barrenness'.[1]

Spencer has gone one better than Malthus. Whereas, it will be recalled, Malthus posited a constant tendency for population to increase; Spencer holds that with increased nutriment there ensues 'a reproductive overflow larger than before'. Yet for Spencer this is no cause for alarm. On the contrary, 'the constant increase of people beyond the means of subsistence (! !) causes, then, a never-ceasing requirement for skill, intelligence, and self-control—involves, therefore, a constant exercise of these and gradual growth of them'.[2]

Indeed, Spencer finds the grand cause of human progress in population pressure:

It produced the original diffusion of the race. It compelled men to abandon predatory habits and take to agriculture. It led to the clearing of the Earth's surface. It forced men into the social state; made social organization inevitable; and has developed the social sentiments. . . . And after having caused, as it ultimately must, the due peopling of the globe, and the rising of all its habitable parts into the highest state of culture—after having, at the same time, developed the intellect into complete competency for its work, and the feelings into complete fitness for social life—after having done all this, the pressure of population, as it gradually finishes its work, must gradually bring itself to an end.[3]

In short, through population pressure we reach the New Jerusalem. Now whatever the rhetorical merits of such lyricism, the fact remains that Spencer does not concern himself with demonstrating the truth of this proposition. On the contrary, the proposition that population growth is the grand cause of human progress rests on nothing more substantial than Spencer's assertion.

To solve the problem of differential fertility among humans, Spencer proceeds by analogy. The infertility of the 'upper classes' is attributable to their greater individuation: 'It is a matter of common remark how frequently men of unusual

---

[1] *The Principles of Biology*, pp. 483-5, footnote.
[2] *Ibid.*, pp. 498, 499.   [3] *Ibid.*, pp. 506-7.

mental ability leave no offspring'; again, 'infertility is generally produced in women by mental labour carried too far'.[1] Here, then, the same laws that govern each movement up the evolutionary scale are invoked to explain intra-species variations. In short, Spencer rejects Doubleday's thesis that increased nutriment decreases fertility and asserts, on the contrary, that increased fertility is the necessary result of an increase in subsistence. The consequent population growth operates in turn as a spur to human progress and is, in fact, the great agency for mankind's advancement. But when population growth tends to become excessive and thereby threatens the extinction of the species, individuation steps in and resolves all difficulties. Differential fertility is attributable to the greater individuation of the 'upper classes'. Evolution is the *deus ex machina* which explains both inter- and intra-species variations. Such are the essentials of Spencer's view on population. Compounded of analogies and dogma, they need not detain us longer.[2]

[1] *The Principles of Biology*, pp. 486-7.
[2] In the United States, Spencer's theory was accepted by such divergent thinkers as the conservative economist H. C. Carey and the 'single-taxer' Henry George (H. C. Carey, *Principles of Social Sciences*, Philadelphia, Vol. III, 1859, Chapters XLVI–XLIX, and Henry George, *Progress and Poverty*, 1879, reprinted 1931, London, p. 101).

CHAPTER THREE

Cultural Theories

UNDER 'cultural' theories are subsumed those explanations of fertility differentials and fertility dynamics which have recourse to a number of factors, both material and immaterial, in the cultural ensemble. In particular, the theories emphasize the importance of psychic factors in determining fertility patterns. In turn, these psychological attributes are regarded as either developed by the present culture, or, if considered part of man's natural inheritance, thought of as receiving sustenance in the present milieu. Although economic considerations are frequently stressed in the various cultural explanations, the economic contribution is recognized as but one of a number of factors operative. That is to say, the economic factor is not regarded as fundamental but, rather, as having co-ordinate significance.

THE VOLITIONAL APPROACH

Under volitional theories are included Dumont's theory of 'social capillarity' and Fetter's principle of 'voluntarism'. Although the doctrines differ in particulars and Dumont emphasizes more the effect of a specific type of civilization, essentially both theories are united in stressing the importance of the will in determining reproductive patterns.

Social Capillarity. Dumont deprecates the contribution of political economists to population theory. He finds that they tend to elevate the purely contingent to laws having universal validity. Moreover, from their habit of reasoning from *a priori* principles, economists continue to repeat the Malthusian argument long after there is empirical evidence to the contrary. So the French economist, Joseph Garnier, published a work on population which completely ignored French statistics demonstrating that population growth did not accompany the increase in wealth. Similarly, John Stuart Mill reproduces the Malthusian argument in his later editions without appreciating the significance of French demographic data.[1]

Economists are also indicted for having for the most part 'contracted an astonishing incapacity to comprehend that it is not production and consumption' which are the mainsprings of human action. Rather, revolutions are caused by a revolt of human dignity, 'an explosion of enthusiasm for truth and justice'. For 'pride and human dignity are the factors which they always forget and nothing is more suitable than this forgetfulness to pervert all their judgments'.[2]

It is not from economists then that Dumont will learn of population. Nor is it sufficient to be thoroughly familiar with the works of historians and philosophers. In addition, the demographer must have statistical data and a first-hand knowledge of the areas under investigation. So for a number of years Dumont spent from three to five months annually visiting and studying in detail the departments, cantons, villages, and communities of France in an attempt to discover the cause or causes determining different fertility patterns.

According to Dumont, there are three principles of population rather than one. The Malthusian principle may be said to hold for animals and men who live like animals, i.e. savages who subsist on what they find rather than on what they produce. At a more advanced stage of human development, Guillard's principle that population proportions itself automatically so that 'where bread is born, is born a man' may govern. In such a society, where labour and accumulation are the sole aim of life, Guillard is correct in holding that natality always proportions itself to available employment and the Malthusian checks of vice and misery are unnecessary. But in a civilized community when 'imagination and the attraction of an ideal enter upon the scene we find ourselves in the presence of a third principle of population which supplants the other two and

[1] Arsène Dumont, *Dépopulation et Civilisation*, Paris, 1890. Preface.
[2] *Ibid.*, p. 13.

which furnishes us with an explanation of the phenomena of depopulation in France'.[1]

The population principle governing civilized societies is 'social capillarity'. This principle recognizes that all societies are virtually unanimous in establishing a social hierarchy of prestige. True, the values differ among the various societies, but the fact remains that in all societies some individuals are given greater recognition than others. Given any hierarchy we find each social molecule striving with all its energy to rise unceasingly to some shining ideal which beguiles and attracts. Now this aspiration or will to advance higher in social status, is not the same as ambition which for Dumont signifies the desire to dominate men by power politics or by wealth. Rather, the aspirations subsumed under the term 'social capillarity' are far more general and may include not only love of pleasure, elegance and luxury but also love of truth, justice, and even the desire to sacrifice oneself for the general good. In short, social capillarity refers to the individual's drive toward recognition according to the values of that society of which he is a member.

But although the principle of social capillarity is manifest in all civilized communities, it does not operate with equal vigour everywhere. On the one hand, it is weakest in those societies where status and caste are rigid barriers to individual advancement. In such communities fertility is always great since the individual is debarred from personal progress. Lacking any motive to deprive himself of the pleasure of paternity and lacking any idea of advancement, he obeys, as would an animal, the impulses of his nature. On the other hand, social capillarity is most influential in communities characterized by great social mobility. Here fertility is low since children are encumbrances which prevent or retard the individual's struggle to advance or 'arrive'. He does not wish to embark on his journey laden with such luggage.

Now the low fertility of the French is not attributable to decadence as some writers have contended. It is rather that in France special conditions exist which tend to emphasize or exaggerate the action of social capillarity. In the political sphere there is a sharp contradiction: historically, political

[1] *Dépopulation et Civilisation*, p. 41.

democracy was exalted and the equality of man loudly proclaimed while simultaneously there was a concomitant growth in government functions, an increase in centralization. A great bureaucracy in which numerous government functionaries wield absolute, although anonymous, power and are responsible only to their superiors, is in fundamental contradiction to formal political democracy. The result has been to elevate Paris, the capital, to a point where it not only dominates the economic but also the political, social, and cultural life of the French nation. In Paris, as nowhere else in France, are to be found the opportunities for satisfying the aspirations for political and economic power, luxury, pleasure, intellectual and aesthetic development. It is the centre of attraction for the aspirant to fame, power or luxury and few indeed are the sacrifices which will not be made in order to become part of this milieu.

Democracy stimulates the ambition of all citizens; while the opportunities for employment in the bureaucracy, formally in reach of all, furnish the means for the realization of this ambition. The result for natality is clear:

If the ideal of all Frenchmen is to be a functionary, that of all functionaries is advancement; but advancement almost always necessitates a change in residence. He who is not married or has no children has a facility for removal which is not possessed by the man in charge of a family. The first is able to accept on demand a post that the second will be forced to refuse. . . .[1]

Again, in France the contradiction between political democracy and economic inequality is most acute. All social power has been suppressed save that of wealth. Moreover, there is in addition the absurd prejudice that wealth spontaneously proportions itself according to the merit of the individual's activity —hence the struggle to accumulate is accentuated and, consequently, the depressing effect on natality.

It is not that poverty is the cause of high fertility. It is, rather, that French demographic data demonstrate that the regions of high fertility are precisely those which are remote from urban centres and are characterized by ignorance and poverty. Considered thus, poverty (like ignorance) is seen as the condition, but not the true cause, of high fertility.

[1] *Dépopulation et Civilisation*, pp. 222–3.

Similarly, wealth is not the cause of low fertility. Rather, they are both common products of the will to advance. So it is that in urban centres where social capillarity is most pronounced, fertility is necessarily low. However, this is not true for every class of urban dweller. The proletariat, whose road to fortune is barred by the insuperable obstacle of a feudal manufacturing system, finds it impossible to elevate his condition and therefore increases in number:

As zero is the only number which, divided by four or six, gives equally zero to its quotient, the proletarian has nothing to bequeath his sons but a patrimony equal to his own, the knowledge in a pair of hands, and, concerning himself, his poverty will be no more irremediable. It is this that explains why the man who lives from day to day is habitually more fecund than any other class in society.[1]

This new principle of population, social capillarity, explains not only fertility differentials within a country but also the low natality of France in comparison with other countries. Abstracting the goal pursued, Dumont formulates the rules of social capillarity:

1. Natality varies inversely with social capillarity;
2. The progress of the individual in either personal worth or enjoyment is in direct proportion to social capillarity;
3. Consequently, the numerical development of the race is in inverse ratio to the development of the individual in worth or enjoyment;
4. The more brilliant the culture, the more it attracts; and the more it attracts, the more brilliant the culture, i.e. it is nourished by its own products;
5. The greater the attraction, the more rapidly consumed are those who submit to its blandishments. The realization of the goal of the ambitious plebeian requires a more intense struggle than that of the son of the aristocrat. He is also more greedy for pleasure when he sets himself this goal;
6. In a democracy, human growth is intensive; whereas in a caste system, growth is extensive.[2]

Voluntarism. According to Fetter, the error of the Malthusian

[1] *Dépopulation et Civilisation*, p. 128. [2] *Ibid.*, p. 130.

doctrine consists in its one-sided emphasis on a single command-ing instinct, sex drive.[1] In reality, man is a much more com-plicated creature whose activities are greatly influenced by his ideals, feelings, desires, and will. So it is that even in the most primitive communities behaviour is determined by other considerations than a mere shortage of food. Infanticide, for instance, seemingly a social response to a threatened shortage of food, is found upon investigation to be traceable to vanity. The mother will not have her beauty sacrificed to the require-ments of nursing. Again, superstition and not food shortage is responsible for the killing of twins. Wars between wild tribes may have as their motive additional hunting territory, but just as frequently they originate from other motives.

For Fetter there is no single population principle adequate to explain the multitude of phenomena. Rather, either several population principles, or none. In the evolution of society, limits to the production of subsistence play an ever-diminishing role so that the explanation of demographic changes must be sought in the multiplicity of motives which determine man's behaviour. Fetter is not arguing that material conditions are unimportant and should be disregarded but rather, that through progress, man achieves a degree of emancipation so that his behaviour is determined more by his will than by the exigencies of physical necessity.

Proceeding to a study of the variety of motives which regulate man's reproductive behaviour, Fetter begins by dividing society into classes. He analyses the function of the family and finds that from the point of view of consumption the family unit fulfils the same function for all classes. Organized along almost communist lines, its income tends to set an upper limit to size. But it does not set an exact upper limit since it is always possible by contracting the consumption of the existing members of the family, to provide for an addition. Now it might be sup-posed that the poorer classes would have a stronger motive than the wealthy to practise family limitation. But, says Fetter, such is not the case. Actually, it is among the well-situated that the fear of hunger is greatest. Their behaviour is characterized by prudence and foresight, by the ability to subordinate present enjoyments to future considerations. The same virtues which

[1] Frank Fetter, *Versuch einer Bevölkerungslehre*, Jena, 1894.

have made them wealthy are the ones which lead them to practise family limitation.

When the family is considered as a production unit, there is absent in the upper classes a motive to procreate which exists among the lower. Whereas among the wealthy an additional child not only increases the family expenditure but also fails to augment the family income for a relatively long period; among the poor, the children frequently supplement the family income at an early age. So it was that in England, with the introduction of machinery and the extensive utilization of child labour, the poor were given a direct incentive to procreate. Again, as Adam Smith long ago recognized, in colonies, children are wealth.

Another motive which leads the well-to-do to practise family limitation is inheritance. The prudent father knows that if his property is too greatly subdivided his children cannot maintain their social position. Thus in Germany it is often remarked that landownership reduces the number of children. Even when the inheritance is not in land the same motive operates, since capital constitutes a certain mass which must be divided among the heirs.

Among the workers there is no inheritance to divide. Further, an additional child can hardly be conceived of as spoiling the labour market for the children already born. Besides, Fetter continues, the burden of large families, so far as it adversely affects the labour market, is shared by the prudent workers. (Curiously, the type of inheritance bequeathed by the educated classes generates a similar attitude toward children. Fetter finds that in Germany, the large families of judges, clergy, and professors may be explained by the fact that the father gives his children good health, good character, and a good education as a legacy.)

Fetter denies that a rapid increase in income will be dissipated by a consequent growth in population. It is true that with the growth in income population will also increase but not, however, to the extent of preventing a rise in the standard of living. Moreover, the motive to maintain the new standard of living will operate as a check to further population growth.

Fetter concludes that although the Malthusian population theory has been shown to be erroneous, this does not destroy the validity of the population argument against socialism. For socialism would remove the responsibility for the care of off-spring from the parents and thus destroy the restraints due to voluntarism, i.e. prudence and foresight; when socialists recognize the necessity for population control and demonstrate that they have means for its solution which are adequate yet not detestable, then the population argument will lose its strength against socialism.

Shortly afterwards in the United States a theory of population identical with that of Fetter's voluntarism was advanced:

It is true that as society exists at present, high comfort and low birth rate are commonly associated, because comfort is made to depend upon prudence. . . . Both are the results of a common cause—the exercise of prudence, which gives high comfort and low birth rate to those who are capable of practising it. . . . It is not that social ambition *in itself* constitutes a greater preventive check to population than the need of subsistence; but that the need of sub-sistence is felt by all men alike, emotional as well as intellectual, while ambition stamps the man or race that possesses it as having reached the level of intellectual morality. Ethical selection can there-fore operate on the latter class as it does not on the former. The intellectual man has possibilities of self-restraint which the emotional man has not. Give the intellectual man the chance to reap the benefit of such self-restraint, and you will find reduced birth rate and increased comfort going hand in hand.[1]

The volitional emphasis of Dumont, Fetter, and Hadley excluded the proletariat from family limitation. Either from lack of prudence and foresight, or the impossibility of bettering their lot, the proletariat were considered incapable of subordin-ating present enjoyment to future welfare.

THE PRINCIPLE OF INCREASING 'INDIVIDUALITY'

In the last decade of the nineteenth century, the Italian econ-omist Francesco S. Nitti also discovered 'a new law of popula-tion', which, in the words of its author, 'we hold to be scienti-

[1] Arthur Twinning Hadley, *Economics—An Account of the Relations Between Private Property and Public Welfare*, New York, 1896, pp. 48-9. Fetter and Hadley's explanation of differential fertility was also accepted by Adna Ferrin Weber in *The Growth of Cities*, New York, 1899, p. 338.

fically unassailable, and largely proved by the most impartial statistics, (and which) gives a deathblow to Malthusianism and to the principle hitherto maintained by the classic school'.[1]

Nitti's work is divided into two parts: Book I constitutes both a critique of the Malthusian theory of population and an historical survey of population theories. The critique of Malthus is neither original nor impressive.[2] In the historical survey Nitti divides population doctrines into two categories, viz. the 'Philosophy of Wealth' and the 'Philosophy of Poverty'. In the first are included all those writers who, like Malthus, speak for and justify the *status quo*. In the second are found thinkers oriented toward the amelioration of man's lot, viz. Herbert Spencer, Karl Marx, Achille Loria, Arsène Dumont, etc.

In Book II, Nitti attempts to synthesize the contributions of the latter group. This leads him to the new law of population:

In every society where individuality will be strongly developed, but where progress of socialization will not extinguish individual activity; in every society where wealth will be largely subdivided and where the social cause of inequality will be eliminated by an elevated form of co-operation, the birth rate will tend to become equal with the means of subsistence, and the regular variations of demographic evolution, will not have, as in the past, an element of fear and terror.[3]

The great contribution of the biological theory 'conceived by Doubleday, afterwards perfected by Darwin, and precisely formulated by Spencer' is that individuation and genesis are in fundamental opposition. This law, which 'has the most absolute confirmation throughout the entire organic world', applies not only to the different species but also to the 'different races of one species . . . consequently the human races which have developed most are the least prolific'. Nitti also agrees with Spencer that 'Excessive fecundity has secured the march of civilization'.

The type of social organization is extremely important for securing the maximum of individuation. So present society is

---

[1] *Population and the Social System*, London, 1894, pp. 191–2.

[2] In particular, his naïve attempt to discredit the Malthusian geometric progression by the *reductio ad absurdum* that if population doubled every 25 years then in biblical times there could have been but one individual (Adam!) in the world (pp. 88–91).

[3] *Population and the Social System*, p. 191.

indicted for suppressing individuality or limiting its growth to the members of the upper classes. For the poverty of the lower classes, which is the major cause of high fertility, has been shown by both Marx and Loria to have its origin in present social institutions and not in the improvidence of the poor.[1] Moreover, Dumont has shown in the course of his discovery of the 'natural law' of social capillarity, that in our society the proletariat are excluded from its action.

What then is the desirable social organization? According to Nitti, neither a highly competitive one which destroys social solidarity by promoting a narrow egotism nor a completely communist society. Regarding the latter, Dumont is absolutely correct in maintaining that 'the socialist principle of the equality of function, if entirely applied, would necessarily imply the destruction of social capillarity and cause a high birth rate'.[2] The ideal society then is one in which wealth is diffused and social capillarity increased.

Such is the synthetic contribution of Nitti. All those who have dissented from the Malthusian school are appreciated.[3] So it is when Guillard states (*Eléménts de Statistique Humaine*, Paris, 1855) that population tends always to proportion itself to the

---

[1] Marx's theory will be discussed in a later chapter. According to Nitti, Marx's contribution was to expose the 'necessity which weighs upon *every capitalist organisation*, at the risk of perishing, of producing a systematic excess of population' (p. 134, emphasis supplied. This is a vulgarization of Marx's theory, completely ignoring the various stages of capitalist development which Marx stressed). Nitti follows Loria in objecting that Marx's theory is too limited by its stress on the technical composition of capital in industry (pp. 83–4, 132–6). Originally, Loria had emphasized overpopulation resulting from the alienation of land. Under the rent system a large amount of land is left uncultivated by the great proprietors, thus creating an artificial food shortage. Further, rent limited food production, since short-term leases provide the tenant farmer with no incentive for increasing efficiency by permanent capital improvements. Also, the system of *métayage* is based on a poor and ignorant class of cultivators who fail to obtain the maximum produce from the land. Later, however, Loria drops this emphasis, holding that it is no longer possible to speak of a shortage of subsistence arising from rent, since we are now confronted with an excess of agricultural production, an acute agrarian crisis, 'the granary of the world contains more provisions than are required for the nourishment of all the inhabitants, but the keys to the garner are held by the rich'. Achille Loria, *Contemporary Social Problems*, London, 1911, pp. 77–8.

[2] *Population and the Social System*, pp. 189–90.

[3] With the exception, however, of Bebel and Kautsky who are dismissed with scorn (*ibid.*, pp. 47–50).

means of subsistence, he (as well as Marx and Loria who show that overpopulation arises from social institutions) is correct; when Thornton states that if the world were inhabited by proprietors only it would soon be depopulated, he is correct. When Dumont traces the fertility decline to social capillarity, he is correct and has discovered the 'natural law' for all societies. However, 'the influences of the psychical-moral order, and the influences of the political order, are but slight compared to influences of an economic kind'.[1] Elsewhere we read that 'the solution of the problem of population, which has been scarcely anything better than utter darkness to the economist, is to be found in the biological theory, which . . . has revealed new horizons to demographic science'.[2]

In summary, Nitti having incorporated into his theory all the explanations adduced by others for the low fertility of the wealthy, finds, as did most of his predecessors, that poverty increases fertility. To this he has grafted Spencer's biological theory, Dumont's theory of social capillarity, and Marx and Loria's indictment of social institutions. In short, an Hegelian synthesis without the dialectic of negation.

THE THEORY OF INCREASING PROSPERITY

According to Brentano, man is essentially a creature of pleasure, and the key to differential fertility is to be found in the various sources of gratification available to the different classes of society. Therefore, the hedonistic principle has a material base —the economic means which greatly extend the range of possible pleasures accessible to the wealthy individual. So it is that 'differences of creed, occupation or domicile, which are adduced to account for differences of fertility . . . appear on closer inspection to reduce themselves to differences in material prosperity'.[3]

[1] *Population and the Social System*, p. 132.   [2] *Ibid.*, p. 167.
[3] L. Brentano, 'The Doctrine of Malthus and the Increase of Population During the Last Decades', *Economic Journal*, September 1910, p. 384. Originally Brentano had emphasized the distinction between the intellectual and non-intellectual individual as an explanation of fertility differences. (*Cf.* Ladislaus Von Bortkiewicz, 'Die Bevölkerungstheorie' in *Die Entwicklung der deutschen Volkswirtschaftlehre im neunzehnten Jahrhundert* (Essays in honour of Schmoller), Leipzig, 1908, p. 53). However, this doctrine was abandoned in favour of the theory of increasing prosperity.

Among the poorer classes, the number of alternative pleasures are strictly limited. So, for example, the high fertility of miners is traceable to their brutal and psychologically restricted existence. Books, travel, intellectual stimulation, and aesthetic appreciation are for the miner obviously not competing sources of satisfaction. Underground all day, spending long hours in arduous toil, he never sees the sun. Returning home late at night to his dismal hovel, the miner tends to find compensation for his deprivations in sexual indulgence.

Among the wealthy, however, the situation is altogether different. The number of competing pleasures are many and, in general, their gratification is found outside the home. Again, among the wealthy the feeling toward children 'takes on a new character of refinement' so that quality is emphasized rather than quantity. Many factors operate: the new status of women makes marriage less attractive to men of the upper classes; with democracy and the separation of the church and state, there is increasing difficulty in finding sinecures for one's offspring; the greater need for education and preparation for a career increases the burden of children, etc.

The general fertility decline is a function of technical, scientific, industrial, and commercial progress which has made new pleasures accessible to an ever larger number of people. But these pleasures can only be commanded if one has the material means. Man is confronted with a choice. He must limit the size of his family if he is to take advantage of the new opportunities for pleasure available in our civilization.

However, in dealing with the wealthier classes, Brentano is careful to emphasize that family limitation is not a virtue as it has been represented by the Malthusians. For when one has a choice between two pleasures and 'prefers one to the other, this is evidently in itself neither moral nor immoral'. Man limits his family when the sum total of his satisfaction would be diminished by an additional member. Moreover, 'the diminution of the birth rate which accompanies increasing prosperity does not imply an increase in sexual continence'.[1]

The difficulty in Brentano's presentation is that he does not differentiate consistently between sexual enjoyment and the pleasure of parenthood. For the miners, sexual indulgence is

[1] *Economic Journal*, pp. 389–90.

apparently identical with the desire for offspring; whereas, for the wealthier classes, the opposite is the case. Brentano might, of course, reply that sexual indulgence is the main pleasure of the poor and that ignorance of contraceptive measures leads to large families. But ignorance rather than pleasure, then, determines fertility among the poor. And since among the wealthy there is no 'increase in sexual continence', the choice is clearly between parenthood and alternative pleasures.

It follows that if Brentano's theory is to have generality the choice for all classes must be between parenthood (not sexual indulgence) and other enjoyments. But if Brentano maintains that parenthood is a positive pleasure for all classes, he must argue on the basis of the calculating hedonic principle that the large families of the poorer classes represent planned increments in pleasure!

RATIONALISM AS THE CAUSE OF THE FERTILITY DECLINE

Writing at a much later date than the cultural theorists previously considered, Ungern-Sternberg necessarily recognizes that a theory of population should explain not only the low fertility of the upper classes but, also, the recent fertility decline among the proletariat. His analysis proceeds on the assumption that since the causes of the fertility decline are not physical (biological), they have 'an entirely mental orgin'.[1]

However, prior to an elaboration of his own theory, Ungern-Sternberg emphasizes that the decline in the birth rate did not result from a shift in the age distribution of the population.[2] Neither has there been a decrease in marriage frequency, nor an increase in the age at which couples marry. On the contrary, in both cases the opposite is true. Further, a decrease in infant mortality is not a satisfactory explanation of the fertility decline, i.e. he rejects the thesis advanced by Wappaüs (*Allgemine bevölkerrungsstatik*, 1859) that with a decrease in infant mortality parents automatically embark upon family

---

[1] Roderich von Ungern-Sternberg, *The Causes of the Decline in the Birth-Rate Within the European Sphere of Civilisation*, Cold Spring Harbor, N.Y., August 1931, p. 86.

[2] *Ibid.*, p. 19. He finds that in most cases the shift in age distribution was favourable to fertility.

limitation: 'The cessation of procreation, in the absence of deaths, certainly presupposes the will not to have any more children than the minimum of 1 or 2 and just this lack of will, this restricted programme, must be solved.'[1]

Ungern-Sternberg denies that wealth or increasing prosperity is a necessary condition for low fertility. On the contrary, the majority of the inhabitants of such countries as Estonia, Norway, Finland, and Latvia are quite poor, yet their fertility is relatively low. And in Germany, after the first world war, both the standard of living and fertility declined together. Nevertheless, he concludes that there may be some connection between decreasing fertility and rising prosperity 'but that the causative factor is not universal'. Here he flirts with the volitional theories discussed above:

An unbiassed observation might tempt us to suppose that rising welfare is not the cause of the decreasing birth-rate but its result. In other words, one limits the number of births in order to be able to obtain prosperity. Prosperity, therefore, is not the cause but the goal, and birth-control the means for the attainment of this goal.[2]

Nor is urbanization a necessary condition for low fertility, since many predominantly rural communities are characterized by low fertility. Nevertheless, it appears that the city

is a particularly favourable soil, we might say a hot-bed, for a mentality which creates a decline in the birth-rate. . . . At the same time we must realize that the mere fact of a low birth-rate in large cities does not admit the conclusion that urbanization in itself is the cause of the declining birth-rate. Urbanization and the fall in the birth-rate may both very well be the result of a common cause.[3]

The decline in fertility within the European sphere of civilization has its origin in the development of a capitalist mentality which has permeated all classes of society. According to Sombart

it is the spirit of the earthly and worldly, a spirit of enormous power directed toward the annihilation of old natural structures, old traditions, old barriers, but also powerful in the reconstruction of new

---

[1] *The Causes of the Decline in the Birth-Rate Within the European Sphere of Civilization*, p. 40.
[2] *Ibid.*, p. 70.
[3] *Ibid.*, pp. 71–83.

Cultural Theories

forms of life, artful and artificial structures of utility. It is the spirit which tears humans from the quiet, organic love-relationship and companionship, and throws them onto the road of restless selfishness and self-determination.[1]

Among the bourgeoisie, the development of a capitalist mentality means that 'Everything impulsive, ecstatic, spontaneous . . . is gradually eliminated more and more under the influence of the developing rationalist spirit'. There develops a non-erotic (where erotic is not the same as sensual) matter-of-fact type of individual who carefully weighs all actions including paternity.

Such was the old type of bourgeois who 'dominated the nineteenth century. His counterpart in the twentieth century, while not possessed with the ideal of saving or earning, is driven by a lust for power. He has little respect for women and his interests lie outside the family. Moreover, the women also are infected by the capitalist mentality and become masculinized in their search for equality and independence. Such is the explanation of the low fertility found among the bourgeoisie.

Among the proletariat the situation is no different. Recruited from an agricultural population, the immigrants to the city consist largely of a group of individuals who desire to elevate themselves socially. These immigrants are an 'unsentimental, robust people, whose intelligence is awakened and who easily break off with their past, and usually adapt themselves to the city'.[2]

Further, while it is true that Marx, Engels, Lassalle, Bebel, and Clara Zetkin were all opposed to Neo-Malthusianism, with the growth of Revisionism under Bernstein there was a rejection of 'orthodox Marxism', a turning away from 'revolutionary methods to opportunism, to social reform'. This change signalizes 'the "embourgeoisment" of the socialistic movement'. The reluctance of the proletarian masses of western Europe to engage in revolutionary activity leads to 'a gradual synthesis between socialism and Neo-Malthusianism'.

Moreover, within the European proletariat there has developed a 'distinct upper class, an aristocracy of the working

[1] W. Sombart, *Der Moderne Kapitalismus*, Vol. I, Chapter 62, quoted by Ungern-Sternberg, p. 87.
[2] *The Causes of the Decline in the Birth-Rate . . .*, pp. 107 ff.

class' which, even if it does not vote for middle-class parties, 'shows arrivistic inclinations in all fields of its daily life, and quite particularly in its attitude toward the child-question'.

The proletariat follows the standards of the upper class. It 'has restricted itself in its entire style of living, to imitating in a general way what the bourgeois is doing'. Undoubtedly, this intensive desire for imitation has also, he believes, had a strong influence on their sexual behaviour.

But the explanation of the reproductive pattern of the proletariat is not found solely in their imitation of the upper classes. Rather, the turn from revolution to revisionism meant that the optimism engendered by Marxism, materialism, and reverence for knowledge, has been supplanted gradually by an increasingly sceptical attitude toward the future. 'Only the rationalistic conception of life remains unchanged and represents the most striking characteristic of the modern urban proletariat.'

In short, the explanation for the fertility decline during the last fifty to sixty years is to be found in the development of the 'striving, arrivistic tendency, the effect of a capitalist mentality'.[1]

It is clear that Ungern-Sternberg has but generalized the volitional approach of Dumont and Fetter. In order, however, to account for the decline in fertility among the proletariat, recourse is had to a capitalist mentality or spirit operating in all classes.

Obviously, it is impossible to confute an idealistic interpretation or theory which invokes an unquantifiable 'spirit' to explain historical changes in fertility patterns and existing fertility differentials. But the theory is open to criticism from the point of what it overlooks or fails to illuminate. Here it is of value to recall that Ungern-Sternberg rejected both urbanization and wealth as causes *per se* of low fertility. He emphasized the low fertility of many rural communities and, also, that poverty and low fertility were frequently concomitant phenomena. Now it might be thought that this recognition by Ungern-Sternberg of the failure of urbanization or material prosperity to provide a satisfactory explanation of fertility patterns would lead him to undertake such an explanation, consistent, of

---

[1] *The Causes of the Decline in the Birth-Rate . . .*, p. 131.

course, with his own theory of capitalist mentality. Such, however, is not the case. On the contrary, the reader is left to wonder how it is that at times the capitalist mentality penetrates more deeply the poor and rural areas and, at other times, dominates the wealthy and urban communities.

Finally, it should be remarked that, contrary to Sombart and Ungern-Sternberg, there is no evidence of a Paradise Lost—a period of 'quiet, organic love-relationship and companionship' —existing prior to the triumph of the capitalist mentality.[1] However, this will be discussed in a later chapter on the evolution of the family.

SOCIO-ECONOMIC STATUS

Regardless of whether it is asserted that increasing wealth lowers fertility by developing a more mature and deliberate mentality; or that wealth lowers fertility by furnishing the individual with the opportunity to experience new sources of satisfaction; or that wealth and family limitation are both effects of the will to advance: all these theories are united in recognizing that progress in socio-economic status necessarily implies a decrease in fertility.

Yet the inverse relationship between socio-economic status and fertility is not the simple relation it was once thought to be; and those who find their explanation of demographic phenomena in the general evolution of the mental processes of society, where the wealthy and cultured represent the vanguard of the movement, have not only to reckon with the fact that low fertility is a phenomenon frequently encountered in regions of poverty and ignorance, but also that increasing prosperity may lead to an increase rather than a decrease in fertility.

Investigations into the relation beween fertility and socio-economic status are complicated by the difficulty of obtaining adequate financial data:

Since fertility data have only rarely been available for groups distinguished by income or property, various indirect measures of

---

[1] Ungern-Sternberg waxes eloquent over a non-existent past when romantic love and marriage went hand-in-hand. He forgets that romantic love and adultery were inseparably associated in the pre-capitalist era.

'wealth' have been used. Moreover, the primary interest of some of these studies is a more general distinction between 'upper' and 'lower' classes of society—a distinction which involves other elements such as power or prestige in addition to purely economic factors.[1]

The difficulty, then, arises from attempting to combine in the socio-economic classification a qualitative judgment, social status, with a fairly precise quantitative measurement, income or property. For example, are professional people, earning approximately the same salary as those engaged in business, to be put in a higher or lower classification? Further, there would appear to be some difficulty in separating social from economic status in a 'pecuniary society' where, by and large, the two are identified in the public mind.

Studies on the relation between fertility and economic status, using such criteria as the average of assessed taxes or the proportion of 'professional' occupations, indicated that the poorer districts of Paris, Berlin, Vienna, and London had a much higher crude birth rate than the richer districts. But, on the other hand, other studies of a similar nature showed that the 'wealthiest districts had more children than those next below them in the economic scale'.

Studies of urban fertility based on income, revealed a decreasing fertility with increasing income up to a certain point, beyond which, however, the opposite was true. Again, some studies on fertility and income among the rural population show that 'the lowest fertility is that of a middle group, both the poorest and the wealthiest groups having larger families; in others there is a continuous decrease in fertility with increasing wealth'.

Nor are uniform results obtained from studies on fertility and occupation. While manual workers generally show a higher fertility than non-manual, nevertheless, 'the various groups of manual workers apart from those engaged in agriculture, forestry and mining differ widely in their fertility'. Further, studies 'in several countries during the 1930's showed that the old pattern of occupational fertility had changed. The lowest fertility was no longer found among "professional workers",

[1] United Nations, *The Determinants and Consequences of Population Growth,* New York, 1953, p. 86. The following material and quotations on fertility and socio-economic status are from the same study (pp. 86–90).

but rather among some other categories of the "white collar" group generally believed to have a lower income and "social status"—e.g. clerical workers, officials in public administration, owners of business'.

Other studies may be briefly noted. In urban areas, employed married women have generally a somewhat lower fertility than housewives. But in rural areas the opposite is true. Some studies suggest that with increased education fertility decreases. Other studies indicate the opposite. Religion seems to exert some influence on fertility, but is not of primary significance since fertility patterns vary greatly among people professing the same faith.

Such are the data on socio-economic status and fertility. What, then, are we to conclude from the contradictory results of these investigations? One possible explanation is that the fertility decline of the last quarter of the nineteenth century was essentially a cultural revolution, a transition from a large to a small-size family. In this evolution, the wealthier and more educated classes took the lead in the transition to the small-size family, and this explains the past inverse correlation between socio-economic status and fertility. Seen thus, the fertility decline of the last quarter of the nineteenth century constituted a shift to a different size family, the establishment of a new optimum. Now it might be further argued that this transition to a new optimum size family has been largely completed for a number of classes in society. In other words, speaking generally, whereas a hundred years ago the ideal size family was (say) eight children, it is now less than four. During the period, then, of the transition to a smaller size family, the wealthy and educated classes were in the vanguard, hence their lower fertility. But given the general adoption of a new optimum size family, economic conditions play an increasingly important role, i.e. those who are able to afford children now have them, and this explains the breakdown in the inverse relation between fertility and socio-economic status. Considered thus, the inverse relation between fertility and socio-economic status was a phenomenon of the transition only. Such an interpretation would explain the contradictory results of recent investigations on fertility and socio-economic status. The differences would be explained by differences in the stages of development. Thus, on the one hand, the inverse relation would dominate where the cultural transition was still in process; and, on the other hand, a breakdown of the inverse relation would signify the completion of the cultural transition or the general adoption of a new optimum size family. In the latter case, material wealth would determine the extent to which a family could realize this optimum. This, of course, involves the assumption of a historically determined standard of living, in the absence of which people refrain from having as many children as they would otherwise have.

But the plausibility of the above argument rests on the use of the term 'culture' which is invoked as the *deus ex machina*. It has already been noted that culture refers to an ensemble of material and non-material factors, in which the specific contribution of the members of the ensemble is left undetermined. Since the word 'culture' includes everything, it tells us nothing. In fact, the application of the cultural theory to demography leads to a special theory for each particular phenomenon. At one time the cultural explanation stresses education; another time—urbanization; another time—wealth; another time—decadence, e.g. the fertility decline among the wealthy Romans; another time—economic conditions, e.g. the abolition of child labour. In short, there are as many theories as there are cases, and the apparent generality is only achieved by subsuming all these different explanations under the general heading of 'culture'.

Another explanation of the contradictory results of the investigation on fertility and socio-economic status—and the one favoured by this writer—is that the criteria of wealth or income and occupation do not sufficiently distinguish the determinants of fertility differences. However, this will be considered later.

URBANIZATION

The influence of urbanization on the individual's attitude toward parenthood is a factor in the cultural ensemble accorded general recognition by cultural theorists. So, for example, in Dumont's theory of social capillarity, the flame of attraction burns more brightly in the city and, consequently, with the exception of the proletariat, fertility is low; whereas, in rural areas, where poverty, ignorance, and superstition abound, natality is high. And another French writer, Leroy-Beaulieu, attributing the decline in fertility to a complex of factors which he terms 'civilization', stresses urbanization along with democracy, development of the middle class, increased demand for comfort and leisure, feminism, the soaring of individual ambition, etc.[1]

In general, such urban characteristics as wealth, luxurious living, increased competition for social advancement, greater diffusion of knowledge, etc., are emphasized. So urban life is thought to develop a more rational, hedonic, self-seeking individual who, less fettered by tradition, naturally pioneers in the practice of family limitation. On the other hand, ignorance and an economic motive, absent among urban dwellers, maintain rural fertility:

> In most countries . . . there are very large differences between the fertility of urban and rural populations. The position in England is peculiar in that this difference hardly exists; but in England the rural population is largely suburbanized. Elsewhere, the rural population is more or less isolated and has less opportunity of acquiring birth-control information; moreover, where farms are owned by their occupiers a large family provides a cheap supply of labour.[2]

Again, high rents are recognized as increasing the burden of parenthood in the city.

To the extent that demographers stress social ambition, luxurious living, increased desire for comfort and leisure, conspicuous consumption, knowledge, etc., they are obviously committed to a theory which holds that rural fertility rates *ought* to be higher than urban. This, of course, does not cast doubt on the validity of their findings but, rather, tends to explain the great number of studies on urban fertility (i.e. true fertility after allowance has been made for the more favourable to fertility age composition generally found in urban areas). In other words, if, as the present writer believes, a theory has practical consequences and influences modes of investigation, an adherent of the cultural school of demography will tend to

---

[1] Joseph J. Spengler, 'French Population Theory Since 1800', *Journal of Political Economy*, October and December 1936.

[2] Carr-Saunders, *World Population*, Oxford, 1936, p. 103.

focus his attention on the significance of rural-urban differences in his study of differential fertility. But selection implies rejection and it is just this preoccupation with rural-urban fertility differences which may lead demographers to overlook more rewarding approaches to the problem of fertility patterns.

Writing in 1899, Weber summarized the available information on rural-urban fertility. For the United States, 'Dr. F. S. Crum has shown that in Massachusetts the fecundity of marriage increases with the density of population, and reaches a maximum in the largest city'.[1] While not subscribing to this theory, Weber's own investigation showed 'that whereas the number of births to 1,000 women aged 14–45 years was about 110 in Massachusetts in 1894–5, it was about 125 in Boston'. Nor was the difference in fertility due to the number of foreigners in the cities. 'That foreigners have larger families than the American is well-known ... (but) ... statistics show that native, as well as foreign women, have more children in the cities than in the country.'[2]

Nor did the European data indicate a generally higher rural fertility. For example, in Denmark (with the exception of Copenhagen) urban fertility exceeded rural. In short, Weber concluded that statistics did not justify the 'generalization that city marriages are less fruitful than country marriages. Indeed, the opposite is true in several countries, if the great cities are excepted.'[3]

For England during the period 1851–1931, Glass found

the highest fertility rate has not been associated with agricultural districts. ... The persistence of high fertility rates in Durham and Monmouth would seem to suggest an important connection with heavy industry, and perhaps also with the growing demand for labourers in the industrial areas. ... Other areas of relatively low fertility throughout the period were the Home Counties and the

---

[1] Adna Ferrin Weber, *The Growth of Cities*, New York, 1899, p. 333.
[2] *Ibid.*, p. 334.
[3] *Ibid.*, p. 333. Marital fertility, rather than the gross reproduction rate, is the appropriate measure of rural–urban fertility differentials since the gross reproduction rate tells us nothing about the sex ratio of a community. For data showing the predominance of women in urban populations in France and other countries, see Jean Daric, 'La Répartition des sexes dans les population urbaines. Cas de Paris et du départment de la Seine' *Population*, October–December 1952.

Cultural Theories

counties of the South-west (with the exception of Cornwall in 1851). In the Home Counties this might well have been due to metropolitan influences (though London itself was not generally the area of lowest fertility) but the South-west counties have long been agricultural. Among the counties the lowest rate has generally been found in Cardigan, another almost agricultural county.[1]

The Swedish data on rural-urban fertility are not conclusive. For 1895, Thomas found that the crude birth rate in predominantly agricultural communities was lower than that of all other communities.[2] Further, the data available for a number of counties on marital fertility for women aged 15–50 for the period 1901–10 confirm the findings based on the crude birth rate. However, to determine the effect of differences within the broad classification 15–50, Thomas calculated age-specific fertility rates for a single county, Västmänland, for the 1901–10 period:

... 'rural industrial communities are shown to have had a fertility rate 2·9% lower than agricultural communities. . . . To generalize for the whole of Sweden from a single county would be quite unjustified. The reversal of the differential in Västmänland, however, raises serious doubts about the validity of inferences derived from either the crude birth rate or the crude fertility rate for other counties or for Sweden as a whole.[3]

French demographic data do not support the theory of separate and distinct rural and urban fertility patterns. From Ariès we learn:[4]

1. That a comparison of natality by departments for the period 1801–10 with the 1938 rates reveals that natality has not fallen everywhere in the same proportion;
2. Departments with a high natality rate in 1801–10 were generally found south of a line drawn from the bay of Mont Saint-Michel to Lake Geneva where a 'combination of industry and agriculture permitted a high density in an

[1] D. V. Glass, 'Changes in Fertility in England and Wales', *Political Arithmetic: A Symposium of Population Studies*, London, 1938, p. 174.
[2] Dorothy Swaine Thomas, *Social and Economic Aspects of Swedish Population Movements, 1750-1933*, New York, 1941, pp. 323-30.
[3] *Ibid.*, pp. 331-2.
[4] Philippe Ariès, *Histoire des Populations Françaises et de Leurs Attitudes Devant la Vie Depuis le XVIIIᵉ Siècle*, Paris, 1948, pp. 386-417.

age when population was pressing hard, and sometimes exceeded, the level of resources';[1]

3. That by 1938 departments with relatively high fertility were no longer to be found in the south but, rather, in the north. Although there are exceptions, there is a large geographical coincidence between the regions of great industries of the north and east and the areas of high natality;

4. A comparison of a map of natality with a map showing the distribution of habitations indicates that regions with large village groups have generally sustained a smaller fertility drop than regions without large villages. In general, areas with the greatest decrease in natality are characterized by mono-culture, particularly the wine areas; whereas, relatively high birth rates are found in the great areas of poly-culture and crop rotation;

5. There is a close relationship between the mode of exploitation and fertility, viz., low fertility where production is carried out by the individual peasant proprietor, and high fertility on capitalist farms—both renters and agricultural labourers having large families.

Such is the evidence. Nevertheless, with reference to France it is held that 'an extremely rural composition of population is much more favourable to fertility than an extremely urban one'.[2]

Again, Whelpton made a study in which he divided the United States into agricultural, semi-industrial, and industrial states. Using the ratio of the number of children age 0–4 per 1,000 women 16–44, he found that *since 1800* agricultural states always had the highest fertility, next came the semi-industrial states, and last the industrial states.[3]

A United Nations' publication states:

The process of industrialization and urbanization which has characterized the development of many countries since about the

[1] *Ibid.*, p. 390.
[2] J. J. Spengler, *France Faces Depopulation*, Durham, North Carolina, 1938, p. 88.
[3] P. K. Whelpton, 'Industrial Development and Population Growth', *Social Forces*, 1928, Vol. VI, Numbers 3 and 4.

middle of the 19th century has been accompanied by marked reductions in fertility. There are adequate statistical data to demonstrate that fertility is lower in urban industrial countries, and that it is lower in urban than in rural parts of the same country, whether the country be industrially advanced or not.[1]

There is no point in multiplying examples of demographers who contend that 'one of the most important differentials in the birth-rate is that between country and city people'.[2] It is not a question of the accuracy of their calculations; rather the difficulty is one of definition. In some countries all communities in excess of (say) 2,500 are considered urban and aggregate urban fertility is found to be less than aggregate rural fertility.[3] Or the fertility of the 'great cities', commercial rather than industrial centres, is contrasted with aggregate rural fertility in order to demonstrate a lower urban fertility pattern.[4]

In summary, there is no evidence of separate and distinct rural and urban fertility patterns. Moreover, this customary division is indefensible since it abstracts from demography significant differences requiring investigation. Generalizations about urban centres indiscriminately lump together all localities with a population of more than some arbitrarily specified numerical value. Significant distinctions are obscured, e.g. the extent to which a city is a commercial, industrial or even *rentier* or tourist centre. Again, under the heading of rural fertility, *intra-rural* differences arising from size of farm and mode of exploitation are ignored.

Instead of such an analysis, we are presented with the idealistic notion that urbanization *per se* removes the clouds of ignorance by making available birth-control knowledge; or, that the civilizing effect of urbanization produces a more enlightened and responsible individual who, sensible of the parental

[1] United Nations, *Demographic Yearbook*, New York, 1952, p. 15. More cautiously another United Nations' publication states 'the relation between the process of urbanization and low fertility is complex. Families tend to be larger in certain highly urbanized countries than in some other less urbanized countries.' *The Determinants and Consequences of Population Trends*, p. 78.

[2] Warren S. Thompson, *Population Problems*, New York, 1942, p. 207.

[3] '. . . definitions of urban and rural population differ markedly in the various countries . . .' *Demographic Yearbook*, 1952, p. 15.

[4] See, for example, A. J. Jaffe, 'Urbanization and Fertility', *American Journal of Sociology*, July 1942.

obligation, limits his offspring in order to more adequately satisfy the needs of the first- or second-born; or, that workers in the city imitate their 'betters' and thus adopt the practice of family limitation, etc.

We conclude the discussion of urbanization with the following definitive formulation:

The idea that it is the 'urban mentality' rather than mere residence in cities which is responsible for declining family size has been advanced by some writers as an explanation of the earlier decline in fertility in France as compared with England, although the proportion of population living in cities was much higher in England than in France.[1]

[1] *The Determinants and Consequences of Population Trends*, pp. 78-9.

CHAPTER FOUR

The Economic Analysis: Classical and Neo-Classical Theories

HISTORICAL SURVEY

PRIOR to a consideration of Classical and Neo-Classical economic analysis and the implications for population theory, some preliminary observations are made regarding the general content of economic theorizing on the population problem in the post-Malthusian period.

The contribution of economic theory to population doctrine in England is well summarized in the following:

. . . when the Malthusian theory had once become fairly settled on its career it was found that the economists had absorbed it, and the study of population was by emphasis and tendency a quantitative comparison of human power to produce with human need to consume. The ranks of the opposition which launched its criticisms at the orthodox theory were on the other hand by no means regularly mustered from among economists. For a time their critical suggestions were utilized in rounding out the details of an analysis which might be called essentially economic; but before long the economic theory showed signs of saturation and absorbed little more . . . economic treatises on population more and more confined themselves to guarding the mummy of the Malthusian theory—revered, traditional, but lifeless because it did not continue to change to meet new conditions.[1]

---

[1] James Alfred Field, *op. cit.*, p. 83. For the sociological explanation of the almost immediate success of the Malthusian analysis in England, see H. L. Beales, 'The Historical Context of the Essay on Population', *Introduction to Malthus* (edited by D. V. Glass), London, 1953.

Similarly, German national economists remained through-out the nineteenth century under the dominant influence of Malthus.[1] True, some writers questioned the geometric progression on the grounds that it was not necessarily true that population has everywhere and at all times a tendency to increase at a constant rate; and, further, there was almost unanimous agreement in rejecting the arithmetic progression. However, the rejection of the arithmetic progression did not constitute a repudiation of the Malthusian doctrine but, rather, only meant, as in England,[2] the substitution in its place of the more carefully formulated law of diminishing returns. Consideration also was given to the counteracting tendencies which hindered the operation of the law, i.e. improvements in agricultural technique and the development of farm machinery; foreign trade or the drawing on the subsistence of another country; the possible increase in subsistence consequent upon social reform. It was also recognized that population itself was a stimulus to greater production since it made possible a greater division of labour. But, in general, these were recognized as qualifications which did not affect the substance of the Malthusian analysis. The German national economists also devoted much time and energy to a consideration of under and overpopulation. In general, they concluded that these concepts were necessarily relative.

In France, where widespread poverty and a dense population insured its success, the contemporaries of Malthus accepted the doctrine in full. So the economist J. B. Say, who 'was Malthusian even before he had read Malthus', believed that population proportioned itself to its products and substituted for 'means of subsistence' the term 'means of existence' which included everything capable of satisfying human wants. The French liberals also were Malthusian, but stressed the importance of education and the establishment of social conditions conducive to the exercise of volitional control among the general population. So Joseph Garnier, editor of the *Journal des*

---

[1] The following brief summary is based on Bortkiewicz, *op. cit.* The almost immediate success of the Malthusian analysis in Germany may also be attributed to social and economic conditions. *Cf.* D. V. Glass, 'Malthus and the Limitation of Population Growth' in *Introduction to Malthus.*

[2] E.g. John Stuart Mill, *Two Speeches on Population* delivered in 1825.

Economistes, was active in advocating the dissemination of birth-control information.[1]

But, as has already been noted, French natality was falling throughout the nineteenth century and it soon became obvious that the Malthusian analysis was not relevant here. So over-population came to be considered a remote possibility and instead the benefits of population growth were stressed.

But if orthodox economic theory added nothing of substance to population theory, neither did the pre-Marxian socialists. The majority indeed found further confirmation of the need for socialism in the Malthusian doctrine. In brief, they argued that since excessive poverty led to excessive fertility, it was only by eliminating poverty that the threat of excessive population could be surmounted. A few like Rodbertus denied the law of diminishing returns and, as had Engels before him, stressed the point that progress in science and production was geometrical. But while all has something to say regarding Malthus, there was no attempt to develop a general theory of population.[2]

But if neither the orthodox economists nor the pre-Marxian socialists made any notable contribution to population theory, the work of the economist Richard Jones deserves honourable mention. For, writing at a much earlier date and before the observed fertility decline in industrialized countries, Jones anticipated and discussed many of the points which were later emphasized in cultural theories of population.

To Jones belongs the distinction of first subjecting the

[1] Joseph J. Spengler, 'French Population Theory Since 1800', *Journal of Political Economy*, October and December 1936.
[2] *Cf.* Heinrich Soetbeer, *Die Stellung der Sozialisten zur malthus'schen Bevölkerungslehre*, Gottingen, 1886. Karl Kautsky at first accepted the Malthusian dilemma. In *Der Einfluss der Volksvermehrung auf den Fortschritt der Gesellschaft*, Wien, 1880, Kautsky granted it was indisputable that every attempt to improve the conditions of the lower classes would result in a great increase in population. Further, neither an increase in welfare nor intelligence would counter this tendency. For with increased welfare, the birth rate rises; and with increased intelligence, mortality declines. In short, on the one hand, Kautsky contended that only through socialism would it be possible to eliminate vice and misery; but, on the other hand, Kautsky acknowledged that the gains of socialism would soon be dissipated by excessive population growth. Hence, birth-control was essential to counter the threat of absolute overpopulation. Later, however, in the *Economic Doctrines of Karl Marx* (translated by H. J. Stenning, London, 1925, Chapter V), Kautsky no longer speaks of absolute overpopulation but confines his analysis to Marx's doctrine of relative overpopulation under capitalism.

Ricardian theory of rent to a searching critique, thereby demonstrating its historical character. Proceeding inductively, Jones argued that the methodological error of the Ricardian analysis was the tacit assumption that the laws regulating the distribution of national income in a capitalist economy had general validity. On the contrary, it is only in a capitalist country that the workers' subsistence depends upon the outlay or previous accumulation of capital. For more than nine-tenths of the world's population, wages did not vary inversely with profits, as Ricardo had contended, but, rather, varied inversely with rent. Now the importance of this objection for population theory lies not in the limitations imposed on the Ricardian theory of rent, which Ricardo doubtless would have conceded, but rather that Jones's inductive bias made him suspicious of any general or universal law of population.

Further, although Jones acknowledged the validity of the Ricardian theory of rent for capitalism[1] he objected to the use which both Ricardo and Malthus made of the law of diminishing returns:

> There is an indefinite point, no doubt, beyond which agricultural production cannot be forced without loss; but we must not, therefore, conclude, that man, with increasing knowledge and means cannot advance from his rudest essays toward this indefinite point without sustaining at each step a loss of productive power, and that he who extracts 40 bushels of wheat from an acre of ground is necessarily worse paid than he who extracts 30; and he who extracts 30 worse than he who extracts 10.[2]

Jones also rejected the Malthusian classification of the checks to population growth of vice, misery, and moral restraint:

> If . . . we include under the head of vice every voluntary habit, however free from moral taint, which increases mortality, and if, under the head of misery we include all causes of increased mortality which arise from the absence of more sufficient means, though free

---

[1] However, Jones denied Ricardo's thesis that the interest of the landlords was always opposed to that of all other classes. For given an increasing population, the *mass* of rent rises with every increase in productivity consequent upon capital accumulation. *An Essay on the Distribution of Wealth and on the Sources of Taxation*, Part I—Rent, London, 1844, Chapter VII. Part II was never published.

[2] *Ibid.*, p. 190.

from conscious suffering, we may certainly extend our notions of the effects of sin and misery to an indefinite extent. . . . In defining moral restraint, Mr. Malthus was unlucky enough to assert that, in all cases of abstinence from marriage, when the chastity of the parties is not absolutely impeccable, the sole cause at work to stay the progress of population is vice.[1]

In general, long before the law of diminishing returns is operative, man's great capacity for natural increase is limited by two characteristics peculiar to *Homo sapiens*: (1) 'knowledge and foresight which can discern coming evil and privation' and (2) tastes and wants which are both primary and secondary.[2]

Foresight and the multiplication of secondary wants ('something beyond mere necessaries'), particularly among manual labourers, means that population is not necessarily regulated by means of subsistence but, rather, by 'means of maintenance' which include both natural and artificial wants.

The conditions favourable to the growth of secondary wants among the working class are increasing prosperity, social mobility, emulation, and imitation which are facilitated by the presence of a large number of intermediate classes, education, etc. Jones concluded:

There seems no reason why abstinence, founded on plenty and on multiplied enjoyments, should not bring the progress of numbers to a stand-still. There are some of the better classes of nations who are confessedly stationary, if not retrograde in their numbers. May not all classes of a prosperous nation be found in this enjoying position? That is possessed of decencies and comforts in sufficient abundance to form efficient motives to restraint, and a sufficient guarantee against haste or imprudence, which would lead to their forfeiture.[3]

THE CLASSICAL SCHOOL

Subject to qualifications regarding the marriage of paupers or those considered likely to become a burden on public relief, mercantilist thought stressed the advantages of a large and

---

[1] *Lectures on Population* in *Literary Remains of the Late Rev. Richard Jones*, London, 1859, pp. 95–6.
[2] *The Political Economy of Nations* in *Literary Remains of the Late Rev. Richard Jones*, London, 1859, pp. 463 ff.
[3] *Ibid.*, p. 536.

growing population. Petty, the founder of political arithmetic, concluded 'that fewness of numbers is real poverty' [1] and before him Harrington had demanded that bachelors above the age of 25 be taxed double, but that the father of ten children should have his name stricken from the tax rolls. Harrington 'shared in the feeling of his time that, though no one knew exactly how many people there really were in England, it was better that the numbers should grow than stand still'. [2]

Along with an appreciation of the advantages of a growing population there was also a recognition of the importance of the demand for labour for population growth. As has already been noted, Arthur Young not only considered population growth an index of economic prosperity but emphasized that 'the demand for hands, that is employment, must regulate the number of people'. [3] Adam Smith, following Cantillon, [4] found the explanation for growth of population in the demand for labour:

Every species of animals naturally multiplies to the means of subsistence, and no species can multiply beyond it. . . . The liberal reward for labour, by enabling them to provide better for their children, and consequently to bring up a greater number, naturally tends to widen and extend those limits. It deserves to be remarked that it necessarily does this as nearly as possible in the proportion which the demand for labour requires. If this demand for labour is continually increasing, the reward of labour must necessarily encourage in such a manner the marriage and multiplication of labourers, as may enable them to supply that continually increasing demand by a continually increasing population. If the rewards should at any time be less than what was requisite for this purpose, the deficiency of hands would soon raise it; and if it should at any time be more, their excessive multiplication would soon lower it to this necessary rate. . . . It is in this manner that the demand for men, like that for any other commodity, necessarily regulates the

---

[1] Quoted by James Bonar, *Theories of Population from Raleigh to Arthur Young*, London, 1931, p. 86.

[2] *Ibid.*, p. 53.

[3] *Supra*, pp. 7–8.

[4] Richard Cantillon, *Essai sur la Nature du Commerce en Général*, 1755, edited with an English translation by Henry Higgs, London, 1931, Chapters IX and XV.

production of men . . . and determines the state of propagation in all the different countries of the world. . . .[1]

In the Malthusian analysis, demand for labour is also the determinant of population growth: 'What is essentially necessary to a rapid increase of population is a great and continued demand for labour; and this proportioned to the rate of increase in the quantity and value of those funds, whether arising from capital or revenue, which are actually employed in the maintenance of labour.'[2] But although Malthus believed that the supply of labour (population) basically was determined by the demand for labour, he also held that through moral restraint, or the prudential check, the supply of labour (population) could be checked so that every increase in the demand for labour would not produce automatically a corresponding increase in population. For Malthus argued that with the progress of civilization the population checks of vice and misery exercised a decreasing influence; whereas moral restraint—abstention from marriage for prudential reasons while continuing in a state of celibacy—became increasingly effective:

From 1720 to 1750 the price of wheat had so fallen, while wages had risen, that instead of two-thirds the labourer could purchase the whole peck of wheat with a day's labour.

The great increase of command over the first necessary of life did not, however, produce a proportionate increase of population. It found the people of the country living under a good government, and enjoying all the advantages of civil and political liberty in an unusual degree. The lower classes of people had been in the habit of being respected, both by the laws and the higher orders of their fellow citizens, and had learned in consequence to respect themselves. The result was that their increased corn wages, instead of occasioning an increase of population exclusively, were so expended as to occasion a decided elevation in the standard of their comforts and conveniences.[3]

---

[1] *Wealth of Nations* (Cannan edition, Modern Library), New York, 1937 pp. 79–80.
[2] *Principles of Political Economy* (second edition), London, 1836, p. 234 (Tokyo Series of Reprints of Rare Economic Works, 1936). *Cf.* also J. J. Spengler, 'Malthus's Total Population Theory: A Restatement and Reappraisal', *Canadian Journal of Economic and Political Science*, February and May, 1945.
[3] *Principles of Political Economy*, pp. 228–9. In the above quotation, one is remained of Schumpeter's comment that 'the only valuable things about

Ricardo also believed that demand for labour governed its supply: 'Every rise of profits is favourable to the accumulation of capital, and to the further increase of population. . . .'[1] But Ricardo was also concerned with the problem of a failure in the demand for labour. He believed that profits and wages were inversely related and, further, because of diminishing returns in agriculture, the natural price of labour must rise, i.e. the workers would have to receive a higher wage than formerly to maintain themselves at their old standard of living. But an increase in wages means that profit, which varies inversely with wages, will fall. However, since the fall in the rate of profit discourages investment there is, consequently, a decline in the demand for labour: 'In the natural advance of society, the wages of labour will have a tendency to fall, as far as they are regulated by supply and demand, for the supply of labourers will continue to increase at the same rate, whilst the demand for them will increase at a slower rate'.[2] Ricardo concluded:

> It is a truth which admits not a doubt, that the comforts and well-being of the poor cannot be permanently secured without some regard on their part, or some effort on the part of the legislature, to regulate the increase of their numbers, and to render less frequent among them early and improvident marriages.[3]

In short, two different approaches to the population problem are found within the Classical school. On the one hand, among the older economists there was the optimistic attitude which

---

Malthus' law of population are its qualifications'. *Capitalism, Socialism and Democracy* (revised, second edition), London, 1947, p. 115, n. 6.

[1] David Ricardo, *The Principles of Political Economy and Taxation* (third edition), London, 1821 (Everyman's Library), p. 281.

[2] *Ibid.*, p. 57. The statement that the 'supply of labourers will continue to increase at the same rate' does not contradict Ricardo's thesis that demand for labour governs its supply. In the former statement, Ricardo is thinking of the Malthusian tendency for population to increase at a geometric rate; whereas, in the latter statement, Ricardo recognizes that accumulation or demand for labour determines *actual* population increase.

[3] *Ibid.*, p. 61. It may be noted, however, on the basis of the Ricardian analysis, that the suggestion that the poor regulate their numbers leads to a dilemma. For suppose that population should limit itself in proportion to the decreasing demand for labour. In such a case, the increase in wages would be sufficient to maintain labour's former standard of living. But this would mean that the whole burden of the niggardliness of nature falls on the capitalist and, consequently, there would be less inducement to invest a further fall in the demand for labour.

saw in population growth an index of economic prosperity. In general, the belief in an automatic adjustment, that 'the demand for men, like that of any other commodity, necessarily regulates the production of men' generated no alarm, no strictures against the large families of the improvident poor. Thus Adam Smith stated:

It is the sober and industrious poor who generally bring up the most numerous families, and who principally supply the demand for labour . . . disorderly persons, however, seldom rear up numerous families; their children generally perishing from neglect, mismanagement, and the scantiness or unwholesomeness of their food.[1]

On the other hand, the Malthusian analysis, in spite of its successive qualifications, coupled with the Ricardian theories of rent and the falling rate of profit, leads to a certain pessimism. Stress is placed on the contradiction between the potentially great increase in population in contrast to the potentially limited increase of the means of subsistence. Doubts arise as to whether, without the checks of vice and misery, population can accommodate itself to the niggardliness of nature.

Finally, in the Classical school there was general recognition that demand for labour determined its supply; demand for labour, however, generally being treated as synonymous with means of subsistence.[2]

NEO-CLASSICAL THEORY

Prior to Keynes, Neo-Classical economists operated within a theoretical framework which, by its acceptance of Say's Law of Markets, postulated a natural tendency toward full employment of all factors of production. Following Adam Smith, capital accumulation was conceived as beneficial to labour since what was annually saved was annually consumed, i.e. all saving is reinvested and constitutes a demand for labour. And although this thesis was qualified by Ricardo when he recognized in the third edition of his *Principles* that machinery could lower the 'gross revenue' of society while simultaneously

[1] *Wealth of Nations*, p. 823.
[2] Among exceptions may be noted Malthus' later advocacy of an underconsumption doctrine which required a distinction between demand for labour and means of subsistence.

increasing the capitalists' 'net revenue', i.e. the income of the capitalist class could rise absolutely while total national income fell; in general, later economists were united in the belief that capital accumulation was beneficial to labour.[1] So in Neo-Classical thought the rate of wages is a function of the supply of labour—population—and the demand for labour—capital. Hence the acceptance of the Malthusian proposition that by limiting the size of the population it is possible to improve the workers' standard of living. That is to say, since wages are determined by the divisor (population) and the dividend (capital) it follows that by decreasing the divisor relative to the dividend, labour's standard of living will rise.[2] Moreover, the acceptance of the law of diminishing returns, coupled with the belief in a natural tendency to unlimited propagation, led to the advocacy of Neo-Malthusian measures.

The conviction as to the niggardliness of nature was not shaken by the existence of temporary periods of increasing real income per head. On the contrary, although the fortunate experience of modern Western European countries during the nineteenth century was recognized and appreciated, it was believed to be attributable to a particularly favourable combination of circumstances, e.g. progress in science, growth of international trade, perfection of other economic techniques, etc. But, according to the consensus of opinion among Neo-Classical economists, it would be Utopian to anticipate a future state of affairs characterized by so favourable a conjuncture.

The attitude of Marshall who exercised so great an influence upon Neo-Classical economics is of interest here, particularly

---

[1] In spite of his repudiation of the Wages-Fund doctrine, John Stuart Mill still concluded in his *Principles of Political Economy* (Book II, Chapter XI) that 'Wages depend mainly . . . upon the proportion between population and capital'. Quoted by Alfred Marshall, *Principles of Economics* (eighth edition), London, 1920, Appendix J, 'The Doctrine of the Wages-Fund', p. 824.

[2] Or alternatively stated: A relative increase in the supply of a factor of production lowers its marginal efficiency since, 'other things being equal, the larger the supply of any agent of production, the further will it have to push its way into uses for which it is not specially fitted. . . . The extra production resulting from the increase in that agent of production will go to swell the national dividend, the other agents of production will benefit thereby; but that agent will have to submit to a lower rate of pay'. Marshall, *op. cit.*, p. 537.

since, as always, Marshall took great pains to qualify his position.[1] With reference to Malthus, Marshall wrote:

His position with regard to the supply of population . . . remains substantially valid . . . it was not Malthus's fault that he could not foresee the great developments of steam transport by land and by sea, which have enabled Englishmen of the present generation to obtain the products of the richest lands of the earth at comparatively small cost. . . . It remains true that unless the checks on the growth of population in force at the end of the nineteenth century are on the whole increased . . . it will be impossible for the habits of comfort prevailing in Western Europe to spread themselves over the whole world and maintain themselves for many hundred years.[2]

In a footnote to the above Marshall estimates that given the present world rate of population increase (about 8 per 1,000 annually) and 'great improvements in the art of agriculture . . . the pressure of population on the means of subsistence may be held in check for about two hundred years, but not longer'.[3] Elsewhere Marshall emphasizes again that there is only temporary escape from the law of diminishing returns.[4] The position of England is especially vulnerable since her 'foreign supplies of raw produce may at any time be checked by changes in the trade regulations of other countries, and may be almost cut off by a great war . . .'[5]

The thesis of the Classical economists that demand for labour regulates its supply was not rejected by Marshall. On the contrary, in spite of the known fertility decline in the western world, the analysis remains valid:

Thus the question how closely the supply of labour responds to the demand for it, is in a great measure resolved into the question how great a part of the present consumption of the people at large consists of necessaries, strictly so called, for the life and efficiency of young and old; how much consists of conventional necessaries which theoretically could be dispensed with . . . and how much is really superfluous regarded as a means towards production . . . . throughout the greater part of the world the working classes can afford but

---

[1] 'It is hard to find any statement in Marshall without such a qualification as "nearly".' Talcott Parsons, *The Structure of Social Action*, Glencoe, Illinois, reprinted 1949, p. 144, footnote 2.
[2] *Principles of Economics*, pp. 179–80.   [3] *Ibid.*, p. 180, footnote 1.
[4] *Ibid.*, pp. 320–1.   [5] *Ibid.*, p. 322.

few luxuries and not even many conventional necessaries; and any increase in their earnings would result in so great an increase in their numbers as to bring down their earnings quickly to nearly the old level at their mere expenses of rearing. Over a great part of the world wages are governed, nearly after the so-called iron or brazen law, which ties them close to the cost of rearing and sustaining a rather inefficient class of labourers.

As regards the modern western world the answer is materially different; so great has been the recent advance in knowledge and freedom, in vigour and wealth, and in the easy access to rich distant fields for the supply of food and raw material. But it is still true even in England today that much the greater part of the consumption of the main body of the population conduces to sustain life and vigour; not perhaps in the most economical manner, but yet without any great waste. . . . It remains true that, taking man as he is, and has been hitherto, in the western world the earnings that are got by efficient labour are not much above the lowest that are needed to cover the expenses of rearing and training efficient workers, and of sustaining and bringing into activity their full energies.

We conclude then that an increase of wages, unless earned under unwholesome conditions, almost always increases the strength, physical, mental and even moral of the coming generation, and that, other things being equal, an increase in the earnings that are to be got by labour increases its rate of growth; or, in other words, a rise in its demand-price increases the supply of it.[1]

Marshall's distinction between efficient and inefficient labour coupled with the recognition that in both cases the earnings received barely cover the expenses of rearing is certainly significant for population theory. The statement that 'in the western world the earnings that are got by efficient labour are not much above the lowest that are needed to cover the expenses of rearing and training efficient workers' suggests an historically determined standard of living to which labour is held; and, further, that the standard of living of efficient labour, as well as inefficient labour, is directly related to the economic needs of society. Thus if a modern industrial community requires a literate labour force then, obviously, there must be some rise above the previously established standard of living which will now permit a worker a sufficient margin of income to support and maintain a child during his period of education.

[1] *Principles of Economics*, pp. 530-2.

Although not developed by Marshall, there is implicit in the argument an explanation of differential fertility. Efficient labour requires an objectively determined higher standard of living to insure its continuous supply, i.e. its replacement in subsequent generations. In terms of cost, the rearing of an efficient (or skilled) labourer will be some multiple (say 2) of the cost of rearing an inefficient (or unskilled) labourer. In order, then, for the fertility pattern of the efficient or skilled labourer to coincide with that of the inefficient or unskilled labourer, the differential in remuneration would have to be such that the efficient worker's higher income would suffice to compensate him for rearing as large a family as that reared by the inefficient labourer. In the absence of the full amount required to compensate him for the expenses of such a large family, we would expect the efficient labourer to limit the number of his progeny.

Subjectively considered, this lack of adequate compensation, or limited demand for skilled labour, reveals itself as a threat to the efficient workers' standard of living, their way of life; to which they respond by curtailing their family size. They, of course, are reacting to an immediate situation and are not concerned with the supply of labour in subsequent generations. But, *objectively considered,* their response means a curtailment of the supply of labour in the following generation.

The mechanism is simple and objective. The demand for labour of a higher skill determines a necessarily higher standard of living for the maintenance and replacement of this class of labour. Subjectively, there is established in the minds of these workers a new standard of living which to them, and rightly so, represents the minimum. A threat to this standard of living leads to family limitation, a curtailment of the supply of labour. It therefore follows that if it can be shown that there was a relative decrease in the demand for labour among industrialized countries beginning in the last quarter of the nineteenth century we have here an economic explanation of the changed fertility pattern which now distinguishes the 'efficient' labour of modern western Europe and industrialized America from that of the 'inefficient' labour of non-industrialized countries.

The emphasis on the importance of demand for labour on

its supply, coupled with Marshall's recognition that in general each quality or type of labour receives but the sum of the necessaries required for its reproduction, throws light on an apparent demographic paradox. For, it will be recalled, demographic investigations indicate that generally the higher the standard of living or income, the lower the fertility; but it has also been demonstrated that when fertility is standardized for occupation it frequently varies directly with income. In terms of demand for labour the explanation would run as follows: A certain historically determined standard of living is required for the reproduction of a certain quality of labour. The poorer members of a given group can only rear one or two children of the quality desired; a larger family would mean a threat to their standard of living and, concomitantly, an inability to furnish their children with the prerequisites for the trade. Obviously, however, the wealthier members of the same occupation can afford to have more children without jeopardizing their standard of living or endangering the reproduction of the same quality of labour.

Income then appears as but an approximate or rough expression of fertility differences. As an index of interoccupational variations, the inverse relation between income and fertility holds since the quality of labour reared usually involves a quantitative sacrifice. But within the occupational group itself, given the historically determined standard of living necessary for the reproduction of a particular quality of labour, the inverse relation between income and fertility is replaced by a direct relation between income and fertility.

But, it should be emphasized, although Marshall remained true to the Classical tradition in his stress on the importance of demand for labour on its supply, he did not draw the above implications nor pursue the line of inquiry further. He could not relate the fertility decline of the last quarter of the nineteenth century to a relative diminution in the demand for labour. His acceptance of a theoretical model which postulated a tendency toward full employment of all factors of production excluded such a possibility. The only explanation possible for him, had he attempted to find such an explanation, would have been to invoke the law of diminishing returns, a shortage of subsistence. But, plainly, this would have been in contradiction to the facts. In short, Marshall was barred from further progress in his study of population along the lines suggested by his own analysis because of the limitations imposed by the theoretical framework of Neo-Classical economics—a theoretical system which owes much to Marshall's articulation.

Neither the contemporaries nor the successors of Marshall made any further advance. The Malthusian analysis was retained as a theoretical framework, but no attempt was made to develop an economic interpretation of population dynamics. Rather, it was tacitly assumed that the demand for labour had been maintained but that somehow or other in civilized countries the causal nexus between demand for labour and its supply had been broken.

Edgeworth, following Sidgwick, brings forward once again the Malthusian spectre as an argument against the redistribution of income by taxation. Cannan in a review of a work on population in 1916, could still find it useful to couch his argument in Malthusian terms, and he omits to generalize for the world economy the trends he had previously forecast for the British economy. In general, therefore, the Malthusian approach was regarded by economists as a useful framework of analysis, and, in the writer's opinion, it is doubtful if it has been superseded—which may be interpreted, perhaps, as a criticism of current economic theory rather than as a commendation of Malthus.[1]

But if in the past the theoretical framework of Neo-Classical economic theory prevented any progress in the explanation of population dynamics, the comparatively recent evolution of orthodox economic thought now makes possible an economic analysis of population growth which is consistent both with the Classical thesis and with Marshall's observations on the importance of demand for labour on its supply.

In social philosophy and in its implications for public policy the fundamental change in formal economic theory may be characterized as the abandonment of a body of presuppositions sanctioning a *laissez faire* approach to economic problems. This revolution in economic theory was heralded by the appearance in the early 1930's of the doctrines of imperfect and

[1] Alan T. Peacock, 'Malthus in the Twentieth Century', *Introduction to Malthus*, p. 64.

97

monopolistic competition,[1] but was only successful following the publication and subsequent general acceptance of the 'neo-mercantilist' economic theory developed by Keynes in *The General Theory of Employment, Interest and Money*.

In the doctrines of monopolistic and imperfect competition it is formally recognized that modern economy does not correspond to the competitive model conceived by earlier Classical and Neo-Classical economists. Rather, attention is focussed on monopoly, duopoly, oligopoly, price leadership, and other forms of imperfect competition which are recognized as inherent features of the modern economy. No necesssarily harmonious result ensues from a struggle of entrepreneurs, or more exactly, organized businesses, to maximize profits. Over a large area of the economy, production is not regulated by a normal or average rate of profit but, on the contrary, is governed by the principle of maximum profits; the realization of which is seldom compatible with full utilization of all factors of production. Production below capacity, idle resources, idle capital, unemployment, social waste in retaliatory advertising which frequently has as its result the mere maintenance of an organization's relative position in the market, are but some of the symptoms. Suggested methods of government interference include nationalization or government regulation of monopolies; establishment of government owned competing plants; fixing of maximum prices to obtain full production by preventing a monopolist from setting a higher price which, while maximizing his profits, restricts production; intricate tax schemes which would penalize firms operating at less than full capacity, etc.

In the Keynesian analysis developed in the *General Theory* there is an explicit repudiation of Say's Law of Markets. Full employment of all factors of production is considered to be but one of a number of possible equilibrium points for the system and, in the absence of appropriate public policy, there is no particular reason why the economy should operate at full efficiency.[2] In fact, a knowledge of the determinants of aggre-

[1] Joan Robinson, *The Economics of Imperfect Competition*, London, 1933, and Edward Chamberlin, *The Theory of Monopolistic Competition*, Cambridge, Mass., 1933.
[2] 'With the passage of time, Keynes' demonstration that the economy is in equilibrium with less-than-full employment is increasingly considered his major contribution.' Seymour E. Harris, 'Ten Years After: What Remains

gate demand for goods and services engenders a certain pessimism. The aggregate demand for goods and services is determined by consumer and investment expenditures. Now, on the one hand, in the short-run period, as society increases its income, consumer expenditures increase absolutely but decline relatively, i.e. each increment to national income gives rise to a less than proportionate increase in consumption, or, in Keynesian terminology, the community's marginal propensity to consume is continuously falling.[1] On the other hand, however, the need for greater investment to counter the consumption lag runs into a difficulty. For the inducement to invest depends upon the marginal efficiency of capital or the entrepreneurs' expected rate of profit from additional investment. But with the movement toward full employment the marginal productivity of capital falls. In brief, in the short-run period, the maintenance of full employment is extremely difficult since consumption decreases relatively while the greater need for investment is handicapped by a fall in the marginal efficiency of capital. And in the long-run period, the situation is no better since although the consumption function remains stable, i.e. consumption rises relatively with the growth in income, a greater *absolute* quantity of investment is required to maintain full employment. Here again, however, the marginal efficiency of capital declines. For with the growth of wealth capital becomes more abundant while, simultaneously, the opportunities for profitable investment decrease. The difficulty arising from the fall in the marginal efficiency of capital is further aggravated by the existence of institutional rigidities which prevent the rate of interest from falling to the level where, given the lower rate of anticipated profit, it would pay an entrepreneur to borrow money to invest.[2] Remedies or meliorative

---

of the *General Theory', The New Economics: Keynes' Influence on Theory and Public Policy* (edited by Seymour E. Harris), New York, 1948, p. 46.

[1] 'All empirical evidence tends to show . . . that as income falls in the business cycle, consumption will fall proportionately *less* than income; and again when income rises cyclically, consumption will rise proportionately less than income.' Alvin H. Hansen, *A Guide to Keynes*, New York, 1953, p. 76.

[2] But note, however, that 'As a result of his [Keynes'] analysis we now place less emphasis than formerly on the rate of interest as a means of increasing the volume of investment . . . the contribution which the secular fall in the rate of interest has made to *annual* investment over the last century is surely negligible. . . . What is needed in order to develop a considerable

policies suggested by Keynes and his followers include an easy money policy to lower the rate of interest; government investment financed by extensive borrowing; progressive taxation with the object of effecting a redistribution of income in favour of those classes in the community with a higher marginal propensity to consume, etc.

For population theory the significance of the recent revolution in Neo-Classical theory is the recognition that the economy no longer corresponds to the competitive model which identified the growth of capital with an increased demand for labour. The formal recognition of the role of monopoly in limiting production and employment, and the Keynesian analysis that there is no inherent tendency toward full employment of all factors of production, make it possible (by recourse to statistical data) to demarcate roughly the historical period when, in general, the economic analysis which proceeded on the assumption of a competitive system had obviously become antiquated as an explanation of contemporary economic phenomena.[1] Moreover, if the general theory formulated by Keynes be made more general, so as to subsume the contributions of the doctrines of monopolistic and imperfect competition, further progress is possible. For instance, while it is generally recognized that the marginal efficiency of capital is crucial in determining invest-

---

flow of investment is a continuing upward shift of the marginal efficiency schedule such as may be caused by technological improvements, the discovery of new resources, the growth of population, or public policy of a character which opens up new investment outlets. The effect of *lowering* the rate of interest would quickly wear off in the absence of an upward shift in the marginal efficiency schedule. Thus, little can be expected for *continuing* investment from progressively lowering the rate of interest, even though this were feasible.' Alvin H. Hansen, 'The General Theory' in *The New Economics* . . ., pp. 138-9.

[1] Michael Kalecki concluded from an historical study of the relative share of manual labour in national income that in England 'the degree of monopoly must have substantially increased' between 1913 and 1935 as compared with the period 1880-1913. Kalecki finds a similar increase in the degree of monopoly for the United States during the period 1909-29. His general conclusion is that 'Monopoly appears to be deeply rooted in the nature of the capitalist system: free competition, as an assumption, may be useful in the first stage of certain investigations, but as a description of the normal state of capitalist economy it is merely a myth.' *Essays in the Theory of Economic Fluctuations*, 1939, pp. 13-41. Reprinted in *Readings in the Theory of Income Distribution* (edited by William Fellner and Bernard F. Haley), Philadelphia, 1946, pp. 197-217.

ment decisions, the rate of interest is not a decisive factor affecting the calculations of entrepreneurs. But if instead of the 'rate of interest' we substitute 'struggle for monopoly profits' the analysis becomes more realistic. Instead, then, of thinking of investment proceeding to the point where the marginal efficiency of capital equals the rate of interest, we recognize that while decisions to invest are governed by the marginal efficiency of capital, the marginal efficiency of capital or rate of profit necessary to induce further investment is itself a function of past monopoly profits. In this way, the Keynesian analysis may be generalized to take cognizance of the special contributions of the theories of monopolistic and imperfect competition. Moreover, the emphasis on the significance of monopoly profits on the decision to invest means that orthodox economic theory is in a better position to appreciate the great and original contribution rendered by Hobson's pioneer work, *Imperialism*.

CHAPTER FIVE

The Economic Analysis Continued: Marxian and Leninist Influence on Soviet Demography

SOVIET demographic theory, as represented in the currently available writings of Urlanis, Boyarski, and Shusherin, is based on Marx's and Lenin's analyses of capitalism. This therefore requires a general knowledge of Marx's theory of capitalist development and, more particularly, familiarity with Marx's doctrine of relative overpopulation under capitalism. But a knowledge of Marx alone is not sufficient, since Soviet demographers stress heavily Lenin's thesis of imperialism as the final stage of capitalism. The procedure followed in this chapter therefore is to begin with Marx, proceed to Lenin and, then only, to consider current population theory in the Soviet Union.

Marx's strictures on Malthus surpass those of Sadler. For whereas Sadler was concerned only to argue that Malthus had plagiarized the population theory, Marx denies Malthus originality in any field. According to Marx, neither Malthus' doctrine of rent nor the theory of population was discovered by him:

Malthus used this theory of rent of Anderson's in order to endow his law of population for the first time with an economic and real, natural-historical foundation, for his nonsense (borrowed) from earlier writers about the geometrical and arithmetical progressions was a purely chimerical hypothesis. Malthus availed himself of the opportunity at once. . . . A careful comparison of their work shows that he knows Anderson and uses him. Malthus was altogether a *plagiarist* by profession. One has only to compare the first edition of his work on population with the work by the Rev. Townsend to become convinced that he does not use the latter as raw material, as an independent producer would, but that he copies and paraphrases him, like a slavish plagiarist, although he *nowhere mentions* him, keeping his existence a secret.[1]

And the doctrine of overproduction has its origin in Sismondi:

Who would think at first sight that Malthus's *Principles of Political Economy* was merely a Malthusianized version of Sismondi's *Nouveaux Principles de l'Economie Politique?* And yet this is in fact the case. Sismondi's book appeared in 1819. One year later Malthus's English caricature of it saw the light of day . . . here too with Sismondi he found a theoretical foothold for one of his bulky economic tracts— in which, incidentally, the new theories which he had learned from Ricardo's *Principles* also came in handy.

Just as Malthus, when opposing Ricardo, fought against those tendencies of capitalist production which were revolutionary in relation to the old society, so with the unerring instinct of a parson he took from Sismondi only what was reactionary in relation to capitalist production, in relation to modern bourgeois society.[2]

As far as Marx is concerned, 'Malthus's only merit, as against the pitiable doctrines of harmony in bourgeois political economy, is precisely his pointed emphasis on the disharmonies'.[3]

Such briefly is Marx's evaluation of Malthus. Regarding population, Marx held that 'every special historic mode of production has its own special laws of population, historically valid within its limits alone. An abstract law of population exists for plants and animals only, and only in so far as man has not interfered with them.'[4] So the law of population under industrial capitalism is the law of a relative surplus population. This law comes into operation at a certain stage in the accumulation of capital, i.e. the law does not hold for *all* stages of capital accumulation. Relative overpopulation can only occur

[1] Karl Marx, *Theories of Surplus Value*, Vol. II, in *Marx and Engels on Malthus*, translated by Dorothea L. Meek and Ronald L. Meek (edited by Ronald L. Meek), London, 1953, p. 116.

[2] *Ibid.*, Vol. III (Meek edition, pp. 158–9).

[3] *Ibid.*, Vol. II (Meek edition, p. 124). Marx, however, could speak favourably of Malthus, e.g. 'all honour to Malthus that he lays stress on the lengthening of the hours of labour . . . while Ricardo and others, in face of the most notorious facts, made invariability in the length of the working-day the ground-work of all their investigations'. *Capital*, Vol. I (Kerr edition), p. 580, n. 1.

[4] *Ibid.*, p. 693.

after a qualitative change has taken place in the organic composition of capital.

Here it is necessary to understand the difference between the Neo-Classical and the Marxian theory of capital. As we saw in the preceding chapter, Neo-Classical economists followed Adam Smith in holding that capital accumulation was favourable to labour since growth of capital constituted an increased demand for labour.[1] Now it is just this thesis that Marx denied; for, he argued, capital accumulation may or may not be beneficial to labour. It all depends on the organic composition of capital, i.e. the ratio of constant to variable capital. For an increase in constant capital does not constitute an increased demand for labour. On the contrary, as defined by Marx, constant capital is that part of the capitalist's outlay which consists of means of production—buildings, machines, raw materials, etc.—whose value is more or less rapidly transferred to new commodities during the process of production. In Marx's terminology it is *dead labour*, i.e. the product of previously expended labour. The living labour expended in *previous periods* on the production of machines and buildings and in the obtaining of raw materials (e.g. the cotton which now appears as constant capital in the textile industry), or in the manufacture of goods destined to be used to further production in a subsequent period, now exists in the *present period* as dead labour, or labour embodied in the existing stock of capital goods. As such, it cannot be considered a demand for current labour. According to Marx, all that happens in the current period is that the value of this embodied labour is transferred to new articles of production. Thus, the value produced in the past reappears in the values of the present as when, for example, a shoe machine costing 1,000 dollars, having a life expectancy of one year, and capable of turning out 10,000 pairs of shoes before wearing out, gives up or transfers $0·10 of its value to each pair of shoes.

Variable capital, on the other hand, constitutes a demand for labour. It is that part of the capitalist's outlay currently expended as wages in the purchase of labour-power. It is the

---

[1] That is, in general, capital growth is considered favourable to labour. However, Neo-Classical economists recognize that labour-saving inventions, although not causing permanent unemployment, lower the marginal productivity of labour and thus reduce labour's share of the national income.

size of this fund which, as its name implies, is not fixed, that determines the demand for labour. Moreover, it is only through the employment of variable capital that profit, interest, and rent are made possible. For in Marxian theory, profit, interest, and rent are but divisions of a surplus yielded by labour over and above its cost of production. They are pipes, differing in size, which are connected to the reservoir of surplus-value. This leads us to the Marxian doctrine of exploitation.

As has been noted, according to Marx, constant capital creates no value, it merely transfers its value to other commodities in the process of production. Therefore, Marx argued, it is only through the purchase of labour-power that the capitalists, as a class, are able to make profits. For the labour-power which the capitalists purchase is a unique commodity which, in the process of production, creates a value greater than its own value, or its cost to the capitalists. The surplus which accrues to the capitalist arises from the difference between the value of labour-power (socially necessary labour-time required for the maintenance of the worker and his family at an historically determined standard of living) and the labour-time value of the commodities produced by the worker for the capitalist.[1] This difference, or surplus-value appropriated by the capitalist, is possible because the capitalist, having a monopoly ownership of the instruments of production, requires that a worker expend (say) 12 hours a day in labour to obtain (say) 6 hours consumption goods necessary for him and his family's maintenance. In short, if a worker requires 6 units a day for maintenance and can produce these 6 units in 6 hours, the capitalist, by virtue of his monopoly ownership of the means of production, will force the labourer to work 12 hours a day by only paying him half a unit per hour. Here, then, surplus-value is 6

[1] In view of the great historical controversy over the labour theory of value, the following comment by Joan Robinson is of interest: 'When you are thinking about output as a whole, relative prices come out in the wash —including the relative price of money and labour. The price level comes into the argument, but it comes in as a complication, not as the main point. . . . You assume away the complication till you have got the main problem worked out. So Keynes began by getting money prices out of the way. . . . But if you cannot use money, what unit of value do you take? A man hour of labour time. It is the most handy and sensible measure of value, so naturally you take it. You do not have to prove anything, you just do it.' *On Re-Reading Marx*, Cambridge, 1953, p. 23.

units, the rate of surplus-value or exploitation being 100 per cent.[1]

Since only variable capital constitutes a demand for labour, and only living labour creates value, it follows that in the Marxian analysis the organic composition of capital is extremely important, i.e. how the total value is divided between constant and variable capital. For, on the one hand, a relative diminution in variable capital means a relative decrease in the demand for labour; and, on the other hand, a relative decrease in the demand for labour, other things being equal, reduces the size of surplus-value, i.e. the reservoir from which rent, profit, and interest are derived.[2]

In order to appreciate the difference between the Marxian and the Neo-Classical analysis of capital and also the implications for population theory, let us consider first a case where the Marxian and Neo-Classical analyses yield similar results. In the first section of Chapter XXV, 'The General Law of Capitalist Accumulation', Vol. I, of *Capital*, Marx considers the growth of capital in the period of 'primitive accumulation'. Here the investigation proceeds on the assumption of a constant organic composition of capital:

Growth of capital involves growth of its variable constituent or the part invested in labour-power. . . . If we suppose that all other circumstances remaining the same, the composition of capital also remains constant (i.e. that a definite mass of means of production constantly needs the same mass of labour-power to set in motion) then the demand for labour and the subsistence-fund of the labourers clearly increase in the same proportion as the capital, and more rapidly, the more rapidly capital increases.[3]

---

[1] For Marx, capital is always a social relation and not merely produced goods used to further production, i.e. the bow and arrow of the savage. Capital to function *qua* capital presupposes a body of workers who, dispossessed of ownership of the means of production, sell their labour-power to the capitalist. Hence capital constitutes a certain historically determined *minimum* quantity, i.e. it must be sufficient to realize through exploitation a mass of surplus value which will not only satisfy the consumption needs of the capitalist but, also, suffice for further accumulation. Also, if the export of capital is a significant factor for a country's economy, it follows from the Marxian definition of capital as a social relation that an investigation of the effect of capital accumulation on labour must take into consideration labour's standard of living both at home and abroad.

[2] The effect of a relative decrease in variable capital on the quantity of surplus-value is discussed below in more detail, see pp. 115 ff.

[3] p. 672.

We can illustrate the importance of population growth in the period of early capitalism or 'primitive accumulation' by the following hypothetical case. First, let us assume for the sake of simplicity that all workers are equally productive and produce in a given period a value of 20 units. It follows that the greater the number of employees, the greater the sum of value produced. Assume further that all workers elect to work so that the wage rate is determined by the amount of variable capital divided by the number of workers. Now proceeding on the assumption of a constant organic composition of capital, (the ratio C/C + V is constant) the importance of the relation between population and variable capital can be shown in the following table where periods IIA, IIB and IIC represent alternative possibilities consistent with period I.

	A	B	C	D	E
Period	Constant Capital	Variable Capital	Population	Wage Rate B/C	Total Value A+(C×20)
I	300	900	90	10·0	2,100
IIA	450	1,350	135	10·0	3,150
or					
IIB	450	1,350	125	10·8	2,950
or					
IIC	450	1,350	145	9·3	3,350

	F	G	H	I
Period	Absolute Surplus (C×20)−B	Rate of Surplus-Value F/B	Consumption* of Capitalists and Retainers	Rate of Profit F⁄A+B
I	900	100·0%	300	75·0%
IIA	1,350	100·0%	300	75·0%
or				
IIB	1,150	85·2%	300	63·9%
or				
IIC	1,550	114·8%	300	86·1%

* To simplify, it is assumed that 300 units of surplus value are always consumed and not invested. Of course, a more realistic model would show that with accumulation consumption rises absolutely although declining relatively.

It follows from the above:

1. If, as in period IIA, population increases at the same rate as variable capital, the mass of surplus-value increases by 450; the rate of surplus-value, rate of profit, and the wage rate remain the same.
2. If, as in period IIB, population increases less rapidly than variable capital, the mass of surplus-value increases by only 250; the rate of surplus-value and the rate of profit both fall; but the wage rate rises.
3. If, as in period IIC, population increases more rapidly than variable capital, the mass of surplus-value soars to 650; the rate of surplus-value and the rate of profit both rise; but the wage rate falls.

It is evident in the above cases, where the organic composition of capital remains constant, that the results would have been identical if we had abstracted all constant capital and dealt purely with variable capital. The only difference, then, would have been that the rate of surplus-value and the rate of profit would have been identical, but so far as changes in the size of population affecting the income of the capitalists is concerned, the result is the same. It is clear, then, that the Marxian analysis of primitive accumulation, or early capitalism, when changes in the organic composition of capital are negligible, gives the same result as the Neo-Classical analysis which considers capital accumulation a growth in the demand for labour.

In the terminology of the Neo-Classicists, the situation IIB, where population increases less rapidly than (variable) capital, would be described as one in which the marginal productivity of labour had risen, or the marginal productivity of capital had fallen. Similarly, period IIC, where population increases more rapidly than (variable) capital, would be described as one in which the marginal productivity of labour had fallen, or the marginal productivity of capital had risen.

The importance of population for profits can be demonstrated more vividly by assuming a period IID in which, because of a plague, half the working population has perished. The amount of variable capital on hand is 1,350 units, but the labour force now consists of only 50 persons. Obviously, wages must now rise since we have assumed that they are determined by the amount of variable capital divided by the number of workers. But it is clear that this assumption about the determination of wages has only *limited* validity and in fact contradicts the other assumption that the workers can produce only 20 units of value during the production period. For the 1,350 units of variable capital divided among 50 workers would give a wage rate of 27 units, i.e. 7 units more than the worker can produce. It is obvious that the employer will not pay even 20 units since, as the saying goes, he is 'not in business for his health'.

The 50 workers can produce a value of 1,000 units (50 × 20) so the wage rate must remain below 20 units. But how far? In the Marxian doctrine of exploitation, the wage rate will be determined by the power position of the respective parties. As Talcott Parsons points out:

> The permanent importance of the Marxian exploitation theory . . . . lies . . . in the fact that, starting as Marx did from the element of class conflict, the centre of his attention was on bargaining power. Thus in a particular case he reintroduced the factor of differences of power into social thinking, which had been so important in Hobbes' philosophy and so neglected since. . . . The Marxian treatment of bargaining power is, however, not merely a revival of the Hobbesian struggle for power. It brings into prominence an element which had been lost to sight in the conflict between the positions of Hobbes and Locke, since this conflict envisaged a rigid alternative between a state of war and a completely noncoercive harmonious order. But actual society is neither. Even though the institutional framework is strong enough to keep the role of force down to a negligible level except at certain special times of crisis, and that of fraud within limits, it still leaves the door open to certain other milder forms of coercion.[1]

The shortage of labour resulting from the plague appears as one of those 'special times of crisis'. Wages cannot remain at their former level of 10 units, as in period I, unless the employers take drastic action. To prevent competition among the capitalists for scarce labour causing a wage rise, recourse is had to the state. New legislation is passed making it illegal for an employer to pay, or a worker to demand, more than a specified maximum wage. Labour pirating is prohibited and the mobility

[1] *The Structure of Social Action*, p. 109.

of the worker restricted. In brief, acts like the Statute of Labourers and the Statute of Apprentices are passed: 'The bourgeoisie, at its rise, wants and uses the power of the state to 'regulate' wages, i.e. force them within the limits suitable for surplus-value making, to lengthen the working-day and to keep the labourer himself in the normal degree of dependence. This is an essential element of so-called primitive accumulation.'[1]

Suppose we make the highly unrealistic assumption that the efforts of the employers are completely successful so that wages do not rise at all; nevertheless, even on this assumption, the capitalists sustain a loss. The 50 workers who remain are paid 10 units as in period I, or 500 units in all, and they produce a value of 1,000 units, or a surplus of 500 for their employers. The rate of exploitation remains at 100 per cent, but the *mass* of surplus-value has fallen from 900 units in period I to 500 units in the subsequent period (period IID) as a result of the absolute decrease in the labour force. Moreover, since variable capital has increased from 900 to 1,350 units in period IID while, simultaneously, through vigorous state action wages do not rise, it follows that 850 units of capital will lie idle $(1,350 - 50 \times 10)$.[2] The situation, of course, is much worse for the employers if, instead of wages remaining fixed, they increase.[3]

In Marxian theory, the importance of population for the profit position of the entrepreneur, then, is that given productivity and the length of the working-day 'Whether its limits are fixed physically or socially, the means of surplus-value can only be increased by increasing the number of the labourers, i.e. the

[1] *Capital*, Vol. I, p. 809. Also, *cf.* Chapter X, particularly section 5, 'The Struggle for a Normal Working-Day . . .'

[2] Actually more than 850 units will lie idle, since included in the 450 units of constant capital on hand are raw materials which, owing to the labour shortage, cannot be worked up.

[3] But, Marx emphasizes, even if wages rise and it is impossible at this stage of development to substitute machinery, the capitalist system remains intact: 'Either the price of labour keeps on rising, because its rise does not interfere with the process of accumulation. . . . Or . . . accumulation slackens in consequence of the rise in the price of labour, because stimulus of gain is blunted. The rate of accumulation lessens, but with its lessening, the primary cause of that lessening vanished, i.e. the disproportion between capital and exploitable labour-power. The mechanism of the process of capitalist production removes the very obstacles that it temporarily creates.' *Capital*, Vol. I, p. 679.

labouring population. The growth of population here forms the mathematical limit to the production of surplus-value by the total social capital.'[1]

As Henryk Grossman puts it: 'Population therefore constitutes a limit to accumulation, but not a limit in Rosa Luxemburg's sense, i.e. that the number of consumers (the customer) limits accumulation but, rather, that population furnishes the limit for value utilization (*verwertungsgrenze*).'[2] Here, then, is found the Marxian explanation of the mercantilist attitude toward population:

Only when one has first recognized the 'ravenous hunger for foreign labour' as the driving factor of the capitalistic mode of production, has one attained a correct theoretical base for evaluating the particular phases of capitalism. . . . For the whole period of early capitalism, for mercantilism, the populationistic orientation is characteristic. . . . In view of the almost constant technique, the expansion of production can only take place on the basis of simple extensive accumulation, consequently only through increased employment of labour-power. . . . From its very beginning it has nothing to do with the mystical question of the 'realization' of capitalist-produced surplus-value, it is not a circulation problem, a problem of markets but, rather, a production problem, a problem of the production of the greatest surplus-value.[3]

So it is that in the period of primitive accumulation, when recourse to machinery is as yet impossible, the problem of underpopulation, on the one hand, is solved by the enclosure movement which 'liberates' the serfs from their instruments of production; and, on the other hand, by 'the turning of Africa into a warren for the hunting of black skins'. Marx emphasizes that the history of Holland, the leading capitalist country of the seventeenth century, is particularly instructive:

Nothing is more characteristic than their system of stealing men, to get slaves for Java. The men stealers were trained for this purpose.

---

[1] *Capital*, Vol. I, p. 336.
[2] *Das Akkumulations—und Zusammenbruchsgesetz des kapitalistischen Systems*, Leipzig, 1929, p. 375. Our summary of the significance of population in Marxian economic theory has been aided materially by Grossman's work which, unfortunately, has not yet been translated into English.
[3] *Ibid.*, pp. 396–8.

The thief, the interpreter, and the seller were the chief agents in this trade, native princes the chief sellers. The young people stolen, were thrown into the secret dungeons of Celebes, until they were ready for sending to the slave-ships. . . . Wherever they set foot, devastation and depopulation followed. Banjuwangi, a province of Java, in 1750 numbered over 80,000, in 1811 only 18,000. Sweet Commerce![1]

Such, briefly, is the Marxian analysis of the significance of population in the period of primitive accumulation. As was shown by the illustrative cases considered above, the Marxian and Neo-Classical analyses of the influence of population on profit and wages yield similar results for the period of early capitalism. Nevertheless, it would be as great a mistake to over-emphasize this area of agreement, as it would be to ignore it.

The differences between the two schools is patent if we consider again the situation IIB above where population increased less rapidly than capital. For Neo-Classicists this is the favourable position for labour and, other things being equal, labour's share of the national income will rise. Marxists, too, would recognize this tendency but would argue that the proviso 'other things being equal' is unrealistic since it abstracts from the problem (or breaks off the analysis just where further inquiry is necessary) the social significance of class conflict. For, as has already been noted, the Marxian doctrine of exploitation with its stress on bargaining position, focuses attention on differences in power. According to Marx, the state is not an independent authority, an impartial arbiter between classes whose function is basically to ensure the continuity of society in general. On the contrary, to employ Laski's expression, it is the supreme coercive power of the dominant class. As such, an unfavourable ratio for the employers between population and capital will lead to action by the state directed toward solving the problem of underpopulation. Evidence for this, of course, Marxists find in the state policies pursued during the period of mercantilism. Hence, it follows that even in the period of primitive accumulation when any large-scale substitution of machinery for men is

[1] *Capital*, Vol. I, p. 824. 'Liverpool employed in the slave trade, in 1730, 15 ships; in 1751, 53; in 1760, 74; in 1770, 96; and in 1792, 132.' *Ibid.*, p. 833. Grossman estimated that at the beginning of the nineteenth century there were 7 million slaves in the European colonial districts. *Op. cit.*, p. 413.

impossible, Marxists would be sceptical of the efficacy of Neo-Malthusian measures to improve labour's standard of living.

In summary, for the period of early capitalism or 'primitive accumulation' the Neo-Classical and Marxian analyses of the population-capital ratio yield similar results. Such, however, is no longer the case when we turn to a later stage in the Marxian schema of capitalist evolution, viz. the period of industrial capitalism when the law of relative overpopulation comes into operation.

Since for Marx only variable capital constitutes a demand for labour it follows that in the period of industrial capitalism, which is governed by the 'law of the progressive increase in constant capital', accumulation and unemployment are inseparably linked together:

> With the advance of accumulation, therefore, the proportion of constant to variable capital changes. It was originally say 1:1, it now becomes successively 2 : 1, 3 : 1, 4 : 1, 5 : 1, 7 : 1. . . . Since the demand for labour is determined not by the amount of capital as a whole, but by its variable constituent alone, that demand falls progressively with the increase of the total capital, instead of, as previously assumed, rising in proportion to it. It falls relatively to the magnitude of the total capital, and at an accelerated rate, as this magnitude increases. With the growth of the total capital, its variable constituent or the labour incorporated in it, also does increase, but in a constantly diminishing proportion. . . . The labouring population therefore produces, along with the accumulation of capital produced by it, the means by which itself is made relatively superfluous, is turned into a relative surplus population ; and it does this to an always increasing extent. This is the law of population peculiar to the capitalist mode of production.[1]

So it is that the mercantilist policies restricting emigration, and establishing minimum hours and maximum wages were no longer necessary. The process of accumulation now solves the problem of a cheap and abundant supply of labour. Wages are held in check

by the expansion and contraction of the industrial reserve army, and these again correspond to the periodic changes of the industrial cycle. They are, therefore, not determined by the variations of the absolute

---

[1] *Capital*, Vol. I, pp. 690–3.

number of the working population, but by the varying proportions in which the working class is divided into active and reserve army . . . by the extent to which it is now absorbed, now set free.[1]

Since wages are not regulated by changes in the absolute number of workers, but by the ratio of employed to unemployed, Marx is contemptuous of 'the economic wisdom that preaches to the labourers the accommodation of their numbers to the requirements of capital'.[2]

Whereas in Classical and Neo-Classical thought the standard of living of the workers is either temporarily or permanently improved by a decrease in the ratio of population to capital; for Marx, a decrease in the ratio of population to capital has no such beneficial results. For although it is true that if the supply of labour is short relative to the demands of variable capital, wages will rise; nevertheless, the rise in wages stimulates the employers to substitute machinery which, in turn, lowers wages. In fact, in the Marxian analysis, a shortage of labour relative to the needs of capital may result in overpopulation. For, on the one hand, high wages lead to the substitution of machinery for labour and therefore unemployment; and/or, on the other hand, high wages lower the tempo of accumulation, capital is withheld from investment and consequently unemployment (overpopulation) results.

Actually the whole Malthusian analysis is reversed. Once it is recognized that accumulation or investment depends on profits, and profits are seen to be greatly influenced by the ratio of population to variable capital, it follows that if it were possible for the workers to heed the advice of the Neo-Malthusians and restrict their numbers, the workers would soon find themselves unemployed. To repeat, in the Marxian analysis, relative underpopulation leads to relative overpopulation.

The model utilized above illustrates the Marxian analysis of the significance of population growth for the profit position of the entrepreneurs in the period of early capitalism. It will be recalled that on the assumption of a constant organic composition of capital we arrived at the following conclusions:

1. The *most profitable* position for entrepreneurs was when

---

[1] *Capital*, Vol. I, p. 699.
[2] *Ibid.*, p. 707. *Cf.* also Vol. III, pp. 260-2.

population increased more rapidly than variable capital (period IIC); and

2. If population increased proportionately with the growth of variable capital (period IIA), the rate of profit remained constant while the mass of surplus-value increased.

The question that now arises is whether the conclusions reached on the assumption of a constant organic composition of capital have value for the period of industrial capitalism which is governed by the 'law of progressive increase in constant capital'. Specifically, what happens to the rate of profit when, given a rising organic composition of capital, population increases proportionately with the growth in variable capital?

It will be recalled that in Marxian theory the rate of profit is determined by the ratio of surplus-value to constant plus variable capital. For example, if constant capital is equal to 500 and variable capital also equals 500, then, assuming the rate of exploitation is 100 per cent, the mass of surplus-value will equal 500. Here the rate of profit is 50 per cent, $\left(\dfrac{500}{500 + 500}\right)$. Now a rise in the organic composition of capital means an increase in the ratio of constant to variable capital, $C/C + V$, which is normally accompanied by an absolute growth in V. If we assume now a 20 per cent increase in constant capital and a 10 per cent increase in variable capital we get the following figures: constant capital, 600; variable capital, 550. Assuming the rate of exploitation remains unchanged at 100 per cent and, further, that population has grown proportionately with the increase in variable capital so that there is no tendency for wages to rise, then the mass of surplus-value will have increased to 550. But this means a fall in the rate of profit from 50 per cent, $\left(\dfrac{500}{500 + 500}\right)$, to 47·8 per cent, $\left(\dfrac{550}{600 + 550}\right)$. It follows then that one of the conclusions reached on the assumption of a constant organic composition of capital is not applicable to the situation where the organic composition of capital is rising. For, given a rising organic composition of capital, it is no longer true that if population increases proportionately with the growth of variable capital, so

115

that the rate of exploitation remains the same, the rate of profit remains stable. Rather, the rate of profit will fall unless the rate of exploitation rises sufficiently to counteract the fall in the rate of profit due to the higher organic composition of capital.

Will the rate of exploitation rise sufficiently to counteract this tendency? Now according to Marx, there are a number of ways by which the rate of exploitation can be raised, viz. lengthening the working-day; increasing the intensity of labour, or the 'speed-up'; depression of wages below their value; an increase in productivity which by cheapening the necessities required for the maintenance of the worker lowers the value of labour-power; foreign trade which also has the same effect since it makes possible the purchase of necessities at a lower price. Also, the fall in the rate of profit may be counteracted by the export of capital which (1) permits a higher rate of exploitation abroad, and (2) reduces the organic composition of capital at home. Further, as Engels pointed out, the rate of profit can be increased by the extension of the market, improvement in transportation, growth of middle-men, only however, in so far as these developments operate to shorten the period of capital-turnover.[1] An increase in productivity, besides cheapening the value of labour-power, also tends to counteract the fall in the rate of profit by cheapening the value of constant capital. That is, through increased productivity the physical or technical increase in constant capital, the ratio $C/C + V$ measured in physical units or what Marx calls the technical composition of capital, is far greater than the increase in the organic composition, i.e. the ratio $C/C + V$ expressed in value terms. Nevertheless, in spite of all these counteracting tendencies, Marx assumed that the rate of profit would fall. His exposition of the tendency for a fall in the rate of profit proceeded on the assumption that the rate of exploitation remained constant.[2]

But writers both sympathetic and hostile to Marx have argued that this was an illegitimate assumption. Their objection

---

[1] *Capital*, Vol. III, Chapter IV. The entire chapter was written by Engels, who stated in the preface that 'Nothing was available for chapter IV but the title' (p. 13).
[2] *Capital*, Vol. III, Chapter XIII.

is that a rise in the organic composition of capital implies an increase in productivity and, therefore, a rise in the rate of exploitation. In brief, it is argued that Marx's assumption of a constant rate of exploitation contradicts the assumption of a rising organic composition of capital.[1] This objection to Marx's assumption of a falling rate of profit has vital significance for the Marxist-Leninist theory of population. For if the rate of exploitation rises *pari passu* with a rise in the organic composition of capital, the conclusions reached earlier on the assumption of a constant organic composition of capital regarding the importance of the population-capital ratio no longer hold for the period of industrial capitalism. For if population fails to increase as rapidly as variable capital (position most favourable to labour in the period of primitive accumulation) entrepreneurs can now substitute machinery which will result either in the rate of profit being maintained or raised. But what does this mean? It would seem to follow that there is no longer a population problem in the period of industrial capitalism.[2] In short, this interpretation of Marx's theory leads to the conclusion that the capitalist system has been immeasurably strengthened by the introduction of machinery. While fluctuations or business cycles are not eliminated, and the rate of profit can fall in the short-run period prior to the introduction of machinery which sets all right again: nevertheless, according to this interpretation, the system is fundamentally stable since it contains within itself a mechanism for the automatic restoration of the rate of profit.[3] It seems desirable, therefore, to consider further the question of productivity and its influence on the rate of profit.

We have seen that according to Marx an increase in

[1] 'It would appear, therefore, that Marx was hardly justified, even in terms of his own theoretical system, in assuming a constant rate of surplus-value simultaneously with a rising organic composition of capital.' Paul M. Sweezy, *The Theory of Capitalist Development*, London, 1946, p. 102.

[2] Substitution of machinery for labour temporarily raises or maintains the rate of profit since the resulting overpopulation either reduces wages or prevents them from rising. But the point is this: Does the substitution of machinery itself tend to lower the rate of profit? If not, then considering production of surplus value only, there can hardly be said to be a population problem in the period of industrial capitalism.

[3] Such essentially is Sweezy's view. *Cf., op. cit.*, Chapter IX, pp. 147 ff. For Sweezy the difficulty of the capitalist system seems to resolve itself fundamentally into a problem of underconsumption. Regarding Sweezy's underconsumption doctrine, see below, pp. 120 ff.

productivity by cheapening the elements of constant capital can counteract somewhat the great increase in the physical volume of constant capital over variable capital, i.e. the technical composition of capital. Nevertheless, increased productivity only operates as a brake on the rise in the organic composition of capital, i.e. the value expression reflects, somewhat imperfectly, changes in the technical composition of capital. The point then is this, given a rise in the organic composition of capital, does increased productivity cheapen the value of labour-power so as to permit a rise in the rate of exploitation sufficient to maintain the rate of profit or raise it above its former level?

On what grounds did Marx assume that the value of labour-power did not fall in proportion to the general increase in productivity? Although Marx did not state specifically his reasons for this assumption, there is, we believe, sufficient evidence throughout *Capital* to indicate his line of reasoning. In the first place, 'an increase in the productiveness of labour in those branches of industry which supply neither the necessaries of life, nor the means of production for such necessaries, leaves the value of labour-power undisturbed'.[1] Would Marx have believed that increased productivity would be reflected equally in both producer and consumer goods departments; or, if not, that the greater gains in productivity accrue to the department supplying means of consumption to the workers? On the contrary, Marx's whole theory of development *in the period of industrial capitalism* assumes a lag in the application of capitalist techniques of production to agriculture.[2] For example, absolute rent is only possible, according to Marx, when the organic composition of capital in agriculture is below that of industry.[3] Again, Marx was at pains to emphasize that while Ricardo was correct in stressing that through the repeal of the corn laws the value of labour-power could be reduced, he argued that Ricardo overlooked an important qualification:

If the value of labour-power be 4 shillings . . . and the surplus-value be 2 shillings . . . and if, in consequence an increase in the

---

[1] *Capital*, Vol. I, p. 346.
[2] '. . . the capture of agriculture by the capitalist mode of production, the transformation of independently producing farmers into wage workers, is in fact the last conquest of this mode of production.' *Capital*, Vol. III, p. 761. [3] Vol. III, Chapter XLV, particularly pp. 885-7.

productiveness of labour, the value of the labour-power falls to 3 shillings . . . the surplus value will rise to 3 shillings. . . . The same quantity, 1 shilling . . . is added in one case and subtracted in the other. But the proportional change in magnitude is different in each case. While the value of the labour-power falls from 4 shillings to 3, i.e. by ¼ or 25%, the surplus-value rises from 2 shillings to 3, i.e. by ½ or 50%. It therefore follows that the proportional increase in the productiveness of labour, depends on the original magnitude of that portion of the working day which embodies itself in surplus-value; *the smaller that portion, the greater is the proportional change; the greater that portion, the less is the proportional change.*[1]

In other words, it follows from Marx's analysis that even *if* every increase in productivity resulted in a cheapening of the value of labour-power this would not lead to a corresponding increase in surplus-value. Rather, we have here a case of the law of diminishing returns.

The fact is that although travelling by different routes both Neo-Classical and Marxiàn economic theory hold that for the period of industrial capitalism, progress in industry surpasses that of agriculture. Both theories acknowledge, of course, such favourable developments as the opening of new areas of subsistence, e.g. the impact of American corn and wheat on the world market. But such favourable conjunctures are recognized as exceptional. According to Marx, agriculture must take the path of capitalist development, but, nevertheless, it lags behind the progress in industry.[2] According to Neo-Classical theory, the law of diminishing returns holds in agriculture:

The law of diminishing returns in primary production is often regarded as axiomatic. Nothing should be regarded as axiomatic in economics, but in this case we have found remarkable evidence from every angle to convince us of its truth. Regarding increasing returns in manufacturing production, the evidence has been found to be generally satisfactory, though by no means without exceptions or qualifications.[3]

---

[1] *Capital*, Vol. I, p. 57 My italics. *Cf.* also Vol. III (p. 269), where Marx considers a hypothetical case where increased productivity could maintain or even raise the rate of profit.

[2] However, Marx did not exclude the possibility of diminishing returns in agriculture. *Cf.* Vol. III (pp. 890-1), where he contrasts social and natural productivity.

[3] Colin Clark, *The Conditions of Economic Progress*, London, 1940, pp. 340-1.

Besides agricultural production, the question of housing which frequently requires an expenditure of more than 20 per cent of a worker's income is important in determining the value of labour-power. But has there been any advance in the building industry comparable to that (say) achieved by the automobile industry? On the contrary, the opposite is the case and it has been estimated by an official in the automobile industry that if American automobiles were produced by methods comparable to those followed in residential construction, the price of a low-cost automobile would be around $60,000.[1]

In summary, it follows both from Marx's specific observations and from his general view of the evolution of industrial capitalism that he could not assume a rise in the rate of exploitation *pari passu* with every increase in the organic composition of capital. It further follows that in Marxian economic theory the population-capital ratio retains its significance in the period of industrial capitalism. But, unlike in the period of early capitalism, if population and variable capital increase at the same rate, the rate of profit tends to fall in the period of industrial capitalism. Finally, the general conclusion still holds that if population grows more rapidly than variable capital, the situation is most favourable from the point of view of investment.

It will be noted that the above discussion of the significance of population for Marxian economic theory has excluded from consideration the effect of population changes on consumption. Our reason for this is that we do not believe that in Marxian economic theory underconsumption plays a leading part. This, of course, is not to deny underconsumption any influence but, rather, to stress the fact that in Marxian economic theory it plays a subordinate and not a crucial role. However, Sweezy recently has attempted to develop a Marxian doctrine of underconsumption which for him appears to be of the highest significance since he does not believe that there is any tendency for the rate of profit to fall in the long-run period. It seems desirable therefore, prior to a consideration of Lenin's contribution to Marxist-Leninist population theory, to consider briefly Sweezy's underconsumption theory.

[1] *Cf.* Charles Abrams, 'The Residential Construction Industry', in *The Structure of American Industry* (edited by Walter Adams), New York, 1950, p. 132.

According to Sweezy, 'capitalism has an inherent *tendency* to expand the capacity to produce consumption goods more rapidly than the demand for consumption goods'.[1] For Marx has shown that the process of accumulation is as follows:

1. Part of the surplus-value extracted from the workers goes to increase the consumption of the capitalist.
2. Another part is utilized to augment the quantity of variable capital, all of which in turn may be assumed to be expended by the workers in the purchase of consumption goods.
3. A third part of the surplus-value is devoted to the increase of constant capital, the corresponding term for which in modern business cycle literature is investment.

Now the consumption of the capitalist class while increasing absolutely, decreases relatively, i.e. represented as a percentage of surplus-value it constantly falls. And the rise in the organic composition of capital means that constant capital (investment) is increasing both absolutely and relatively. But it also means that variable capital is decreasing relatively even though growing absolutely, hence there is a relative decline in the worker's demand for consumption goods. We have then a relative decrease in the demand for consumption goods by both capitalists and workers. But, and here is the difficulty for capitalism, accumulation or the growth in constant capital (investment) leads to a constantly increasing output of consumer goods. For, according to Sweezy, there is a fixed technical relation (which also holds when expressed in value terms) between investment and the output of consumer goods such that every increment to investment gives rise to a proportionate increase in consumption goods. In short, according to Sweezy, the dilemma of capitalism arises from the process of accumulation which, on the one hand, enforces a relative reduction in the demand for consumer goods and, on the other hand, simultaneously generates a constantly increasing output of consumption goods (constantly increasing since there is a fixed relation between constant capital or investment, which is increasing both absolutely and relatively, and the output of consumption goods):

[1] *Op. cit.*, p. 180.

The essence of the underconsumption theory can now be very briefly stated. Since capitalists, who control the direction of resources and funds, act in such a way as to produce a steady decline in the ratio

$$\frac{\text{rate of growth of consumption}}{\text{rate of growth of means of production}}$$

and since the nature of the production process enforces at least approximate stability in the ratio

$$\frac{\text{rate of growth in the output of consumption goods}}{\text{rate of growth of means of production}}$$

it follows that there is an inherent tendency for the growth in consumption to fall behind the growth in the output of consumption goods.[1]

On the basis of this analysis, Sweezy concludes that population growth is extremely important since it tends to counter the underconsumption tendency:

... the strength of the tendency to underconsumption stands in inverse relation to the rapidity of population growth, being weak in periods of rapid growth and becoming stronger as the rate of growth declines. We may, therefore, for the sake of convenience, speak of the law of inverse relation between population growth and the tendency to underconsumption.[2]

Such is Sweezy's underconsumption doctrine which also leads him to conclude among other things that 'faulty investment' by absorbing 'a part of capitalists' accumulation without adding to the output of consumption goods . . . counteracts the tendency to underconsumption'.[3]

What is the relationship of Sweezy's formulation to Marx's analysis of the significance of population for investment? If Sweezy's underconsumption theory is correct, it leads to conclusions diametrically opposed to Marx's analysis of capitalism.

For it can be shown that Sweezy's underconsumption doctrine, if true, requires a constantly rising rate of profit.[4] This

---

[1] *The Theory of Capitalist Development*, pp. 182–3.
[2] *Ibid.*, pp. 223–4.   [3] *Ibid.*, p. 221.
[4] It is clear that Sweezy was unaware of this implication of his underconsumption doctrine, since he wrote (p. 104) that '. . . Marx's formulation of the law of the falling tendency of the rate of profit is not very convincing. At the same time we may remark that attempts which have been made to demonstrate that a rising organic composition of capital must be accompanied by a rising rate of profit are equally unconvincing.'

is evident from the following: In Marxian economic theory, total output in value terms (TO) equals the value output of Department I, means of production, plus the value of the output of Department II, consumer goods, i.e. Dept. I plus Dept. II equals TO. But in Marxian theory total output is also equal to the *sum* of the constant capitals plus the *sum* of the variable capitals plus the *sum* of the surplus-values of Departments I and II, i.e. C plus V plus S equals TO. Now by definition C, the *sum* of the constant capitals of Departments I and II, is equal to investment. C therefore is equal to the value of Department I. But if C is equal to the output value of Department I, then V plus S equals the output value of Department II.

Sweezy holds: (1) The value of investment output is in fixed proportion to the value of consumption goods. But, as we have just seen, this means that C is in fixed proportion to V plus S; and (2) The organic composition of capital is continuously rising, i.e. V is always decreasing relative to C. But this must mean a rising rate of profit. For if (1) C is fixed relative to (V plus S) and (2) V is decreasing relative to C, then S must be rising relative to C and, also, relative to (C plus V). But if S is always rising relative to (C plus V) then the rate of profit is continuously rising.

It follows then that Sweezy's underconsumption doctrine is not in the main stream of Marxist theory and, further, that his conclusion regarding the importance of population growth for maintaining the market for consumption goods places the wrong emphasis. Rather, the significance of population growth in Marxist theory lies in the process of production where a cheap and abundant labour force makes possible a high rate of exploitation.[1]

[1] At the time the above was written, I had not seen Professor Y. Yoshida's criticism of Sweezy's underconsumption doctrine (summarized in English in the bilingual Japanese periodical, *The Economic Review*, April 1950, and reprinted in Sweezy's *The Present as History*, Monthly Review Press, New York, 1953, pp. 360–1). Professor Yoshida apparently did not discuss the implications of Sweezy's theory for the rate of profit, but pointed out the incompatibility of the assumption of a stable relation between stock of means of production and output, given a rising organic composition of capital. Although recognizing the inadequacy of his formulation, Sweezy continues to emphasize underconsumption and, in particular, the significance of the rate of population growth 'in determining the relative size and rate of growth of consumption'. *Ibid.*, p. 359.

For Marx, the basic problem of political economy was to discover the laws of motion of capitalism. In a sense the approach is biological. From whose loins sprung the lusty infant, capitalism; was it begot by men and, as such, mortal? Again, like a Greek drama, was parricide also involved? If capitalism did not always exist and if, further, its parents were also mortal, must it not, like everything which is mortal, first grow with boundless energy until it reaches a state of maximum strength, following which decay sets in? In the Marxian analysis, the evolution of capitalism is similar to man's cycle as summarized in Shakespeare's *As you Like It*: 'And so, From hour to hour, we ripe and ripe, And then, from hour to hour, we rot and rot; And thereby hangs a tale.'

But analogies are tricky things. Old men do not willingly depart from the scenes of their triumphs to rest peacefully among the bones of their ancestors. According to the Marxist-Leninist school, we have here to deal with an aged but very resourceful and cunning individual, jealous to the last of his prerogatives. Besides, being diabolically clever, he insists that his preservation is necessary or all will perish. Frequently his eloquence is convincing and since, moreover, he usually contrives to involve his family in difficulty with their neighbours, his plea for family unity in the face of mutual danger is often successful. Again he is not above selecting certain members of the family for rewards and special favours, thus splitting them off from the rest of the family. They become the old man's allies and are convinced that their fate is united with his, their success or failure intimately related to the welfare of the old man.

The Old Man of capitalism is, of course, imperialism. For just as concentration of capital—the coalescence of the pigmy property of the means of production held by the many into the hands of the relatively few, and the consequent growth of a large class of workers divorced from ownership of the means of production—was necessary for capital to function *qua* capital; so concentration has the further result of inevitably leading to monopoly. For with the concentration we have, on the one hand, not only an absolute growth in the mass and number of capitals but, on the other hand, an opposite tendency in that the growth of capital leads to an intestine struggle for domination. Other things being equal, that capital which is relatively larger will be more efficient since the large capital can produce its commodities more cheaply, temporarily sell them above value, and thus augment itself more rapidly than its smaller counterpart: 'the battle of competition is fought by cheapening of commodities. The cheapness of commodities depends, *ceteris paribus*, on the productiveness of labour, and this again on the scale of production. Therefore, the larger capitals beat the smaller.'

The absolute growth in the mass and numbers of capital is countered then by centralization which differs from concentration in that it is not limited by accumulation but 'only presupposes a change in the distribution of capital already to hand. . . . Capital grows in one place to a huge mass in a single hand, because it has in another place been lost by many. This is centralization proper, as distinct from accumulation and concentration.' But although centralization is independent of accumulation it 'supplements the work of accumulation, by enabling the industrial capitalists to expand the scale of their operations', since accumulation,

the gradual propagation of capital by a reproduction passing from a circular into a spiral form, is a very slow process as compared with centralization, which needs but to alter the quantitative grouping of the integral parts of social capital. The world would still be without railroads, if it had been obliged to wait until accumulation should have enabled a few individual capitals to undertake the construction of a railroad. Centralization, on the other hand, accomplished this by a turn of the hand through stock companies. Centralization, by thus accelerating and intensifying the effects of accumulation, extends and hastens at the same time revolutions in the technical composition of capital, which increase its constant part at the expense of its variable part and thereby reduce the relative demand for labour.[1]

Later on in another chapter in Volume I of *Capital* Marx again emphasizes how concentration leads to centralization and centralization is qualitatively different from concentration. In fact, it might be argued that the substance of Lenin's theory of modern imperialism is foreshadowed in the following:

. . . as soon as the labourers are turned into proletarians, their means

---

[1] *Capital*, Vol. I, pp. 686–9.

of labour into capital, as soon as the capitalist mode of production stands on its own feet, then . . . expropriation . . . takes a new form. *That which is now to be expropriated is no longer the labourer working for himself, but the capitalist exploiting many labourers.* This expropriation is accomplished by the immanent laws of capitalistic production itself, by the centralization of capital. One capitalist always kills many.[1]

Considered abstractly, centralization or monopoly could proceed to the point where 'the entire social capital would be united, either in the hands of a single capitalist, or in those of one single corporation'.[2] In fact, however, centralization does not proceed to such an extreme. Within a country, the largest aggregates of capital reach a point where mutual repulsion becomes almost as strong as attraction. To some extent, the large corporations pursue a policy of live and let live toward their powerful rivals. In other words, it is easier to come to an agreement with a large competitor (e.g. an expressed or tacit understanding not to engage in a price war) than to risk everything on a knock-down-drag-out struggle for absolute domination. Besides, according to Lenin, there is another alternative. The large capitals can come to temporary agreement, subordinate their differences to some degree, and unite to invoke state action for the expropriation of the capitalists of another country. Hence imperialism is inevitably bound up with monopoly capitalism.

It is not proposed here to consider in detail the characteristic features of imperialism as set forth by Lenin, i.e. wars for the territorial redivision of the world, the export of capital, the union of banking and industrial capital into a financial oligarchy, growth of parasitism, etc., but it is important to emphasize that in the period of monopoly capitalism, although concentration is both logically and historically considered prior to centralization, both processes continue and constitute important sources of revenue. So it is that the export of capital not only attracts to its orbit the small capitals of the 'backward' areas, but accumulation as represented by concentration in the early stage of capitalism continues, i.e. the export of capital finds its reward not only in the swallowing of existent capitals but, also, in the separation of the small producer from ownership of the means of production, e.g. the destruction of handi-

[1] *Capital*, pp. 835–6, My italics. [2] *Ibid.*, p. 688.

craft production along with the alienation of the natives' rights in land.

Thus, considered from the point of view of its importance for population, the export of capital under imperialism means that monopoly capitalism gains access to a cheap and abundant supply of labour which yields profits far above those to be realized by the employment of capital in an already industrialized area where an historically determined standard of living has been evolved during the period of 'progressive capitalism'. But the export of capital finds its reward not only in the super-profits obtained in colonial areas but, also, because capital export reduces the competition of capitals for the purchase of labour-power and thus makes it possible for the capitalists to purchase this labour-power at home at a lower rate.[1]

The relative reduction in the demand for labour that accompanies accumulation is, then, aggravated by the export of capital.[2] Further, since in the period of monopoly capitalism, production is not regulated by the average rate of profit but, on the contrary, is limited by the need of monopoly capitalism for maximum profits, it follows that full employment in the period of imperialism is an exceptional case usually referable to either existing or anticipated wars, or to the new activity generated by the need for reconstruction following a war.

Such, briefly, is the Marxist-Leninist theory of capitalist evolution which determines the presuppositions of Soviet demographers. Thus Soviet demographers stress the correlation between the fertility decline during the last quarter of the nineteenth century and the transition from competitive industrial capitalism to monopoly capitalism or imperialism. In their

[1] *Cf.* Maurice Dobb, *Political Economy and Capitalism*, London, 1937, pp. 234–5.

[2] 'It is of the greatest importance, finally, to understand that export monopolism injures the workers far more unequivocally than the capitalists. There can be no dumping of labour power, and employment abroad or in the colonies is not even a quantitative substitute.' Joseph A. Schumpeter, 'The Sociology of Imperialisms', *Imperialism and the Social Classes*, edited by Paul M. Sweezy, Oxford, 1951, p. 112. Schumpeter, however, argued that '*it is a basic fallacy to describe imperialism as a necessary phase of capitalism, or even to speak of the development of capitalism into imperialism*'. (p. 118.) Rather, imperialism is a hangover from the ideology of 'the war-oriented nobility', a survival of precapitalist elements in the system which 'the climate of the modern world' will inevitably destroy. For export monopolism is 'untenable even from the capitalist point of view'. (pp. 118–30.)

view, the fertility decline is a symptom of the general crisis of capitalism whose essential features are depression, stagnation at less than full employment, followed by wars for the territorial redivision of the world.[1] Essentially, the analysis is based on the relative reduction in the demand for labour. In other words, although the Marxist-Leninist school denies the possibility of the workers improving their economic position by recourse to Neo-Malthusian measures; it recognizes that in the period of the general crisis of capitalism the decrease in the relative demand for labour has as its result family limitation among the proletariat.

As has already been noted, in Marxist-Leninist theory population is the dependent variable. So the Soviet demographer, Urlanis, in a work which he describes as an 'experiment in dynamic calculation', proceeds on the assumption that population growth is a function of changes in the economic and social development.[2] Urlanis starts his analysis with the Middle Ages and divides the period of European economic development as follows:

1. The age of Feudalism,
2. The period of early capitalism or primitive accumulation, i.e. the sixteenth, seventeenth, and eighteenth centuries,
3. The period of industrial capitalism, or the nineteenth century, and
4. The twentieth century, or the era of imperialism.

Although Urlanis makes use of such data as tax rolls, numbers in the armed forces and numbers of households which furnish an indirect measure of population, church statistics on confirmation, birth and death registers, etc., he quotes with approval those writers who have stressed that population calculations based on the number of persons who could subsist on a given territory at a given level of economic and social development have approximate accuracy. So changes in agricultural technique make possible a greater population density, e.g. the

[1] In his last work Stalin predicted that with 'the disintegration of the world market' the industries of the major capitalist countries 'will be operating more and more below capacity'. *Economic Problems of Socialism in the U.S.S.R.*, Foreign Languages Publishing House, Moscow, 1952, p. 36.

[2] B. T. Urlanis, *The Growth of Population in Europe* (in Russian), Moscow, 1941, pp. 10–11.

transition from the two to the three field system meant that the productive area under cultivation increased from one-half to two-thirds.

Therefore, those writers who assume that the population of Europe was the same in 1300 as in 1600 are in error. For although it is true that the period of Feudalism was one of uninterrupted warfare, hunger and epidemics, peasant revolts, etc.; nevertheless, there was a gradual progress in agricultural technique. Urlanis notes that progress was both extensive and intensive: extensive, through the clearing of lands and the draining of swamps; intensive, through the improvement of soil cultivation with the adoption of the three field system which had become general by the fifteenth century. Also, the sowing of winter in place of summer corn significantly increased food production. Further, the increased importance of wheat and rye in place of oats and barley augmented the food supply. Similarly, there was a gradual improvement in agricultural equipment. Whereas under Charles the Great agricultural implements consisted of shovels, picks, sickles, and mattocks; in the fifteenth century the plough and harrow were extensively, if not universally, employed. Again, in the tenth and eleventh centuries animals were but slightly used as a motive force, whereas in the fifteenth century the horse was no longer limited to purely military purposes but hauled the plough and was harnessed to the wagon for various economic purposes.[1]

Using the statistical data mentioned above but relying more on the level of economic development, Urlanis places the population of Europe at 56·4 millions in the year 1000.[2] From 1000 to 1500 population grew from 56·4 to 90·7 millions, or an average annual increase of 0·09 per cent which, however, is not to be understood as a constant or even progression. On the contrary, according to Urlanis, there were periods of rapid growth such as from 1350 to 1400 when the rate increased to 0·20 per cent; as well as periods where growth was below the average annual rate of increase, e.g. the period from 1300 to 1350 when population decreased absolutely.

But, in general, Urlanis argues, there is a relation between

[1] *The Growth of Population in Europe*, Chapter II.
[2] Including European Russia as defined by the 1914 boundaries.

the rate of economic development and the rate of population growth which may be summarized as follows:[1]

Period	Average Annual Rate of Population Growth in %	Average Annual Rate of Growth in % for	
		Agriculture	Industry
Feudalism	0·09	0·12	—
Primitive Accumulation	0·22	0·3	0·5
Industrial Capitalism	0·69	0·9	3·0
Imperialism	0·64	0·7	1·3

So it is that Urlanis finds that a chart of the coefficient of natural increase (second order parabolic curve) for the period 1880–1940 reveals a crisis or turning point between 1900 and 1901 when population growth for western capitalism as a whole takes the descending road. Now this crisis point almost coincides with the entrance of capitalism on a new phase, the phase of monopoly capitalism leading to the most destructive world wars and to more profound economic crises than have ever previously been experienced.[2]

It is clear that the above analysis finds the explanation for the fertility decline among the proletariat in the relative decline in the demand for labour. True, Urlanis recognizes that the fertility decline in England and Wales in the last quarter of the nineteenth century is partially a function of the abolition of child labour. Again, it is also related to the employment of women in industry; however, the fundamental emphasis is on unemployment and wars which destroy the vital impulse to reproduce.

Such is the explanation of the changed fertility pattern of the proletariat. What then is the explanation of the fertility pattern of the other classes in society? According to Urlanis, any form of private property in the instruments of production reduces fertility. Thus peasants who possess small plots of land strive to avoid further subdivision. They marry late and limit the number of their heirs. This is the explanation for the low fertility

---

[1] *The Growth of Population in Europe*, Chapter VII.
[2] *Ibid.*, pp. 391–2. *Cf.* also A. Ya. Boyarski and P. P. Shusherin, *Demographic Statistics* (in Russian), Moscow, 1951 (second edition), Chapter IV, pp. 113 ff.

found among the French peasants. Similarly, the Russian data demonstrate that growth in private property in land leads to a reduction in fertility. Thus, although generally the Stolypin agrarian policies were unsuccessful in destroying communal ownership, Urlanis finds statistical evidence that those regions where private ownership in land greatly increased were also regions where fertility declined. He concludes that if the Tsarist government had embarked on the programme of dividing communal property several decades earlier, the fall in fertility in Russia would have been much more pronounced.[1]

Not only private ownership of land but *any kind of private ownership reduces fertility*. This, Urlanis asserts, explains the low fertility found among the bourgeoisie of both large and small towns.[2] Apparently, it is sufficient for Urlanis to affirm that private ownership *per se* reduces fertility. He appears to believe that the proposition is self-evident and incontestable. At least, such is the implication since Urlanis does not pursue the subject further. But, is not the statement too general since, other things being equal, will not the size of a landholding affect the proprietor's fertility pattern?

In summary, although Marx limited his investigation of population to the formulation of the law of a relative surplus population following the establishment of industrial capitalism; Soviet demographers apply Marx's theory of economic development along with Lenin's elaborations to explain changes in the rate of population growth. With Adam Smith and others it is recognized that population growth is a function of the demand for labour. There is an explicit repudiation of any identification of subsistence with the demand for labour which can be traced back in Marxist theory to as early as 1844 when Engels wrote:

That population always presses against the means of employment, that the number of people who are propagated corresponds to the number who can be employed, in short, that the propagation of labour power has up to now been regulated by the law of competition and has therefore also been subject to periodical crises and fluctuations—all these are facts, the establishment of which stands to the

---

[1] *The Growth of Population in Europe*, pp. 409 ff.
[2] *Ibid.*, p. 408.

credit of Malthus. But means of employment are not means of subsistence.[1]

The recent fertility decline among the proletariat is traceable to the relative diminution in the demand for labour which occurs in the period of imperialism. But, as has already been noted, the Malthusian and Neo-Malthusian thesis that population can regulate its supply to the extent of improving its position under capitalism is denied.[2]

Finally, the Marxist-Leninist school holds that population is the dependent variable and, as such, is incapable of determining the type of social organization.[3] Nevertheless, it is recognized that, given the social organization, population may be extremely important in determining the general efficiency of society. Other things being equal, the growth in population tends to increase productive efficiency. It makes possible a greater division of labour, a larger labour force, a greater interchange of skills and knowledge, etc. Moreover, it is held that population becomes increasingly a greater asset with the growth of the productive forces of society. In other words, Engels' thesis that progress in science and knowledge follows a geometric progression means that each productive individual becomes progressively more valuable to society.[4]

An evaluation of Soviet demographic theory herein cited would be as follows. The emphasis on the importance of demand for labour in determining its supply is correct and,

---

[1] *Outlines of a Critique of Political Economy* (Meek edition), pp. 60–1.

[2] 'We are unconditional opponents of Neo-Malthusianism, of that direction which suits some little petty-bourgeois couple who, stupid and self-centred, whisper in panic: "If we can only keep ourselves, with God's help, above water; but children we cannot do with" . . . this does not prevent us in the slightest from demanding the abolition of all laws which place penalties either upon abortion or upon the circulation of medical writings dealing with methods of preventing conceptions or similar laws. . . . But freedom of hygienic instruction and the protection of elementary democratic rights of men and women is one thing. Another thing, and a very different thing, is the social thinking of Neo-Malthusianism. The class-conscious worker will always wage the most relentless fight against the attempts to impose this reactionary and cowardly teaching upon the most progressive, strongest class of modern society, which is prepared to carry through great transformations of this society.' N. Lenin, 'Neo-Malthusianism and the Working Class', *Pravda*, June 16, 1913. Translated into English in the *Labour Monthly*, October 1927, pp. 597–9.

[3] Stalin, *Problems of Leninism*, cited by Urlanis, *op. cit.*, p. 369.

[4] *Outlines of a Critique of Political Economy* (Meek edition), p. 63.

as we saw in the preceding chapter, not only follows Classical economic theory but, also, is consistent with Marshall's analysis. However, in Soviet demographic theory the argument is developed completely on the basis of the correlation between the fertility decline and imperialism. No attempt is made to pass beyond this correlation to an analysis of the causal nexus or the *modus operandi* by which demand for labour governs its supply. For instance, it is not clear whether the relative decline in the demand for labour is to be interpreted as resulting in an absolute or relative decline in the standard of living, i.e. relative in the sense that historically determined expectations of a continuing rise in the standard of living are no longer being fulfilled. The mechanism by which demand for labour regulates supply remains obscure.

Differential fertility analysis is limited to a consideration of differences in fertility patterns between the rich and the poor, and the solution offered is the bald statement that wealth *per se* limits fertility. Intra-rural fertility differences arising from size of farm and mode of exploitation are not considered. Again, no attempt is made to consider the problem of intra-labour fertility differences. For example, in reviewing Marshall's approach to the problem of population, it was suggested that demand for different types or qualities of labour leads to objectively determined differences in living standards; that these differences in the standard of living were necessary for the reproduction of different grades of labour; and that the standard of living represents the subjective corollary or ideological duplication of the objective needs of the market. Hence it was possible to explain differences in fertility patterns between the 'efficient' labour of western European countries and the 'inefficient' labour of non-industrialized countries, i.e. given a relatively smaller demand for skilled labour. Further, it was possible to explain the apparently curious paradox encountered in demographic investigations, viz. that within a country fertility is found to vary inversely with income; but when fertility is standardized for occupation, it is found to vary directly with income.

The overemphasis on the correlation between the fertility decline and the demise of competitive capitalism excludes from consideration yet another question of practical significance.

For instance, would Soviet demographers contend that if demand for labour had not fallen relatively with the transition to monopoly capitalism, there would have been no fertility decline among the proletariat? In other words, suppose the demand for labour in England to have been maintained throughout the period from 1870 to the present. Are we to conclude that the fertility pattern of the proletariat would have remained the same? Or should we not consider the evolution in the economic function of the family for the poor consequent upon industrialization?[1] Again, suppose England to become a socialist state and that this results in a great increase in the demand for labour. Would this mean a revival of the fertility pattern found among the English proletariat during the mid-nineteenth century?

In short, objection is made not to the emphasis on demand for labour, but the failure to pursue this line of inquiry further. The exclusive preoccupation with the correlation between the fertility decline and a certain stage in the evolution of capitalism leads to sins of omission—a neglect of other problems.

[1] Undoubtedly, the evolution in the economic function of the family can itself be shown to be largely determined by the demand for labour. For the demand for more efficient labour (a better educated working class) means that the economic function of the family, as a unit engaged in direct co-operative production, is supplanted by a new economic function where the family becomes the labour reservoir for industry. *Cf.* Marshall, *op. cit.*, p. 564.

PART II

The Economic Interpretation

CHAPTER SIX

The Problem

PART I consisted of an exposition and evaluation of demographic theories adduced to explain fertility differentials and the comparatively recent fertility decline among the poorer classes in industrialized countries. The procedure followed was critical and necessarily polemic since the object of Part I was not only to achieve familiarity with the various alternative explanations of fertility patterns but, also, to gain an appreciation of the complexity and diversity of phenomena requiring elucidation in a general theory of population dynamics.

In Part I both biological and cultural theories of population growth were judged to be inadequate; however, the economic analysis based on the Classical school's thesis that demand for labour governed supply was recognized as valid but requiring further elaboration. The Classical thesis was accepted by Marshall who argued that demand for labour regulated not only the supply of 'inefficient' labour but, also, that of 'efficient' labour, i.e. demand for labour determines the fertility pattern of the proletariat of modern industrialized countries. However, this recognition of the importance of demand for labour on its supply did not lead Marshall to undertake an economic explanation of the recent fertility decline of the proletariat in modern industrial communities. It was suggested that Marshall was precluded from pursuing a fruitful line of inquiry by his adherence to the theoretical framework of Neo-Classical economics which, by its acceptance of Say's Law of Markets, did not consider the problem of a general failure in the demand for labour. Further, it was pointed out that Marshall's recognition that demand for labour governed its supply in modern industrial communities was exceptional rather than typical of Neo-Classical thought on the population problem. For the general tendency among Neo-Classical economists was to assume the validity of the Malthusian theory with respect to 'backward' areas of the world, but to deny its applicability to modern industrialized communities, i.e. it was believed by Neo-Classical economists that somehow in modern industrialized communities the causal nexus between demand for labour and its supply had been broken.

Further, it was pointed out in Part I that the comparatively recent evolution of orthodox economic thought, specifically the doctrine of monopolistic or imperfect competition, coupled with the Keynesian contribution, now makes possible the formulation of an economic theory of population growth which is consistent with the Classical school's thesis that demand for labour governs supply. Again, it was noted that this principle of the Classical school constituted the major assumption of Marxist-Leninist population theory.

Before proceeding with the exposition of the economic interpretation of demography, it should be emphasized that the approach is theoretical rather than empirical. The method followed is to take the facts of demography, previously established by empirical investigations, and relate them to changes in economic development. The object is to provide a conceptual scheme or *general theory* of population dynamics which will explain and integrate both long- and short-run phenomena. Interest is in the general pattern of economic development and demographic change *common to a number of countries*. Hence, no attempt will be made to apply in detail the economic interpretation of demography to a specific country whose peculiar conditions must, of course, be the subject of a special inquiry. However, this does not detract from the practical value of the present work since an adequate theoretical framework is a necessary prerequisite for the analysis of particular countries if the pitfalls of a blind empiricism are to be avoided. In short, an attempt is made to satisfy the following need:

Population study has developed no conceptual framework for investigating short-run variations in marital and childbearing patterns. In addition, theoretical consideration of the long-run, as distinguished from the short-run, aspects of population change is likely to be an increasingly important prerequisite to the refinement of future empirical research.[1]

The exposition of the economic interpretation of demography proceeds with the summary of the phenomena requiring illumination by way of a theory of population oriented to a materialist interpretation of fertility differentials and fertility dynamics. Unavoidably, the summary involves a repetition of some of the material covered in Part I as well as other demographic findings as yet unmentioned in this work. The following demographic facts are of major significance:

1. Historical evidence indicates that at one time women and children were prized economic possessions. The wealthy man had a large family.

2. Nevertheless, since the time of the Greeks and Romans, the wealthy classes have generally been characterized by a relatively low fertility.

3. Prior to the industrial revolution, family limitation among the poorer classes was not unknown. In Sweden, for example, 'conscious family limitation must have been practised in earlier times. . . . The general low level of Swedish fertility in the preindustrial period in comparison with other countries would otherwise be difficult to explain.'[2]

4. In general, mortality and fertility vary directly and not inversely.

5. The evidence does not support the theory of a common pattern of demographic evolution. True, some countries passed through the first stage of the so-called 'vital' or 'demographic revolution' when mortality declined but fertility remained constant. However, there were exceptions, e.g. in France the decline in mortality during the last quarter of the eighteenth century was accompanied by a concomitant, but not proportionate, fertility decline.[3] Again, in the United States

---

[1] Quoted above, Introduction, p. 2.

[2] Alva Myrdal, *Nation and Family*, London, 1941, p. 50. See also Norman E. Himes, *Medical History of Contraception*, London, 1936.

[3] *Cf.* J. Bourgeois-Pichat, 'Évolution de la population française depuis le XVIIIe siècle', *Population*, October–December 1951.

fertility declined throughout most of the nineteenth century.[1]

6. In the last quarter of the nineteenth century, fertility fell in a number of western European countries. Even in France there was an acceleration in the decline of the gross reproduction rate during the last quarter of the nineteenth century.[2]

7. In some regions rural fertility exceeds urban, in others the opposite is the case. Fertility rates vary also between industrial and commercial cities.

8. Fertility varies inversely with income; however, there is some evidence that when fertility is standardized for occupation, fertility varies directly with income.

9. Fertility varies inversely with education; however, there are exceptions.[3]

10. Fertility appears to vary inversely with social status of women; however, in the United States fertility is higher than in England where women's status is not so high.

11. The wealthy or more industrialized countries generally have a lower fertility than poorer and less industrialized countries. However, a comparison of two industrialized countries with similar social and economic institutions (United States and England) shows that the wealthier country (United States) has a much higher birth rate.

12. In periods of prosperity, the birth rate rises; in periods of depression, it falls. Nevertheless, there has been a secular decline in the birth rate among the major industrialized countries. On the other hand, in recent years, the birth rate for these same countries has risen significantly above the low level of the 1930's. E.g. in the United States in 1933 the birth rate reached an all-time minimum; since then fertility has risen sharply and

[1] Warren S. Thompson and P. K. Whelpton, *Population Trends in the United States*, New York, 1933, p. 310.

[2] *Cf.* Pierre Depoid, *Reproduction nette en Europe depuis l'origine des statistiques de l'état civil*, Paris, 1941, p. 17.

[3] United Nations, *The Determinants and Consequences of Population Trends*, New York, 1953, Chapter V. The economic interpretation does not regard education *per se* as a causative factor but rather its economic implication.

maintained a level far above the expectations of demographers.

Consideration of the above findings suggest that the inverse relation between fertility and such variables as social status of women, education, wealth, and income may be subsumed under the general inverse relation between economic status and fertility—education and social status being regarded as generally concomitant phenomena of high economic status.[1]

With reference to differential fertility, the analysis must provide an economic explanation of the apparent paradox that those less able to afford children make a proportionately greater contribution to population growth; where, by 'an economic explanation', it is understood that we are precluded from having recourse to putative psychological attributes distinguishing social classes and determining differences in fertility patterns.[2] Further, the economic analysis of differential fertility must pass beyond the broad division between rich and poor and inquire into inter-occupational fertility differences.

Again, differential fertility requires an investigation into geographical variations in fertility, traditionally analysed under the heading of 'rural-urban differences'. But as we saw in Part I there is no justification for the belief in a peculiarly rural or peculiarly urban fertility pattern.[3] Rather, the evidence indicates that demand for labour is crucial in determining *intra-rural* fertility differences. Thus Ariés has shown that *intra-rural* fertility differences can be related to demand for labour by investigating agricultural areas according to the prevailing mode of exploitation and type of proprietorship which, of course, are generally related to the size of the farm. In France, the general association of monoculture with poverty limits fertility.[4] Similarly, demand for labour is the significant factor determining *intra-urban* fertility differences. For the low

[1] The relation between social status and fertility will be discussed further in the next chapter.
[2] This, of course, is not to be construed as a denial of psychological differences distinguishing social classes, but rather as the methodological requirement for the economic interpretation at this level of analysis.
[3] *Supra*, Chapter III, pp. 78 ff.
[4] *Ibid.*, p. 80.

fertility of the great cities or commercial centres has no analogue in those urban centres where manufacturing and heavy industry are the mainstay of the economy.[1]

Geographical variations in fertility also include international differences in fertility patterns. Here, also, demand for labour analysis must be invoked to explain fertility variations between two countries characterized by similar economic and social institutions, e.g. the much higher birth rate of the United States in comparison to England in the post-war II period.

With reference to fertility dynamics, exceptions to the observed direct relation between mortality and fertility rates require clarification. Specifically, there should be an explanation why in the period of the industrial revolution in England, decreasing mortality did not occasion a decline in fertility, whereas in France there was a concomitant fall in both rates. Or, in other words, under what conditions is Wappaus' thesis valid that with a decrease in infant mortality, parents automatically embark upon family limitation?[2]

Further, with reference to fertility dynamics, the evidence indicates that at one time there was a direct relation between wealth and fertility. In this period, women and children were prized economic possessions, constituting a major portion of man's wealth. In a subsequent period, however, the economic value of women and children is depreciated. This depreciation is evident in the transition from bride-price to dowry where recognition is given to the metamorphosis of the wife from a value-yielding asset to an economic liability, compensated for by a dowry. It is also evident in the reluctance of the wealthy citizens of the Roman Empire to assume the burden of marriage and procreation. This changed fertility pattern will be analysed in terms of the evolution in the economic function of the family for the wealthy.

But an analysis of the economic function of the family for the rich is not sufficient. It is also necessary to consider the evolution in the economic function of the family for the poorer classes. For even if it should be possible to relate the fertility decline among the lower classes beginning in the last quarter of the nineteenth century to a relative diminution in demand for

---

[1] *Supra*, Chapter III, p. 78.
[2] *Ibid.*, p. 69.

labour, there is still another question, viz. whether in the absence of a decreased demand for labour, the fertility pattern of the proletariat would have remained the same?

In other words, there is the hypothesis to consider that the evolution in the economic function of the family for the poor was inevitably such as to induce some family limitation, even in the absence of a decreased aggregate demand for labour. Moreover, such a proposition would be compatible with the view that a decreased demand for labour was the major or immediate cause which induced the observed fertility decline. That is to say, these two propositions are not irreconcilable. For it might be contended that the economic evolution of the family towards a smaller size was inevitable, but that this evolution was obscured, hastened and distorted by the decline in the rate of economic development among the major capitalist countries during the last quarter of the nineteenth century. 'Obscured' in the sense that it was impossible to observe this transition freed from extreme economic insecurity and, therefore, the transition appears as due only to a decreased demand for labour; 'hastened' in the sense that the impact of unemployment accelerated the transition; and 'distorted' in the sense that severe economic crises (e.g. the period of the 1930's) forced the 'lower classes' to the temporary adoption of a lower fertility pattern than that which would have resulted in the absence of such economic insecurity. This same evolution in the economic function of the family may also be considered in terms of changes in the quality of labour demanded. For the change in the economic function of the family from a production unit to a labour reservoir for the needs of industry is but a reflection of economic development and, in particular, a qualitative change in the demand for labour.

Again, with reference to fertility dynamics, the economic interpretation must define its attitude toward the following thesis. According to Himes, 'the desire to control conception is a well-nigh universal phenomenon' and 'fragmentary knowledge of contraceptive means has existed in all major cultures throughout the entire range of social development'.[1] However, and this for Himes is the fact of major significance, it is only in comparatively recent times that knowledge of effective

[1] Norman E. Himes, *op. cit.*, p. 333.

means of contraception is being diffused in all classes in societies. This progress in the diffusion of contraceptive knowledge means that there will be an 'international convergence of birth rates'.

All are approaching, or tending to approach with some delay (as in the case of Russia and south-eastern Europe) *what might be called the level of controlled fertility. Thus the democratisation process is not culture-bound; it is not applicable only to one or two Western societies. With the exceptions already noted, it is characteristic of all important Western civilisations.* I predict that within fifty years, certainly within a century, the exceptions in Europe will fall into line, and it is only a question of time before the process will be repeated in Oriental societies. This seems to me one of the most certain of sociological predictions.[1]

Similar to the above thesis of Himes and also requiring comment is the view that depressions do not result in a net fertility loss:

All that seems to happen is that under worsened conditions some married couples postpone having a child, and some who would have married and had a child postpone doing so. But they do so sooner or later and, if the number of children aimed at in the family is limited, then it makes little difference in the long run whether the children come sooner or later. Indeed, the broad conclusion to be drawn from these observations is that, while changing economic conditions may cause some fluctuations in the birth-rate, they do not affect the general trend.[2]

Our investigation will proceed first with an analysis of the economic evolution in the function of the family for the rich and the poor. This is followed by a review of historical changes in the quantity and quality of labour demanded and their effect on population growth. Finally, there is a consideration of the implications of the conceptual framework proposed.

[1] Norman E. Himes, *op. cit.*, p. 390.
[2] A. M. Carr-Saunders, *World Population*, Oxford, 1936, p. 116.

CHAPTER SEVEN

The Evolution in the Economic Function of the Family

IT was stated above that the inverse relation between income and fertility was subject to exception. In particular, it was noted that when fertility was standardized for occupation, the correlation between income and fertility was found to be positive. However, in spite of such exceptions, the fact remains that *in general* there is a fairly well-established inverse relation between income and fertility. But it does not follow that simply because there exists such an inverse relation that income is the causal mechanism determining fertility patterns. Rather, the association between low fertility and high income may be considered as having no direct relation, i.e. both phenomena may be common products of something else. Thus differences in income may merely reflect differences in the mode of obtaining a livelihood among the various classes. If such is the case, and if it can be established that differences in the manner of gaining a livelihood are significant in determining fertility patterns, then we have an explanation of the inverse relation between income and fertility which does not imply that income is the significant factor determining fertility differentials.

Again, the inverse relation between income and fertility also appears to give sustenance to a cultural explanation of fertility differences which is based on the observed inverse correlation between women's status and their fertility pattern. Such a cultural explanation emphasizes the fact that among the wealthier and better educated classes woman is regarded as an individual with her own unique personality and hence entitled to develop her full potentialities. Naturally, however, to realize these potentialities she must be relieved from the burden of bearing a child every year or so. But, again, this inverse relation between woman's social status and her fertility pattern may imply no direct relation and, as in the case of the inverse relation between income and fertility, respect for women's rights and low fertility may be considered as common products of a more fundamental economic change.

This chapter, then, proceeds to consider the economic function of the family for the rich and the poor. The evolution of the economic function of the family for the rich is traced, particularly with reference to those developments which transformed its economic function. Next, a similar procedure is followed in reference to the family of the poor. Finally, consideration is given to the determinants of women's social status in order to ascertain what relation, if any, exists between women's social status and their fertility pattern.

THE CHANGED ECONOMIC FUNCTION OF THE FAMILY AMONG THE WEALTHY

Regardless of the actual order of development followed in the evolution of sexual relations, we can best appreciate the economics of differential fertility by confining ourselves to a consideration of the evolution of the family in the history of European civilization.

With the Romans, following the dissolution of the clan, patriarchal families were formed to utilize women's labour and that of their offspring for the accumulation of wealth:

> . . . *famel* meant originally the equivalent of *slave*, and *familia meant property in and over persons, whether related biologically, or hired for service, or bought or captured in war as slaves.* And *Pater* did not originally express the *organic* relationship as *begetter* that is denoted by the term *genitor*. It was a synonym for *rex*, or *basileus*, and in its original sense was *Ruler, Master.* Paterfamilias was first and foremost *the lord of his household*, his *familia*, his slaves.[1]

---

[1] Müller-Lyer, *The Family* (translated by F. W. Stella Browne), London, 1931, p. 194. 'The original meaning of the word "family" (*familia*) is not that compound of sentimentality and domestic strife which forms the ideal of the present-day philistine; among the Romans it did not even refer to a

The Economic Function of the Family

According to Roman law, the rights of the paterfamilias over his wife, his children and his children's children were as follows: to inflict punishment, including the death penalty; to sell into slavery or give as security for debt; to force them into marriage or divorce; and control and disposition of all family wealth, including that of his sons even if obtained independently by them. 'In the Civil Wars, fathers were habitually betrayed to death by their sons. Slaves were more loyal and dependable, for their lord's death did not liberate them.'[1]

In the economics of production, the early Roman period is comparable to Melanesian society in the twentieth century, as described by H. J. Nieboer:

> Purchase of wives is in vogue; and most of the women are bought by the rich, many of whom possess a larger number of wives. . . . The wife is the slave of her husband. . . . Women are degraded to the level of brute beasts, doing all the hard field work, and being made to carry loads which appear quite disproportionate to their ugly-shaped bodies and thin legs. . . . Melanesian wives supply the place of slaves. They are bought like slaves; and their labour, like that of the slaves, increases the wealth of their lords.[2]

Nieboer suggests that the low status of Melanesian women might be attributed to the fact that 'male slaves are impossible or difficult to procure, or because the coercive power of these tribes is not strong enough to admit the keeping of slaves'. Again, the men captured may be required as warriors and hence adopted into the tribe.[3]

The Roman economy, however, progressed beyond the point reached by Melanesian society. The *full* development of slavery was realized and, consequently, a large family ceased to be an economic asset. Class and caste differences were accentuated. The family as the economic unit of production was superseded by a more efficient exploitation system. A new principle comes into operation. Divorced from production, the wealthy family is now analogous to a modern holding company. Through the

---

married pair and their children, but only to slaves.' Frederick Engels, *The Origin of the Family, Private Property and the State*, Lawrence & Wishart (fourth edition), London, 1940, p. 60.

[1] Müller-Lyer, *The Family*, pp. 182–3.

[2] *Slavery as an Industrial System* (second, revised edition), The Hague, 1910, pp. 389–92.   [3] *Ibid.*, p. 393.

dowry, family fortunes are merged while, simultaneously, through family limitation, the integrity of the patrimony is preserved in subsequent generations.[1]

Thus, the economic explanation of the low fertility of the wealthy stresses the functional relation between fertility patterns and modes of gaining a livelihood. The key to the problem of differential fertility, then as now, is to be found in the economic function of the family for the wealthy, i.e. its evolution from an economic unit of production under the direction of the paterfamilias to a non-producing unit obtaining its income through a monopoly ownership of the instruments of production—in the case of the Romans, these being the land and slaves.[2]

THE ECONOMIC FUNCTION OF THE FAMILY FOR THE POOR

It remains to consider the evolution in the economic function of the family for the poor. However, our knowledge is limited here since it was not until a comparatively recent period that

[1] Explanations of the transition from bride-price to dowry typically have an idealistic bias, the argument resting on the putative psychological state of the father, e.g. 'The fathers, whose sentiment was refined by growing culture . . . did not wish to think of their daughters being treated as wares. The upper classes took the first step by renouncing the purchase price . . . either wholly or in part and bestowing it upon the daughter . . . and the great mass followed after.' (F. Müller-Lyer, *The Evolution of Modern Marriage*, translated by Isabella C. Wigglesworth, London, 1930, p. 128). A similar explanation is given by Max Radin ('Dowry', *Encyclopaedia of Social Sciences*, Vol. V, pp. 230–3). An *economic* explanation, however, was suggested by Lewis Morgan, viz. the dowry originally represented the resolution of a conflict which arose during the transition period from agnatic inheritance through male descent to the newly evolved principle of inheritance by the children of the deceased only. Upon the complaint of the tribe of Israel that they would lose their inheritance if the daughters of Zelophehad (there being no male offspring) should marry outside the tribe, Moses set aside the rule of exogamy and decreed that the daughters must marry within the tribe (*Ancient Society*, 1877, pp. 546 ff.). According to this analysis, the dowry system would not only strengthen individual family rights but also remove the moral stigma on marriage within the tribe. Hence, the tendency for the dowry system to prevail, including its adoption by the 'great mass'.

[2] As is obvious, the economic explanation of the low fertility of the Romans is not based on their immorality, worldliness, sensuality, decadence, etc., though these were the symptoms. Moreover, according to the economic interpretation, any nostalgia for a bygone period when large families were the rule is not only Utopian but, from a moral point of view, ridiculous. In effect, what is glamorized is a period when man's chief source of exploitation was the labour-power of his wife (wives) and children.

the 'simple annals of the poor' were recognized as affording a valuable insight into the forces at work in history.

Among the Romans, the concept of the family was confined to the patricians or property-owning classes. Since the proletarians owned no property they were considered to be without families and the juridic relations governing them had reference only to the clan. And in the sixth century, when the Christian Church adopted the legal definition of marriage as contained in Roman law, its concern was with the marriages of the nobility and not with marriages among the 'common people'.

During the Medieval period the serf continued to be part of the lord's property. His offspring and the offspring of the lord's horse and cattle 'were both designated by one word (*sequela*), and were looked upon as possessions'.[1] Generally the serfs were free to marry on the manor, but the right to marry off the manor had to be purchased (*redemptio*). In the latter case, with reference to the issue of such a marriage, it appears that the custom was to divide the offspring equally between the two manors. Further, marriage among the serfs was frequently involuntary, the serf being commanded by his lord to take a certain woman as his wife.[2] Sometimes the serfs paid fines rather than marry as demanded by their lords.[3]

There is then an ambiguity in speaking of the 'family' of the poor in the Medieval period if by 'family' is implied either that patriarchal, organized property arrangement bequeathed by Roman institutions, or an autonomous, voluntary, monogamous association for joint housekeeping. Since the serf possessed

---

[1] H. S. Bennett, *Life on the English Manor*, Cambridge, 1948 reprint, p. 241.

[2] *Ibid.*, pp. 242-4. In the early fourteenth century, the Franciscan, Alvarus Pelagius, who was penitentiary to the Pope, drew up a series of indictments against the peasantry. Among the twenty-two faults mentioned was that 'they often abstain from knowing their wives lest children should be born, fearing that they could not bring up so many, under the pretext of poverty . . .' Quoted by G. G. Coulton, *The Medieval Village*, Cambridge, 1925, p. 243.

[3] Of course, there was an evolution in the sexual relations among the poor in the Medieval period. For example, in the twelfth century, 'the church ventured to declare the binding force of marriages between two slaves, even against the will of their lord or lords'. (Coulton, *op. cit.*, p. 493). Again, in the thirteenth century, the Church came out for the serf's right to make a will (Bennett, *op. cit.*, p. 249). Similarly, the gradual growth of a class of freemen also operated to establish the family among the poorer classes.

neither property rights nor personal freedom, he had, strictly speaking, no family. Again there were a number of countries where the clan and not the family remained the important economic and social unit till the end of the Middle Ages.[1] In such areas, the clan not only fulfilled many of the functions commonly associated in the present period with the family, but also the democracy and egalitarianism of the clan retarded the progress of the Feudal system.[2]

But whatever the details of the evolution of the family among the poor in its early history, the important point is that following its constitution the family of the poor was a joint economic enterprise united in production and consumption. Woman made a significant contribution. Prior to the industrial revolution, her work included 'brewing, dairy-work, the care of poultry and pigs, the production of vegetables and fruit, spinning flax and wool, nursing and doctoring'.[3] Unknown was the modern division of labour between the sexes where the married woman, unless employed in industry, is limited to the preparation of the meals, house cleaning, laundry, and the care of the children. In an earlier period, these tasks were frequently performed by unmarried girls under the direction of the housewife, thus freeing her for more productive economic activities.

In the pre-industrial period, then, women and children were employed both in agriculture and industry. However, with industrialization their economic contribution was magnified. For although it is true that the introduction of machinery meant the destruction of domestic industry; nevertheless, the increased demand for women and children in the factory more than compensated for their economic depreciation in the home. Simultaneously, the absolute value of male labour-power was depreciated:

---

[1] 'In Denmark, signs of the partial survival of the kindred are not wanting even at the dawn of the 17th century. . . . In Schleswig the old customs defy legislation levelled at them by king, duke or *Landtag* for another century still. In Holstein . . . certain of their functions continued to be exercised until near the end of the 18th century, and indeed even into the 19th century. . . .' Bertha Surtees Phillpotts, *Kindred and Clan in the Middle Ages and After*, Cambridge, 1913, pp. 245–6.

[2] *Ibid.*, p. 256.

[3] Alice Clark, *Working Life of Women in the Seventeenth Century*, London, 1919, p. 5.

Machinery by throwing every member of that family on the labour market spreads the value of the man's labour-power over his whole family. It thus depreciates his labour-power. To purchase the labour-power of a family of four workers may, perhaps, cost more than it formerly did to purchase the labour-power of the head of the family, but, in return, four day's labour takes the place of one, and their price falls in proportion to the excess of the surplus-labour of four over the surplus-labour of one.[1]

Along with the reduction in the cost of male labour-power the relative value of women and children rises, since frequently, as in the cotton industry, they could perform the work more efficiently than men.

In fact, from the point of view of population dynamics, the significant immediate effect of the industrial revolution was to provide a stimulus to increased fertility:

> The demand for children's labour often resembles in form the inquiries for negro slaves, such as were formerly to be read among the advertisements in American journals. . . . In the notorious district of Bethnal Green, a public market is held every Monday and Tuesday morning, where children of both sexes from 9 years of age upwards, hire themselves out to the silk manufacturers. 'The usual terms are 1s. 8d. a week' (this belongs to the parents) and '2d. for myself and tea'. The contract is binding for only a week. . . . Whenever the law limits the labour of children to 6 hours in industries not before interfered with, the complaints of the manufacturers are always renewed. They allege that numbers of the parents withdraw their children from the industry brought under the Act in order to sell them where 'freedom of labour' still rules. . . .[2]

The evolution of industrial capitalism which at first, particularly in England, enhanced the economic value of women and children but later resulted in the economic depreciation of children will be considered more fully in the following chapter on 'Demand for Labour', where demand for labour will be analysed not only quantitatively but also qualitatively, i.e. with reference to what Colin Clark has termed the 'morphology of economic growth'.

For the present, however, it is sufficient to realize that the

[1] Karl Marx, *Capital*, Vol. I, p. 431.
[2] *Ibid.*, pp. 393-4. Marx was quoting from the *Children's Employment Commission*, Third and Fifth Reports, London, 1864 and 1866.

economic function of the family for the poor has undergone an evolution. Women's economic contribution in the home has been depreciated and transformed while, simultaneously, children are an economic liability. Purely as wife and mother in the home, woman is divorced from direct productive activity. Her function now is one of conserving or maintaining rather than value-producing or surplus-yielding. Practically every productive activity previously performed by women in the home can be accomplished more economically in the factory. In short, woman's work, whether indifferently performed or not, resolves itself into catering to the needs of the producer, the wage-worker, e.g. preparation of meals, mending and cleaning of clothes, keeping the house tidy, and the care of the children.

Nevertheless, the wife in the family of the poor makes a greater economic contribution than her counterpart among the wealthy. For the worker needs companionship, someone to prepare his meals, maintain his clothes and look after his children.[1] On the other hand, considered purely from an economic point of view, the function of the wife among the wealthy resolves itself essentially into being the vehicle for the perpetuation of the patrimony through, it is hoped, legitimate heirs, or in the frequently quoted words of Demosthenes:

For we have the Companions for the sake of pleasure, the concubines for the daily care of the body, and the wives that genuine children may be born to us, and that we may have a trustworthy guardian of our household property.[2]

---

[1] It should be obvious that the economic interpretation does not assume (regardless of the past economic foundation of the family) an existing economic motivation for procreation. Rather, in general, the evidence indicates that children are considered as desirable, a good. The point, however, is that the economic interpretation attempts to throw light on fertility differences or 'corruptions' traceable to economic conditions, e.g. excessive fertility stimulated by the economic value of children; or sharply curtailed fertility resulting from an economic desire to maintain intact an estate or patrimony in subsequent generations; or, in the case of the poor, reduced income which prevents them from having the number of children desired.

[2] According to the Greeks, all citizens were 'connected by ties of blood more or less distant; they all had the same divine ancestor; they all worshipped the same gods in the same temples'. Also, 'they possessed many rights, properties, and privileges in common. It was therefore of supreme importance that in the continuation of the State only true citizens should be admitted, and, accordingly, the general principle was laid down that none could become citizens but those whose fathers and mothers had been the

The Economic Function of the Family

The analysis of the economic function of the family for the rich and the poor provides an explanation of the historically observed differences in their respective fertility patterns. Moreover, the analysis suggests the explanation of the recent fertility decline among the poorer classes. However, a 'demand-for-labour' analysis is required for a further understanding of family limitation among the poor; of inter-occupational differential fertility or why among the propertyless masses (i.e. those not deriving income from ownership), the strata least able to afford children make a relatively greater contribution to population growth; and, finally, of the recent population upsurge among the industrialized countries of the west. Such an analysis will be presented in the next chapter.

WOMEN'S SOCIAL STATUS AND FERTILITY

Since the status of women is closely associated with the evolution of the family and, further, since women's social status is frequently emphasized in cultural theories of population as a significant variable determining fertility patterns, it is desirable to consider briefly the relation between woman's economic value, her social status and her fertility pattern.

For although it is not believed that the status of women is a *basic factor* determining fertility patterns; nevertheless, there appears to be some relation such that when women's status is high there is a *tendency* toward family limitation.[1] But, of course, this relation is not universal. Thus, among the wealthy Athenians, low fertility did not have as its concomitant high social status for women; whereas, under the Roman Empire,

---

children of citizens. From this it followed that the utmost care should be taken that no spurious offspring should be palmed upon the State. The women could not be trusted in this matter to their own sense of propriety. It was natural for women to love. . . . Means must therefore be devised to prevent the possibility of anything going wrong, and, accordingly, the citizen-women had special apartments assigned to them, generally in the upper storey, that they might have to come downstairs, and men might see them if they ventured out.' James Donaldson, *Woman: Her Position and Influence in Ancient Greece and Rome, and among the Early Christians*, London, 1907, p. 50.

[1] That the status of women is not fundamental in determining fertility differences is evident in the higher fertility of women of the U.S.A. as compared to English women.

the low fertility of the wealthy did have as its concomitant high social status for women.[1] A conclusion based on these two cases alone would indicate that woman's status was largely irrelevant with respect to her fertility pattern.

But the problem is not so easily disposed of. There are grounds for believing that where women have a high social status and this status, in turn, is directly related to their high economic contribution, fertility will be curtailed. That is to say, the association between status and fertility is not direct. It is, rather, that when women's labour is especially productive their social status is not only high, but economic factors operate to reduce their fertility. Moreover, the relation may be complex and does not necessarily imply conscious family limitation, i.e. the very nature of women's employment, if especially arduous, may reduce their fertility.[2] On the other hand, family limitation may be deliberate since many confinements reduce women's economic value. For if, as in present times, woman labours in the factory, the rearing of children obviously entails a great financial sacrifice.[3] Therefore, it seems probable that where woman's high social status is a function of her economic contribution, there will be a general association between high social status for women and family limitation. But this discussion has been conducted on the assumption that woman's status is

[1] Given the Roman heritage in which women and children were regarded as the property of the father of the family, women's rise in social status under the Empire was truly remarkable. Brooks Adams explains the development as follows: 'When wealth became force, the female might be as strong as the male; therefore she was emancipated. Through easy divorce she came to stand on an equality with the man in the marriage contract. She controlled her own property, because she could defend it; and as she had power, she exercised political privileges. In the third century Julia Domna, Julia Mamaea, Soaemis, and others, sat in the Senate, or conducted the administration.' *The Law of Civilization and Decay*, New York, 1910, pp. 43–4.

[2] 'It is known that the load carrying and agricultural work undertaken by many African women is detrimental to health and childbearing, and tends to induce abortions.' C. J. Martin, 'Some Estimates of the General Age Distribution, Fertility and Rate of Natural Increase of the African Population of British East Africa', *Population Studies*, November 1953, p. 199.

[3] There is no contradiction in recognizing that fertility is diminished by both the reduction of the family to a consumption unit and by the employment of women in modern industry. In the former case, the economic liability of the wife and children is the decisive factor; in the latter case, the significant factor is the financial loss resulting from confinement and nursing.

largely determined by her economic contribution.[1] Let us consider this further and attempt to establish to what extent such an assumption is justified.

The generalizations suggested by history and comparative anthropology regarding the status of women are as follows:

1. Differentiation of labour leads to differentiation of status between the sexes.
2. Provided differentiation of labour is not so extreme as to constitute class exploitation of one sex by another, sex status is determined by productivity or social utility of labour.[2]
3. Where there is little differentiation of labour, or where no labour at all is performed, differences in sex status are at a minimum.

The statement that 'differentiation of labour leads to differentiation of status between the sexes' is not only the postulate of the economic interpretation but, also, is implied by the evidence supporting the second proposition that sex status is a function of the productivity or social utility of labour. The first generalization is, of course, not susceptible to inductive proof since there are no communities now extant lacking a division of labour between the sexes. But unless we are prepared to imagine that simultaneously with the origin of *Homo sapiens*, division of labour between the sexes sprung up, absence of inductive proof will not disturb us:

The first primeval phase must have been as devoid of labour, in the sense of *continuous purposive activity*, as animal life. There could have been no *product of labour*. Like animals, our earliest forefathers took their food straight from Nature, were it animal or vegetable. . . . Any economic dependence of women on men will have been as

---

[1] There is one generalization upon which all social anthropologists agree; namely, woman's execution of arduous labour in no way indicates a low status for her.

[2] The qualification having to do with 'class exploitation' refers to the low status of women in early Roman history as well as in Melanesian society. In such cases, considered collectively, women's economic contribution is great. But here, of course, differentiation of 'labour' ('function') is at a maximum. Further, although the collective contribution of women is high, considered individually she is dispensable since, like a slave, she can be replaced in the market.

unlikely at this stage as the economic dependence of the hind on the hart, or the she-wolf on her mate.[1]

Whether the first division of labour between the sexes resulted in the subordination of women since 'man enslaved his unarmed mate and founded *the family; his domain, his property*';[2] or whether with the first division of labour, woman's economic contribution on a co-operative basis was sufficient to insure her equal status is a point of controversy, the resolution of which does not concern us here.[3] Whatever the evolution in the division of labour between the sexes, and there seems no compelling reason why it must have been unilineal in all societies, the significant point that emerges is that given differentiation of labour, sex status is determined by the productivity of the labour performed.

This second proposition has received general recognition and does not require special labouring. Early in the nineteenth century, Lewis and Clark noted:

Where the women can aid in procuring subsistence for the tribe, they are treated with more equality, and their importance is proportioned to the share which they take in that labour; whilst in countries where subsistence is chiefly procured by the exertions of the men, the women are considered and treated as burdens.[4]

Nieboer explained the higher status of the Indian women of western Washington and north-west Oregon in comparison to that of the native women of Australia on the basis of their greater economic contribution.[5] Even Lowie, who cannot be suspected of any economic bias, wrote as follows:

There is one gross correlation, nevertheless, that has considerable support and has been repeatedly emphasised. Among stock-raising populations the status of woman is almost uniformly one of decided and absolute inferiority. Thus Professor Hobhouse finds that the

---

[1] Müller-Lyer, *The Family*, p. 105.   [2] *Ibid.*, p. 105.
[3] An early but good summary of divergent theories of the evolution of sexual relations is given in George Elliot Howard's *History of Matrimonial Institutions* (Chicago, 1904, Vol. I). At present, anthropologists and sociologists of the West, while not committed to a unilineal theory of development, tend to emphasize the primacy of the family. However, the theory that a matriarchal organization always precedes the patriarchal family was again advanced by Robert Briffault in *The Mothers* (London, 1927, 3 vols.).
[4] *Expedition up the Missouri*, Vol. II, pp. 334–5. Quoted by H. J. Nieboer, *op. cit.*, p. 222.   [5] *Ibid.*, p. 221.

percentage of cases in which woman occupies a low rung in the social scale is 73 among cultivators of the soil, but rises to 87·5 among pastoral tribes. On economic grounds the matter is readily explained. The domestication of animals was undoubtedly a masculine achievement and practically everywhere the care of the herds has remained a masculine occupation. But such complete dissociation of woman from productive toil is bound, according to the argument, to lead to her social degradation. In my opinion this consideration should be extended to agricultural (as distinct from horticultural) tribes. For, as Hahn has taught, it is not merely domestication but also plough-culture that is linked with masculine effort.[1]

The recognition of the importance of the division of labour and how it determines the status of the sexes has been interpreted to imply that women's status is necessarily low in a military society. Overemphasis on the 'manly' virtues of destructiveness implies a subordination of feminine excellencies, and it is not necessary to cast our eyes backwards to Feudalism to convince ourselves of the truth of the proposition. It is sufficient to recall the ideology of Fascism which not only glorified war but deprecated the feminine contribution. However, war *per se* does not necessarily imply that women's status will be low, and it is incorrect to conclude as Simone de Beauvoir does,[2] that women's status under the Spartan and Nazi regimes was equally low:

The Spartans wanted brave men; the mothers must be brave. . . . They believed, with intense faith, that as are the mothers, so will be the children. And they acted on this faith. They first devoted all the attention and care they could to the physical training of their women . . . the women engaged in gymnastic exercises; and when they reached the age of girlhood, they entered into contests with each other in wrestling, racing, and throwing the quoit and javelin. . . . But it was not only for the physical strength, but for the mental tone, that the girls had to go through this physical exercise. They mingled freely with the young men. They came to know each other well. . . . And in the games nothing inspirited them so much as the praise of the girls, and nothing was so terrible as the shouts of derision which greeted their failures.[3]

---

[1] Robert H. Lowie, *Primitive Society*, London, 1921, p. 144.
[2] *The Second Sex* (translated and edited by H. M. Parshley), London, 1953, p. 84.
[3] James Donaldson, *op. cit.*, pp. 25–6.

The point is this: disregarding the values of the particular society, woman's status is higher where her contribution is valued and she is allowed to participate. So in militarist Sparta where, according to Aristotle, women possessed two-fifths of all the land,[1] they yet attained to a higher status than their Athenian sisters whose duties, because of a sharper division of labour, 'lay entirely within the house' and 'were summed up in the words "to remain inside and to be obedient to her husband" '.[2]

The significance of the economic contribution is also emphasized by the rise in the social status of women in the post-Feudal period. During the Middle Ages the attitude toward woman, as expressed by the only articulate group in society, the clergy, was a 'theory of her essential inferiority'.[3] The influence of the Roman concept of the family as a property arrangement is evident in a Theological Dictionary of the fourteenth century which stated:

> Moreover a man may chastise his wife and beat her by way of correction, for she forms a part of his household; so that he the master may chastise that which is his, as it is written in the Gloss (Canon Law).[4]

Not much later, St. Bernardino of Siena recognized the same marital right but admonished the male members of his flock to practise restraint:

> There are men who can bear more patiently with a hen that lays a fresh egg every day than with their own wives. . . . O raving madmen! who cannot bear a word from their wives, though they bear them such fair fruit. . . . Consider, rascal, consider the noble fruit of the wife, and have patience; it is not right to beat her for every cause, No![5]

---

[1] James Donaldson, *op. cit.*, p. 25. [2] *Ibid.*, p. 52.

[3] Eileen Power, 'The Position of Women' in *The Legacy of the Middle Ages* (edited by C. G. Crump and E. F. Jacob), Oxford, 1926, p. 403. The Medieval period, however, was characterized by a peculiar ambivalence toward woman, for although deprecated on earth woman was exalted in the empyrean realm through the cult of the Virgin.

[4] Quoted by G. G. Coulton, *Chaucer and His England*, London (sixth edition), 1937, p. 214.

[5] *Ibid.*, p. 215. However, in another sermon, speaking of woman's extravagance and immodesty, St. Bernardino remarks ' . . . if I were your husband, I would give you such a drubbing with feet and fists, that I would make you remember for awhile'. *Ibid.*, p. 215.

While it would be a mistake to form a judgment on the status of women based entirely on the statements of the clergy since, as Eileen Power has shown, women frequently made a great economic contribution during the Medieval period and, thus, probably occupied a higher position than that indicated by the writings of the cultured ecclesiastics; [1] nevertheless, reiterated propaganda on women's inferiority must have had a noticeable effect.

Such was the legacy of the Middle Ages. The importance of woman's economic contribution in determining her status now becomes evident when we contrast Feudal ideology toward women with that of the English middle-class in Elizabethan England. In an extremely interesting chapter on 'The Popular Controversy Over Women', Louis B. Wright stated:

... woman became the theme of many popular poems and pamphlets, which vigorously attacked her weakness or with equal vigor defended her virtue. . . . Stories mocking the vanities of women still excited the laughter of the man in the street. . . . Yet, despite the recrudescence of medieval condemnations of the female sex, a new note of respect was creeping into the popular literature, as writers reflecting the trend of middle-class opinion arose to defend woman against her traducers. [2]

Two pamphlets which were widely circulated in this period are especially informative. The first, *Hic Mulier: Or, the Man-Woman: Being a Medicine to cure the Coltish Disease of the Staggers in the Masculine-Feminines of our times,* savagely attacked the insolence and vanity of women. However, a rejoinder *Haec Vir: Or the Womanish-Man: Being an Answere to a late Booke intituled Hic Mulier,* reflected the 'opinion of the more advanced social thinkers among the bourgeoisie, it is a document whose significance has been overlooked'. [3] In this pamphlet, a woman and a man argue over the respective merits of women and men, and the argument reaches a climax in the following statement of women's rights:

We are as free-borne as Men, haue as free election and as free spirits, we are compounded of like parts, and may with like liberty

---

[1] *Op. cit.,* pp. 410 ff.
[2] *Middle-Class Culture in Elizabethan England,* University of North Carolina Press, 1935, p. 465. [3] *Ibid.,* p. 494.

make benefit of our Creations: my countenance shal smile on the worthy, and frowne on the ignoble, I will hear the Wise, and bee deafe to Ideots, giue counsell to my friend, but bee dumbe to flatters, I haue hands that shal bee liberal to reward desert, feet that shal moue swiftly to good offices, and thoughts that shal euer accompany freedome and seuerity. If this bee barbarous, let me leaue the Citie, and liue with creatures of like simplicity.[1]

It is not difficult to relate the rise in the status of woman to her economic contribution. Whereas under Feudalism, differentiation of labour was extreme since 'as the military tenure of land increased, the powers and rights of women, who could not perform military service, decreased';[2] with the growth of trade in the subsequent period women could make a valuable contribution in the same field as men:

The relation between husband and wife which obtained most usually among the upper classes in England at the opening of the seventeenth century, appears indeed to have been that of partnership ... in business matters she was her husband's lieutenant. The wife was subject to her husband, her life was generally an arduous one, but she was by no means regarded his servant. The ladies of the Elizabethan period possessed courage, initiative, resourcefulness and wit in a high degree ... perhaps it was partly the comradeship with their husbands in the struggle for existence which developed in them qualities which had otherwise atrophied.[3]

During the seventeenth century, English women managed the estates of their husbands who were frequently absent for months; were active in politics; obtained patents and monopolies from

---

[1] *Middle-Class Culture in Elizabethan England*, p. 497. Even prior to the Elizabethan age, the woman question had been agitated. Christine de Pisan (1363–1420) argued in *La Cité des Dames* that although physically inferior, women were neither morally nor mentally inferior to men. Male champions of women's rights in the sixteenth century included Martin Le Franc, Provost of the Church at Lausanne, who wrote a poem (1540) defending women; an Italian historian, Capella (1476–1535) who denied that women were inferior to men; Cornelious Agrippa who in a Latin treatise (1532), which was translated into English in 1670, argued that women should not be excluded from public offices. For a more detailed discussion of the above mentioned authors, as well as a number of other women writers active in promoting the feminine cause in the sixteenth and seventeenth centuries, see the chapter 'The First Feminists' in G. W. Johnson's *The Evolution of Woman*, London, 1926, pp. 92 ff.

[2] Ernst R. Groves, *The American Woman*, New York, 1944, p. 31.

[3] Alice Clark, *op. cit.*, pp. 40–1.

the court; managed salt mines; acted as pawnbrokers; engaged in shipping, trade and commerce; dealt in insurance; contracted to supply the army and navy with apparel, etc.[1]

Similarly, in the highly developed capitalist country of Holland, according to an English traveller writing in 1622, the status of women was high:

. . . in *Holland* the wif's are so well vers'd in bargaining, cifring and writing, that in the absence of their Husbands in long Sea-Voyages, they beat the trade at home, and their words will pass in equal credit: These women are wonderfully sober, though their husbands make commonly their bargains in drink. . . .[2]

But the promise of a new and richer life for women, following the collapse of Feudalism, was prevented from being realized by the very nature of capitalist development. For whereas in its initial stage, capitalism enhanced the economic value of middle-class women and brought them into co-operative activity with men; in the succeeding period, women's economic value was again depreciated by developments leading to her isolation from productive activity. In England, for example, following the Restoration, the growth of capitalist organization of industry 'made possible the idleness of growing numbers of women':

Simultaneously, the gradual perfecting by men of their separate organizations for trade purposes rendered them independent of the

---

[1] *Ibid.*, Chapter II, pp. 14 ff. Joan Dant who, starting as a peddler, saved sufficient capital to enter the wholesale trade is a case in point. Joan died in 1715 at the age of eighty-four after having accumulated a fortune of £9,000. When asked how she proposed to dispose of her property, she stated: 'I got it by the rich and I mean to leave it to the poor'. *Ibid.*, p. 33.

[2] James Howell, *Epistolae Ho-Elianae-Familiar Letters* (fifth edition), London, 1678, p. 87. Howell is also interesting for his attitude toward marriage. Although business-minded, and not a poet, Howell repudiated the traditional separation of marriage from love. In a letter to his cousin (1635) Howell wrote: 'If you are resolv'd to marry . . . let love, rather than *lucre*, be your guide in this election, though a concurrence of both Be good, yet for my part, I had rather the latter should be wanting than the first, the one is the Pilate, but the other the Ballast of the ship which should carry us to the *Harbour* of a happy life: if you are bent to wed, I wish you another wife than Socrates had; who when she had scoulded him out of doors, as he was going through the Portal, threw a Chamber-pot of stale Urine upon his head, wherat the Philosopher having bin silent all the while, smilingly said, "*I thought after so much Thunder we should have rain.*" ' *Ibid.*, pp. 159–60.

services of their wives and families for the prosecution of their undertakings.[1]

Such was the effect of capitalist development upon the status of women of the upper classes. With reference to the lower classes, we have already seen that women's status was not affected until the time of industrial capitalism which, on the one hand, by depreciating the value of man's labour-power, raised the relative contribution of women in industry, but, on the other hand, through the destruction of domestic industry, rendered the wife in the home an economic liability.

In the third generalization regarding the determination of women's status, it was stated that where no labour at all is performed, differences in sex status tend to be at a minimum. Evidence for this is found in the high status of Roman women under the Empire. The point is not particularly significant, but it does enable us to understand how among purely non-productive classes, i.e. those receiving their income from the mere fact of ownership, the women of this class, which is divorced from direction or even minor superintendence, can enjoy a high social status and reach near equality with men.

Such are the economic determinants of women's social status. The laws governing her social status are not the same as those determining her fertility pattern. The wife of the rich man may or may not enjoy high social status, depending on the extent of the differentiation of labour between the sexes. But whether a wealthy Greek or Roman wife, whether enjoying a high or low social status, her fertility pattern is dictated by the economic function of the family for this class. *Her social status is largely adventitious but seems to be causally connected to her fertility pattern since, in general, among the wealthy, differentiation of labour is at a minimum and thus the women of this class enjoy a high social status.*

Among the poorer classes, high social status for woman is seen to be connected with her economic contribution. However, when women's economic contribution is high, there are obvious reasons for family limitation. So, in a sense, there is a relation

---

[1] Alice Clark, *op. cit.*, p. 41. In the manner of Lewis Carroll, Janet Dunbar describes the education of the eighteenth century: 'religious instruction, needlework and resignation seem to have been the chief subjects for girls'. *The Early Victorian Woman*, London, 1953, p. 144.

between social status and fertility, *but the association is indirect and rests fundamentally on the nature of her work.*

The importance of women's economic contribution and its influence on fertility may, perhaps, have contributed to the continued fertility decline in the United States from the beginning of the nineteenth century.[1] As we saw above, the women of Elizabethan England, as well as the women of Holland, enjoyed a high social status in the seventeenth century. They not only participated in the economic affairs of the country but frequently managed their husbands' businesses during long periods in which the men were absent. This trend toward a higher status for women was carried over into the American culture by the early colonists and was not reversed, as in England following the Restoration.[2] On the contrary, the activities of the colonial women and their successors were such as to enhance their economic contribution and, consequently, their social status. Women were engaged in fighting Indians; managing households, farms, and in the south, plantations; ferry transportation; tavern keeping; running boarding houses, etc. The importance of the contribution of American women was fully appreciated by Alexis de Tocqueville:

> If I were asked now that I am drawing to the close of this work, in which I have spoken of so many important things done by the Americans, to what the singular prosperity and growing strength of that people ought to be attributed, I should reply, to the superiority of their women.[3]

It seems probable that the high social status of American woman, a function of her economic contribution which included hard labour, may have resulted in either voluntary or involuntary family limitation, or both.[4]

[1] The United States and France were, apparently, the only two countries which experienced a fertility decline throughout the whole of the nineteenth century.

[2] The influence of the Dutch in New York has been noted: 'During the New Netherlands era women profited from the relative freedom enjoyed by their sisters in Holland. Legally husband and wife were equals who, without an ante-nuptial contract, enjoyed a community of possession. Such contracts permitted husband and wife to inherit separately.' Ernst R. Groves, *op. cit.*, p. 48.

[3] *Democracy in America*, quoted by Mary R. Beard, *Woman as Force in History*, New York, 1946, pp. 74-5.

[4] In the next chapter, the influence of immigration on fertility in the United States will be considered, i.e. the substitution effect.

In summary, in this chapter the economic function of the family for the rich and poor has been contrasted. The evolution in the economic function of the family for the wealthy indicated that at one stage in the process of accumulation of wealth, when the family was the productive unit, fertility must have varied directly and not inversely with material fortune. However, following the full development of slavery or the derivation of income from the mere fact of a monopoly ownership of the instruments of production (land and labour), there is a change in the economic function of the family for the wealthy. From a production unit it is transformed into a vehicle for the transmission of property rights. Family limitation is the effective means for preserving intact the patrimony in subsequent generations.[1]

In the case of the poor, the economic function of the family was originally the co-operative satisfaction of production and consumption needs. Although the industrial revolution meant the destruction of domestic industry and the elimination of the co-operative production function of the family, nevertheless, the increased industrial demand for the labour of women and children more than compensated for their economic depreciation in the home. However, a subsequent stage in the evolution of capitalism, including the legal limitations imposed on child labour, meant that children are transformed from economic assets to liabilities. The adage, 'Children are the poor man's wealth', no longer holds true. In this stage, the economic contribution of women in industry remains high but the activities of the wife of the poor man (when she remains in the home) are reduced to catering to the consumption needs of the husband and the rearing of children. Developments subsequent to the industrial revolution which have made children progressively more expensive must be considered in the next chapter on qualitative and quantitative changes in the demand for labour.

Differences in the economic function of the family for the rich and poor furnish the explanation for the first great fertility differential. As yet, however, there is no explanation of fertility differentials within the large class who, divorced from owner-

---

[1] The children of the wealthy may also fulfil another need, e.g. when the rearing of a large family is a form of conspicuous consumption.

ship of the instruments of production, gain a livelihood from some type of labour or another. The economics of *inter-occupational* differential fertility as well as the recent fertility decline among the poorer classes of industrialized countries will be considered in the next chapter on demand for labour.

Finally, in this chapter there was an inquiry into the determinants of woman's social status and its relation to her fertility pattern. It was found that the laws governing woman's social status were not the same as those determining her fertility pattern. Hence social status was *not* fundamental in determining fertility. Nevertheless, it was recognized that when high social status for woman was a function of her economic contribution, high social status and low fertility or, at least, some family limitation, tended to be associated together. But the association was indirect and not causally connected since both high social status and low fertility were recognized as common products of woman's valuable economic contribution.

CHAPTER EIGHT

The Demand for Labour

THE importance of demand for labour in determining population distribution both nationally and internationally is generally recognized. Growth of cities, the rural exodus, and emigration are readily comprehended as population responses (changes in supply of labour) to shifts in demand for labour.[1] Similarly, cyclical variations in fertility are also attributed to short-run fluctuations in demand for labour.[2] However, with regard to secular changes in population growth, specifically the birth rate, the tendency of Neo-Classical economists was to ignore long-run changes in demand for labour when considering the population problem with reference to modern industrialized communities. Therefore, it is proposed in this chapter to provide a theoretical framework for the long-run analysis of population changes which is consistent with the short-run analysis based on geographical and cyclical changes in demand for labour.

The abandonment of the Classical thesis that demand for labour regulates supply was sanctioned by the realization that population did not increase *pari passu* with the growth in real income. Obviously it would have been ridiculous, in view of the actual developments in the last quarter of the nineteenth century, to have maintained in the original Malthusian version the thesis that the population of modern industrialized communities was always pressing against the means of subsistence.

[1] Students of population movements stress the 'push' (low local demand for labour) and 'pull' (high foreign demand for labour) factors influencing migration. *Cf.* United Nations, *The Determinants and Consequences of Population Trends*, Chapter VI.

[2] For a short summary of studies on the influence of the business cycle on fertility, see United Nations, *op. cit.*, Chapter V.

But means of subsistence and demand for labour must be distinguished; and Malthus, himself, made just such a distinction when he turned to a consideration of the problem of effective demand.[1] However, in Neo-Classical thought this distinction was not made clear. On the contrary, since Neo-Classical economists did not recognize the problem of effective demand, the analysis of population growth was conducted within the framework of a 'natural' rather than an institutional context, i.e. in terms of the ratio of numbers to physical resources. Hence, the failure of population growth to keep pace with the increase in real income meant not only the rejection of the Malthusian analysis for modern industrialized communities but, also, the more or less explicit repudiation of the thesis that demand for labour governed supply. Thus were economists frequently led to the acceptance of a volitional theory of population growth.

So it is that in the contemporary period, economists and demographers stress the importance of demand for labour as the determinant of population distribution and cyclical changes in fertility, while simultaneously minimizing its influence on overall population growth. But the lack of correspondence between the short- and long-run theory does not bridge the gulf nor subsume the phenomena of demography under a general theory of population growth. However, the necessity for developing a *general* theory of population dynamics which will explain both long- and short-run phenomena originates not merely from a recognition of the formal inadequacy, or inelegance, of contemporary population theory. On the contrary, as was noted in the introductory chapter, the need arises from the failure of demography as a science of prediction.

The following analysis proceeds on the assumption that demand for labour governs its supply both in the long- and short-run. However, since there is general recognition of the importance of demand for labour in determining short-run fertility phenomena, the analysis will be concerned with demonstrating how secular changes in the demand for labour may influence population growth by effecting basic and relatively permanent changes in fertility patterns.

[1] *Supra*, Chapter IV, p. 89.

Although recognizing that the production period for labour-power was a relatively long one in comparison to that of other commodities; nevertheless, the population theory of the Classical school premised that laws regulating its production were basically no different from those for any other commodity. Thus, an increased demand for labour, like that for any other commodity, was reflected in the market by a rise in price. The rise in wages, however, leads to an increased supply of labour which, in turn, counters the wage rise. Wages are thus restored to their 'natural' level, i.e. the amount required to cover the cost of production of labour-power.

The tendency of Classical economic thought was to consider labour in terms of the aggregate supply and, therefore, to neglect qualitative differences; but it is essential for the present argument to bear in mind that the demand for labour is not homogeneous. Demand for labour must be analysed in terms of the amount of labour demanded of a particular grade or skill. Given an equal demand for skilled and unskilled labour, where the cost differential for the production of these two grades of labour-power is in the ratio (say) of one to one-and-a-half, the amount of skilled labour forthcoming will be sufficient provided only that the cost differential is paid. Viewed dynamically, the actual mechanism for obtaining the required quantity and quality of labour is as follows: that grade of labour which is in relative short supply is temporarily paid a premium over and above its cost of production; while, simultaneously, that grade of labour which is in relative oversupply suffers a depreciation below its cost of production. In such a way, the supply of labour is regulated and diverted into the appropriate channels according to the needs of industry.

Recognition of the importance of demand for labour, how it regulates the supply and determines the allocation, does not imply a normative evaluation. The equilibrium achieved may or may not be desirable even under competition, depending on the criteria employed. Further, in most cases, both the demand for and the supply of labour are subject to some degree of monopsony and monopoly. Again, although above, wages were spoken of as being 'restored to their "natural" level' this does not imply an external sanction in nature for the existing distribution of income. All that the statement asserts is that, *in general*, in a capitalist society there is a tendency for wages to equal the cost of production of labour-power.[1]

Application of the demand for labour analysis to population growth is complicated by the fact, as already indicated, that demand for labour must be considered both quantitatively and qualitatively. *On the assumption of no changes in the normal supply price of labour*, the quantitative possibilities of changes (*shifts*) in demand for labour are:

1. Demand for labour may be increasing at an increasing rate;
2. Demand for labour may be increasing at a constant rate;
3. Demand for labour may be increasing at a decreasing rate;
4. There may be an absolute decrease in demand for labour.

Along with the above possible changes in the quantity of labour demanded, there may be concomitant changes in the quality of labour demanded. Such changes in the quality of labour demanded may either increase or reduce labour's normal supply price. Obviously, various combinations are possible; however, they need not be detailed here. But for population growth, the situation most favourable would be one in which demand for labour was increasing at an increasing rate (number 1, above) while simultaneously, there was a great relative increase in the demand for labour of a lower quality. For a decrease in the quality of labour demanded is tantamount to a reduction in the production period of labour-power. That is to say, the more unskilled the labour, the shorter is the period of time required for it to reach the market, and the lower its supply price.[2] An extreme example of such a situation was the utilization of child labour at the time of the industrial revolution.

Conversely, the situation most unfavourable to population growth would be one in which the demand for labour fell absolutely while, simultaneously, there was a shift in demand to a higher quality of labour. But it is obvious that even if demand for labour were increasing at a decreasing rate (number

---

[1] 'Thus we may conclude that, *as a general rule* . . . the longer the period, the more important will be the influence of cost of production on value.' Marshall, *op. cit.*, p. 349.

[2] '. . . the supply price of a certain kind of labour may for some purposes be divided up into the expenses of rearing, of general education and of special trade education'. *Ibid.*, p. 340.

3, above) and this was accompanied by a relative increase in the demand for skilled labour, the rate of population growth would tend to decline. Recognizing, then, that demand for labour must be considered both quantitatively and qualitatively, we proceed now to a consideration of population growth and the evolution of capitalism.

THE INDUSTRIAL REVOLUTION

The crux of the population controversy in the latter half of the eighteenth century was whether the number of people in England and Wales had increased since the time of the Glorious Revolution.[1] Today there still remains the question of what happened to fertility during the period of the so-called industrial revolution. On the one hand, the majority of demographers believe that the population upsurge of this period must be attributed almost wholly to a decline in mortality; on the other hand, the great increase in the demand for labour suggests the possibility of an increase in fertility.[2] Absence of reliable statistics precludes a definite answer.

However, it is possible to approach the fertility question in the period of the industrial revolution by a different method. As T. H. Marshall pointed out, a decline in mortality which is not accompanied by a fall in fertility is, in effect, tantamount to the adoption of a new fertility pattern.[3] The conclusion follows even if it should be established absolutely that people neither married earlier nor had more children. This apparently paradoxical result is justified by the following considerations:

Assume a society in population equilibrium, where equilibrium is interpreted broadly to include either a stationary population, or a population increasing at a moderately constant rate. In the absence of either emigration or immigration, population size is determined by the existing mortality and fertility rates. Now, on the assumption of such an equilibrium, it follows that any change in one rate will effect a corresponding change in

[1] *Cf.* D. V. Glass, 'The Population Controversy in Eighteenth-century England, Part I, The Background', *Population Studies*, July 1952.
[2] *Cf.* H. H. Habakkuk, 'English Population in the Eighteenth Century', *The Economic History Review*, December 1953.
[3] 'The Population Problem During the Industrial Revolution', *The Economic Journal* (Economic History Series, No. 4), January 1929.

the other rate.[1] Thus if mortality rises, fertility also must rise in order to maintain the previous adjustment; and, *vice versa*, if mortality falls, fertility must also decline in order to preserve the previously established equilibrium.[2] Equilibrium then is maintained by compensatory movements in mortality and fertility rates or, in other words, by a cancelling out process.

This analysis suggests that a change in one rate which is not followed by a compensatory change in the other rate indicates that the previously established equilibrium between population and environment is being supplanted by a new equilibrium. In short, the situation is dynamic and there is in progress a movement toward a new equilibrium which, until realized, permits of a change in one rate which does not result in a compensatory change in the other rate.

With reference to England, the decline in child mortality meant that the number of children per family rose. In effect, as already suggested, since the fall in mortality did not lead to a compensating fertility decline the result was tantamount to the introduction of a new fertility pattern. For, objectively speaking, the increase in average family size consequent upon the reduction of child mortality amounts to the toleration, if not the conscious adoption, of a new fertility pattern.

So the problem of population growth in the period of the industrial revolution must be analysed in terms of economic

---

[1] In an investigation of twenty-two countries at about the same stage of economic development, G. Udny Yule obtained a positive correlation (plus 0·81) between birth and death rates for the period 1901–10. 'The Growth of Population and the Factors Which Control It', *Journal of the Royal Statistical Society*, January 1925.

[2] The adjustment is not immediate and, in fact, the relation between mortality and fertility might be the very opposite of that stated above. For example, in India, during periods of famine, high mortality and low fertility are concomitant phenomena. However, here the complicating factor may be the loss of a large number of women in the reproductive age group which would include the destruction of numerous unborn babies as well as 'the debilitating effect of disease and food shortage upon the physiological capacity to bear children' (Carr-Saunders, *World Population*, p. 272). Again, the relation between fertility and mortality is complex, and the above discussion must not be construed as maintaining that every increase in mortality which is accompanied by an increase in fertility necessarily indicates the existence of a compensatory action for the maintenance of a previously established adjustment between population and environment. Thus increased mortality may itself be a function of increased fertility simply because the first years of life have been extremely hazardous.

development, changes in the demand for labour, which permitted the 'toleration of a new fertility pattern' following the decline in infant mortality. Here it should be noted that, as stated above, the situation most favourable to population growth is one in which a great increase in the quantity of labour demanded is accompanied by a reduction in the quality demanded.

As is known, the spread of the factory system meant a great increase in the quantitative demand for labour. Simultaneously, however, there was a reduction in the quality of labour demanded:

... wherever a process requires peculiar dexterity and steadiness of hand, it is withdrawn as soon as possible from the *cunning* workman, who is prone to irregularities of many kinds, and it is placed in charge of a peculiar mechanism, so self-regulating that a child may superintend it. ... On the handicraft plan, labour more or less skilled, was usually the most expensive element of production ... but on the automatic plan, skilled labour gets progressively superseded, and will, eventually, be replaced by mere overlookers of machines.[1]

Again:

It is, in fact, the constant aim and tendency of every improvement in machinery to supersede human labour altogether, or to diminish its costs, by substituting the industry of women and children for that of men; of that of ordinary labourers, for trained artisans.[2]

The characteristic features of the growth of the factory system were the destruction of handicraft production, or the elimination of ancient skills which had formerly required a considerable period of time for their mastery; the utilization and sometimes even the substitution of the unskilled labour of women and children for that of adult male workers; the reduction in individual differences among workers or, as the saying goes, 'All men are equal before the machine'.[3]

The establishment of the factory system lowers the cost of labour-power in two ways: In the first place, the reduction in

[1] Andrew Ure, *The Philosophy of Manufactures*, London, 1835, pp. 19–20.
[2] *Ibid.*, p. 23.
[3] See the chapter 'Machinery and the Quality of Labour', in John A. Hobson's *The Evolution of Modern Capitalism* (revised edition), 1916, pp. 335 ff.

the demand for skilled labour shortens the production period of the worker, i.e. the time and expense required in preparing him for productive labour. Secondly, simultaneously with the increased demand for unskilled labour, the employment of women and children further lowers the cost of a man's labour-power, or in the previously quoted words of Marx: 'Machinery by throwing every member of that family on the labour market, spreads the value of the man's labour-power over his whole family'.[1]

The economic explanation of the population upsurge in the period of the industrial revolution, then, is found in the growth in the aggregate demand for labour, simultaneously accompanied by a reduction in the quality of labour demanded.[2] Such were the economic developments which in England permitted the 'toleration of a new fertility pattern'.

Consider now the question raised in a preceding chapter, viz. can decreased fertility 'be viewed in part as a social adjustment to the improvement of mortality'? According to the demand-for-labour analysis, the answer must be 'Yes'. For in the absence of any great change in either the quantitative or qualitative demand for labour, the previous adjustment between population and environment could only be maintained by a decrease in fertility. In other words, decreased mortality does not necessarily engender decreased fertility; however, in the absence of any increase in the demand for labour or any reduction in the quality required, such will be the tendency. Here, then, is suggested the explanation for the difference in the demographic history of France and England. For, it will be recalled, whereas in England decreased mortality was not accompanied by an observed fertility decline; in France, on the contrary, there was a concomitant fall in mortality and fertility. But not only did French industrial development lag far behind that of England but, also, the system of peasant proprietorship was already well established prior to the French revolution, especially in the east. In short, according to this analysis, the slow growth in the demand for labour in France, while per-

---

[1] Quoted above, Chapter VII, p. 151.

[2] '. . . in the broader applications of economic science it is sometimes necessary to . . . take account of the slow changes that in the course of centuries affect the supply price of the labour of each industrial grade'. Marshall, *op. cit.*, p. 365, n. 1.

mitting an absolute increase in population, was not sufficient to maintain the previous fertility level following the decline in mortality.

THE EVOLUTION OF CAPITALISM AND THE FERTILITY DECLINE

It was pointed out above that a decrease in the rate of growth in the demand for labour is unfavourable to population increase. It was also recognized that the situation would be further aggravated by a shift in demand from a lower to a higher quality of labour. Therefore, the economic explanation of the fertility decline in the last quarter of the nineteenth century should establish that qualitative and/or quantitative changes in the demand for labour were such as to induce family limitation.

Although the immediate result of the industrial revolution was the substitution of unskilled for skilled labour, this process was in turn negated. In contrast to the early period of industrial capitalism, mature capitalism demands labour of a higher quality. This is true not only with reference to the shift in demand from a lower to a higher quality of labour but also holds with respect to the quality of 'unskilled' labour itself.

With reference to the qualitative change in unskilled labour, it will be recalled that Marshall distinguished between the 'efficient' labour of western industrialized communities and the 'inefficient' labour of the non-industrialized east. This distinction holds for a comparison of the unskilled labour of both communities. Historically, it has been recognized in the progressive modification of the mercantilist doctrine of the 'economy of low wages':

Lord Brassey . . . found that English navvies employed upon the Grand Trunk Railway in Canada, and receiving from 5s. to 6s. a day, did a greater amount of work for the money than French-Canadians paid at 3s. 6d. a day; that it was more profitable to employ Englishmen at 3s. to 3s. 6d. upon making Irish railways than Irishmen at 1s. 6d. to 1s. 8d; that 'in India, although the cost of dark labour ranges from 4½d. to 6d. a day, mile for mile the cost of railway work is about the same as in England.'[1]

---

[1] Hobson, *op. cit.*, p. 355.

Marshall, in his testimony before the Royal Commission on the Aged Poor (1893), emphasized the increased efficiency associated with a rise in labour's standard of living.[1] As Francis A. Walker put it: 'With more fuel, the engine will do more work. With more food, the man will do more work.'[2]

The doctrine of the economy of high wages, of course, has only limited validity and, as Hobson rightly emphasizes, must not be interpreted to imply 'a direct arithmetical progression in the relation of wage and work such as would . . . be reflected in an exactly correspondent difference of output of productive energy'.[3] Obviously, such an assumption would be ridiculous and, moreover, would fail to explain the phenomenon of capital export in a number of cases.

The importance of the doctrine of the 'economy of high wages' for population theory lies in its recognition of the increased demands on labour associated with the progress of machine production, i.e. the qualitative evolution in the demand and supply of unskilled and semi-skilled labour.[4] And although it would be false to assert that every increase in productivity arising from the more extensive application of machinery implies a 'speed-up' for labour; nevertheless,

. . . the history of the factory system, both in England and in other countries, clearly indicates that factory labour is more intense than formerly, not, perhaps, in its tax upon the muscles, but in the growing strain it imposes upon the nervous system of the operatives.[5]

Besides increased intensity of labour which *raises the cost of maintenance*, consideration must also be given to the *increased cost of labour-power* arising from modern industry's need for a literate labour force. For example, the driver of a truck in America (in England, lorry) must be able to read, merely to qualify for an operator's licence. Moreover, his duties may frequently involve some paper work; at a minimum he should at least be

---

[1] Cited by Alan T. Peacock, *op. cit.*, pp. 62–3.
[2] *Political Economy* (third edition), London, 1896, p. 47.
[3] *Op. cit.*, p. 356.
[4] In view of the frequently arbitrary division between unskilled and semi-skilled labour (sometimes having its origin in the necessities of collective bargaining) the above remarks should be understood as referring to a large class of manual labourers whose actual duties on the job can be performed satisfactorily following a brief period of instruction.
[5] Hobson, *op. cit.*, p. 371.

able to read maps. Thus, in the United States, according to a recent census publication, the median number of years of education for unskilled labour is now about eight.

Even more significant than the historical improvement in the quality of unskilled and semi-skilled labour has been the *rise in the average cost of labour-power* consequent upon the shift in demand to labour of a higher quality or grade of skill. This relative increase in the demand for a higher quality of labour is attested by occupation statistics of major capitalist countries. The statistics exhibit both an absolute and a relative growth of a 'new middle class'—a salaried group of white-collar workers divorced from ownership of the instruments of production.[1]

The evolution of capitalism which led to the destruction or relative subordination of an old middle class possessing ownership of the instruments of production is part of the history of centralization or the decline of competition. However, centralization of capital, alone, is not sufficient to explain fully the growth of a new class of salaried employees. Consideration must also be given to what Colin Clark has termed the morphology of economic growth or historical changes in production.

With industrialization, the number employed in primary production declines relatively; the proportion of the 'working population engaged in secondary industry' rises 'to a maximum' and then begins to decline relative to tertiary production. The occupational changes associated with this evolution are 'the gradual elimination of the manual worker, particularly the unskilled, and the rapid growth of the numbers of clerical and professional workers'.[2]

[1] 'In terms of property, the white-collar people are *not* "in between Capital and Labour"; they are in exactly the same property-class position as the wage-workers.' C. Wright Mills, *White Collar*, New York, 1951, p. 71. In popular writings, it is frequently stated that the German middle class supported Hitler. The thesis should be qualified. It was true of the old middle class, threatened with extinction, rather than of the new middle class of salaried employees. Ideologically, 'a great part of the white-collar workers—probably the majority—more closely resembled the character structure of the manual workers. . . .' Erich Fromm, *The Fear of Freedom*, London, 1942, p. 183.

[2] Colin Clark, *The Conditions of Economic Progress*, London, 1940, p. 7. (*Cf.* also Hobson, *op. cit.*, Chapter XVI, 'Occupations of the People', pp. 383 ff.) To avoid misunderstanding, it should be emphasized that centralization of capital is an important factor in the relative increase of tertiary over secondary production. For centralization of capital means monopoly restrictions

176

Statistics on occupational changes in the United States are revealing and also illustrative of the general pattern:

The Labour Force	1870 %	1940 %
Old Middle Class	33	20
New Middle Class	6	25
Wage-Workers	61	55
Total	100	100

Changes in the composition of the middle classes were as follows:

Old Middle Class	1870 %	1940 %
Farmers	62	23
Businessmen	21	19
Professionals	2	2
	85	44
New Middle Class		
Managers	2	6
Salaried Professionals	4	14
Sales People	7	14
Office Workers	2	22
	15	56
Total	100	100[1]

Thus, whereas in 1870 wage-workers constituted 90 per cent of all employees, in 1940 they comprised less than 70 per cent. The new middle class rose from less than 10 per cent in 1870 to more than 30 per cent.

As has been remarked, this evolution in the demand for labour was not confined to the United States but is also confirmed by occupational statistics for other industrialized countries. With reference to population growth, the significance of this historical shift in the demand for labour to that of a higher quality is, of course, the lengthened and increased cost of the average period of production of labour-power. For example, in the United States, the median number of years of

---

on production, particularly in secondary industries, as well as increased distribution costs, e.g. advertising. Further, the relative decline of secondary industries within a country is also related to the export of capital. Hence, although Clark's terminology is employed as a description of the actual evolution of capitalism, this does not imply the inevitability of such a pattern of economic growth for every industrialized society regardless of its institutional context.

[1] C. Wright Mills, *op. cit.*, pp. 63 and 65.

education requisite for office workers and sales people is somewhat above twelve, in contrast to slightly more than eight for semi-skilled and unskilled labour.[1]

The average cost of labour-power has been raised by

1. Demand for a better quality or more efficient kind of unskilled and semi-skilled labour, and
2. A shift in demand for labour to that of a higher quality or classification.

The rise in the cost of labour-power is reflected in the absolute increase in labour's standard of living. Speaking generally, *the increased goods and services consumed by the modern labour force are necessary cost elements for the maintenance and reproduction of a higher quality of labour.* This was recognized by Marshall when he stated:

> It remains true that . . . in the western world the earnings that are got by efficient labour are not much above the lowest that are needed to cover the expenses of rearing and training efficient workers, and of sustaining and bringing into activity their full energies.[2]

With the increased cost and lengthened average period of production of labour-power consequent upon a shift in demand for labour to that of a higher classification, there was a concomitant historical development significant for population growth, viz. the gradual decline in the relative earnings of labour of a higher classification (non-manual labour). Thus, in the United States:

> In 1890 . . . the average income of the salaried employee was roughly double that of the average wage-worker. . . . By 1920, the gap between wages and salaries had narrowed; salaried workers in manufacturing were receiving incomes that were only 65 per cent higher than those of wage-workers, compared to the 140 per cent advantage of 1900. Office-men in 1939 . . . received incomes 40 per cent higher than those of semi-skilled male workers; in 1948, only 9·5 per cent higher. Salesmen's incomes in 1939 were 19 per

---

[1] U.S. Bureau of Census, *U.S. Census Publications*, 1950, Vol. IV. *Special Reports*, Part 5, Chapter B. Education, U.S. Government Printing Office, Washington, D.C., 1953.
[2] Quoted above, Chapter IV, p. 94.

cent higher than those of semi-skilled male workers; in 1948, only 4 per cent higher.[1]

The narrowing of the income differential between non-manual and manual labour was not caused by a relative increase in the demand for unskilled and semi-skilled labour. Neither was it due to any shortage in the supply of this kind of labour. On the contrary, the relative decline in the earnings of non-manual labour was caused by a proportionately greater increase in the supply than in the demand for labour of a higher quality:

... between 1910 and 1947, the demand for clerical workers and salesmen in the U.S.A. rose from 10·2 to 18·2 per cent of the occupied population, yet the supply of this labour was so abundant that its relative remuneration was heavily reduced.[2]

Unemployment statistics also demonstrate that the narrowing of the income differential between manual and non-manual labour was not caused by an increased demand for unskilled labour. Thus, the United States' data for 1940 on 'Per cent of the Labour Force Seeking Work or on Public Emergency Work' showed a marked surplus of unskilled labour. Similarly, in England and Wales in 1931, the percentage of unemployed to total occupied male population was 30·5 per cent for unskilled workers as compared to 7·9 for salesmen and shop assistants, and 5·5 for clerks and typists.[3]

The narrowing of the wage differential between manual and non-manual labour has received recognition in the following empirical generalization: in primitive communities or in countries entering the path of industrial development, there are great differences in relative earnings between skilled and unskilled labour; whereas, in long industrialized communities, the

[1] C. Wright Mills, *op. cit.*, pp. 279–80. A more recent study shows that average weekly earnings in 1952 were $69.24 for wage earners as compared to $66.63 for salaried employees. Robert K. Burns, 'The Comparative Economic Position of Manual and White-Collar Employees', *The Journal of Business*, October 1954, p. 260.

[2] Colin Clark, *op. cit.* (second edition, 'completely rewritten'), London, 1951, p. 467.

[3] *Ibid.*, pp. 470–1. 'The increasing surplus of unskilled labour found in nearly all countries should be attributed to a contracting demand for this type of labour, rather than to an excessive supply consequent upon unduly narrow wage differentials' (*ibid.*, pp. 73–4).

differential in relative earnings between skilled and unskilled labour tends constantly to narrow.[1] However, this empirical generalization, itself, requires an explanation. Allowing for the rationalization of production concomitant with industrial progress which tends to eliminate extraordinary rewards or premiums for special or 'unique' skills (e.g. reading, book-keeping, engineering, etc.), there is still the problem of explaining a *continued decline in the relative earnings of non-manual labour*. For it is by no means self-evident that an *increasing demand* for labour of a *higher skill* (non-manual) which is accompanied by a *relative or an absolute decrease* in the demand for labour of a *lower grade* (manual) should have as its result a *continued narrowing* of the income differential between these two groups. However, the resolution of this paradox requires a quantitative analysis of the *total demand* for labour. Prior to proceeding to such a quantitative analysis, it will be helpful now to recapitulate briefly the results of the investigation into comparatively recent qualitative changes in the demand for labour.

Changes in demand for labour have raised the average cost of labour-power and lengthened its production period by

1. Qualitative improvements in the categories of 'unskilled' and 'semi-skilled' labour, and
2. Qualitative improvements consequent upon a shift in the demand for labour from a lower to a higher grade or skill.

The average cost of labour-power rises since Marshall's 'efficient' labour of the West requires more food and more education. Along with the rise in the cost of labour-power, there was a relative reduction in the demand for unskilled and semi-skilled labour. To some extent this relative decrease was compensated by a relative increase in the demand for non-manual labour. Nevertheless, the relative increase in the demand for non-manual labour was in some countries accompanied by a fall in its relative remuneration. In terms of demand for labour analysis, the implications for population growth are:

1. The relative fall in demand for unskilled and semi-skilled labour should result in a relative curtailment of its supply;

[1] *Cf.* Colin Clark, *op. cit.* (second edition), Chapter X, 'Relative Incomes and other Factors Controlling the Supply of Labour to Different Industries and Occupations', pp. 440 ff.

2. The relative and absolute increase in the demand for non-manual labour should result (as it did) in an increased supply;

3. Given an increased demand for non-manual labour relative to manual, a *continued* fall in the relative remuneration of non-manual labour is one indication that the supply of non-manual labour has increased proportionately more than demand and hence a curtailment in the supply of non-manual labour is a necessity.

In short, the analysis indicates that the adjustment of the supply of labour (population growth in the long-run) requires a curtailment of the supply of both manual and non-manual labour.

The necessity for the curtailment of the total supply of labour can be demonstrated as follows: the *aggregate demand* for labour is the sum of the total demands for manual and non-manual labour. It follows, then, that to *maintain a previous rate of growth in the total demand for labour*, a relative decrease in the demand for manual labour must be offset by a *proportional increase* in the demand for non-manual labour. In the event that the increase in the demand for non-manual labour is less than proportional to the relative decrease in the demand for manual labour, the rate of growth in the total demand for labour has decreased. As previously noted, the historic decline in the relative demand for manual labour was accompanied by a relative increase in the demand for non-manual labour. Simultaneously, however, in the United States there was a continued decline in the relative remuneration of non-manual labour which was caused by a proportionately greater increase in supply than in demand for non-manual labour. Hence the demand for non-manual labour could not have increased proportionately to the relative decrease in the demand for manual labour. Therefore, the rate of increase in the total demand for labour must have fallen.

In other words, the relative decline in the demand for manual labour means the allocation of population increase to non-manual occupations. However, unless the relative increase in the demand for non-manual labour is sufficient to absorb not only its past share of the 'normal' (historic) population increase but, also, the relative increase in the supply of non-manual labour consequent upon the relative reduction in the demand for manual labour, relative overpopulation results. As was indicated, the evidence for this overpopulation relative to the total demand for labour is found in the proportionately greater increase in the supply of than the demand for non-manual labour during the period in which the relative demand for manual labour was declining. A symptom of this overpopulation was, of course, the continued fall in the relative remuneration of non-manual labour.[1]

The resultant overpopulation leading to the fertility decline dating from the last quarter of the nineteenth century is but the expression of the decline in the rate of growth of the long-run demand for labour. Recognition of this decline is, of course, to be found in numerous economic writings on the export of capital, monopoly or the decline of competition, secular stagnation, late capitalism or the mature economy. Since, however, the aim of the present work is but to establish a general theoretical framework for the analysis of secular changes in population growth and fertility patterns which is consistent with the short-run demand for labour analysis of population changes, a review of the literature on the long-run decline in the rate of growth of demand for labour would serve no useful purpose. However, the following remarks from the first edition of Colin Clark's *Conditions of Economic Progress* may be quoted:

> Some explanation must now be sought of the virtual cessation of economic progress in U.S.A. since 1900, and a marked slowing down of the rate of growth of a number of other industrial countries. . . . Some powerful secular force, probably related to the investment and saving tendencies of the community, is acting to steadily keep down

---

[1] The proposition, 'given a decreasing demand for manual labour relative to non-manual labour, a continued fall in the relative remuneration of non-manual labour implies total relative overpopulation', cannot be converted. That is to say, it does not follow that relative overpopulation necessarily leads to a continued fall in the relative remuneration of non-manual labour when the total demand for manual labour is decreasing relative to non-manual. In England, for example, prior to the recent period of full employment, the slowing down in the rate of economic progress did not result in a continued narrowing of the differential between manual and non-manual labour. But this only means that there are a number of factors affecting the distribution of income between manual and non-manual labour, particularly market imperfections arising from imperfect mobility of labour in both the long- and short-run period.

the level of achieved real income, while the potential real income, if all the working population were fully employed, continues to rise.[1]

In summary, the economic analysis proceeds on the assumption that population is the dependent variable reflecting both long- and short-run changes in demand for labour. The long-run decline in the growth rate of demand for labour explains secular changes in population growth, specifically the comparatively recent fertility decline among industrialized capitalist countries. Superimposed on the long-term decline are short-run cyclical variations in demand for labour. These enter as complications and it is sometimes difficult to demarcate the 'short-run period' as, for example, in the United States where a prolonged war and post-war boom has been accompanied by a great population upsurge. Nevertheless, the fact remains that the long-term fertility decline has been accompanied by a relative decline in demand for manual labour, as well as by a shift in demand to labour of a higher quality. But the relative and absolute increase in demand for non-manual labour was not sufficient to maintain the aggregate demand for labour necessary for the continuation of past population growth.

Finally, as in the case of any transition from the general to the particular, application of 'demand-for-labour' analysis to specific countries is not a simple procedure. With reference to aggregate changes in population growth, however, the preceding analysis suggests the following principles:

1. In the absence of changes in demand for labour, mortality and fertility will vary directly and not inversely.
2. Quantitative changes in demand for labour lead to quantitative changes in population growth.
   A. The growth in demand for labour consequent upon industrialization leads to a great increase in population. The following fertility phenomena are consistent with this growth in population:
   (i) An increase in fertility.
   (ii) Mere maintenance of past fertility when mortality declines.
   (iii) A decline in fertility which, however, is less than proportional to the mortality decline.

[1] p. 6.

B. Decline in demand for labour consequent upon a slowing down in the rate of economic progress ('secular stagnation', monopoly, capital export, etc.) leads to a declining rate of population growth and possibly even to an absolute decrease in population. Besides family limitation, emigration and increased mortality resulting from wars and epidemics may be factors contributing to the adjustment of population to a decreased demand for labour.

3. Qualitative changes in demand for labour lead to quantitative changes.

   A. In the initial period of industrialization, there is a great increase in demand for unskilled labour. Thus the growth in the aggregate demand for labour is accentuated by the proportionately greater increase in demand for less costly labour-power.

   B. In the subsequent evolution of industrialism, along with the institutional checks to economic progress, changes in demand for labour retard population growth by raising its supply price, e.g.

      (i) Qualitative improvements in demand for unskilled and semi-skilled labour.

      (ii) Absolute and relative increase in demand for labour of a higher classification, e.g. non-manual labour.

4. Emigration and immigration are obvious factors influencing population and are related to changes in the demand for labour. They also influence other population variables.

   A. Emigration may operate to maintain fertility. That is to say, the adjustment of population to a decreased demand for labour can be achieved by emigration which, in effect, relieves the pressure to lower fertility.

   B. Immigration may operate to lower fertility.

      (i) A vast immigration followed by a relatively great contraction (cyclical or secular) in demand for labour may induce an extremely low fertility pattern in a subsequent period.

      (ii) Given the demand for labour, immigration is a substitute for fertility. Other things being equal, fertility will vary inversely with immigration. Here, then, is an explanation of the fertility decline in the United States throughout most of the nineteenth century. A large part of the demand for labour was supplied by a vast immigration.[1] Similarly, it seems reasonable to 'attribute' part of the high fertility of the recent post-war period to restrictive legislation on immigration.

With reference to fertility differentials within a country, the economic analysis emphasizes the importance of the following:

1. Ratio of income to cost of production of a particular grade of labour-power. As previously indicated, it is significant that there is evidence of a direct relation between income and fertility when fertility is standardized for occupation.[2]

[1] This was recognized by Francis A. Walker, *Discussions in Economics and Statistics*, New York, 1899, Vol. II, pp. 417 ff. Unfortunately, however, Walker's argument was marred by his 'racist' theory of teutonic supremacy.

[2] Assuming mortality differentials to explain the slope of the EE line, the relation between income, cost of labour and fertility can be illustrated as follows:

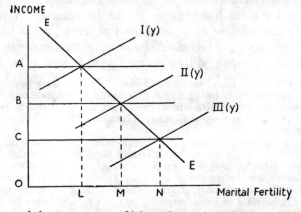

Let OA equal the average cost of labour for grade I, OB for grade II and OC for grade III. Curves I(y), II(y) and III(y) represent incomes for each grade of labour, respectively. Then OL is the average number of children for grade I, OM for grade II and ON for grade III. Line EE shows the traditional inverse relation between income and fertility. However, the graph also indicates that when income is above the average cost of labour for a particular grade, fertility varies directly and not inversely with income. Further, if the relation of income to cost of labour for some individuals in (say) group I is sufficiently favourable, their fertility will exceed that of some of the less fortunate members of group II and even group III.

Regarding the fertility differential between manual and non-manual labour, the fall in the relative remuneration of non-manual labour is significant and should be related to the relative costs of children in different occupational classifications.[1]

2. The relation between mortality and fertility rates. As in the case of whole communities, the direct association between mortality and fertility may influence differential fertility. That is to say, the adjustment of supply to demand for a particular grade of labour is determined by both mortality and fertility rates. Thus, the persistence of a higher fertility among the poor may be partially attributed to the inverse relation between socio-economic status and adult and infant mortality.[2]

3. Social mobility or 'generationwise' occupational changes may also influence differential fertility. However difficult it is to measure its specific contribution, the effect of social mobility is the same as that of immigration. Some appreciation of its influence on differential fertility may be gained from a consideration of the following: In the United States there has been a decline in demand for manual labour relative to non-manual; nevertheless, as has been indicated, the increased demand for non-manual labour was accompanied by a proportionately greater increase in

[1] A. Henderson found that 'middle-class parents make a larger proportionate contraction in their personal expenditures when they acquire a first child than do working-class households, and this may also be true of a second child'. 'The Cost of Children', *Population Studies*, December 1950, p. 273.

[2] *Cf.* Jean Daric, 'Mortality, Occupation, and Socio-Economic Status', translated in United States Public Health Service, *National Office of Vital Statistics—Special Reports*, Vol. 33, No. 10, 1951; also United Nations, *The Determinants and Consequences of Population Trends*, Chapter IV, as well as National Health Assembly, *America's Health* (Official Report), New York, 1949. English data on infant mortality by social class of father for the years 1911, 1921–3 and 1930–2 indicate that although mortality has declined for all groups 'the gradient of inequality has not lessened over the twenty years but has, in fact, tended to increase'. Richard M. Titmuss, *Birth, Poverty and Wealth*, London, 1943, pp. 26–7. A more recent study confirms Titmuss's conclusion, see J. W. B. Douglas, 'Social Class Difference in Health and Survival During the First Two Years of Life; The Results of a National Survey', *Population Studies*, July 1951. The study is a continuation of an investigation undertaken by a Joint Committee of the Royal College of Obstetricians and Gynaecologists and the Population Investigation Committee. For results of the first study, see *Maternity in Great Britain*, London, 1948.

supply. Suppose now that the recent and comparatively long period of prosperity were to be followed by a relatively great fall in the total demand for labour. Other things being equal, non-manual labour whose supply has been increasing proportionately more than manual labour would be harder hit by a fall in the total demand for labour. Hence, the fall in fertility consequent upon the decline in the total demand for labour would be proportionately greater among non-manual employees.

CHAPTER NINE
Summary and Conclusions

IT was stated in the Introduction that the object of the present work was to return population theory to its natural habitat, the field of economics. Part I contained an examination of population theories since Malthus. Both the biological and cultural theories were rejected. It was also seen that Neo-Classical economists had refrained from attempting an economic explanation of population dynamics. Rather, the tendency was to treat population as the independent variable, something given for the analysis; an analysis which might be concerned with either the optimum population (*vis-à-vis* natural resources) or the implications of changes in population growth on the marginal efficiency of capital. Again, it was shown that although Soviet demographers recognized the importance of demand for labour on population growth, their analysis oversimplified the population problem.

The failure of Neo-Classical economists to apply 'demand-for-labour' analysis to population growth originated in the apparent paradox of an historic rise in labour's standard of living accompanied by a fertility decline. It appeared impossible to reconcile these phenomena with a 'demand-for-labour' analysis. Moreover, the assumptions of Neo-Classical economic theory prior to the 'Keynesian Revolution' were such as to preclude an analysis based on a relative decline in the aggregate demand for labour. Again, recognition by the Keynesian school of equilibrium at less than full employment, as well as consideration of the possibility of secular stagnation, did not effect a basic change in the Neo-Classical approach to the population problem. On the contrary, in the Keynesian analysis

188

population remains the independent variable influencing the marginal efficiency of capital.

As to Soviet demographers, it was recognized that the emphasis on demand for labour for population growth was correct and consistent with the Classical school. However, Soviet demographers concentrated almost exclusively on the correlation between the fertility decline and a late phase of capitalism. No attempt was made to pass beyond this correlation to an analysis of how demand for labour governed its supply. In particular, there was no clarification of the relation between a relative decline in the aggregate demand for labour and a given standard of living. Thus, if it were contended that the secular fertility decline was caused by an absolute fall in the standard of living under 'imperialism', the statement would be patently false. On the other hand, if it were argued that there had been a relative decline in the standard of living in the sense that *expectations of a continuing rise* were no longer being fulfilled, then the economic analysis would have to be abandoned. For in place of a demand for labour analysis which relates the standard of living or supply-price of labour-power to changes in the value or cost of labour-power, there would be substituted an analysis which stressed the importance of the subjective factor of 'expectations' in determining fertility patterns. Apparently, Soviet demographers, like Neo-Classical economists, failed to appreciate that an historic rise in labour's standard of living is consistent with the observed fertility decline. That is to say, both Neo-Classical economists and Soviet demographers neglected qualitative changes in demand for labour which raised its supply-price.

In Part II an attempt was made to provide the theoretical apparatus for the economic analysis of population changes and fertility differentials. Long-run changes in the economic function of the family for the rich and poor were first considered. The evolution in the economic function of the family for the rich indicated that the inverse relation between wealth and fertility had not always existed. On the contrary, when a man's family (*familia*) constituted a major source of wealth there was no incentive for family limitation. However, with the full development of slavery (both male and female) and the concomitant concentration of wealth and increasing class differentiation, it was no longer necessary for the rich to engage in direct productive activity. Income now was derived from the mere fact of monopoly ownership of the instruments of production (land and labour). Among the wealthy the family no longer served as a production unit.[1] Its function now was analogous to a holding company. Through the dowry,[2] family fortunes were merged while, simultaneously, through family limitation, the integrity of the patrimony was preserved in subsequent generations. In short, the evolution of the economic function of the family for the wealthy indicates that at one time fertility must have varied directly and not inversely with wealth. Its subsequent evolution furnishes the economic explanation for family limitation among the wealthy.

The evolution in the economic function of the family for the poor was next considered. It was at first a production and consumption unit. This economic function was not basically changed by the impact of industrialization. True, industrialization meant the destruction of domestic industry and, consequently, the depreciation of the economic contribution of women and children in the home. However, their economic depreciation in the home was more than compensated for by the increased demand for women and children in industry. Hence, there was no economic stimulus for family limitation among the poor.

The contrast in economic function of the family for the rich and poor provided the explanation of the first great fertility differential. However, the difference in economic function did not explain the fertility decline among the poorer classes dating from the last quarter of the nineteenth century nor did it explain interoccupational differential fertility. This required an historical review of changes in demand for labour.

Since there had been general recognition of the significance

---

[1] This evolution is analogous to that which occurred in the transition from early capitalism, when the entrepreneur was an active participant in the production process, to late capitalism when, through the rationalization of production and the growth of a skilled managerial class, income is derived merely from a monopoly ownership of the instruments of production (land and capital).

[2] The dowry as an institution, explicable in terms of its historic economic function, may itself at a later stage undergo a corruption, e.g. when the dowried wife dissipates the family income in profligate living.

of changes in demand for labour for cyclical fertility fluctuations and the geographical distribution of population, the main problem here was to demonstrate how long-run changes in demand for labour effect relatively permanent changes in fertility patterns. The point of departure for such an analysis is an equilibrium between population and demand for labour; equilibrium being interpreted broadly to include either a stationary population or one increasing (decreasing) at a moderately constant rate. The equilibrium condition then, assuming no migration, is that mortality and fertility vary directly and not inversely. Absence of such compensating movements means that the situation is dynamic and that the old equilibrium is being supplanted by a new one.

One interesting result of the equilibrium approach is that the question of whether or not fertility in England rose in the period of the industrial revolution is not basic. The significant demographic fact requiring explanation is why the fall in mortality in England did not engender a compensating fertility decline. 'Demand-for-labour' analysis provides the answer and also explains why in France there was a concomitant fall in mortality and fertility. Further, 'demand-for-labour' analysis explains why the fertility decline in France was not sufficient to compensate fully for the mortality decline.

Besides France, the United States was apparently the only other country to experience a fertility decline throughout the nineteenth century. It must be recognized that a number of factors may have operated to reduce native American fertility, viz.:

1. The 'native sons', i.e. second and third generation Americans, were heirs to the more skilled occupations. Their labour-power was of a higher quality (cost);
2. The high social status of American women, a function of her economic contribution (and relative scarcity) may have operated to reduce fertility;
3. The uneven distribution of women (variations in the sex ratio) throughout the United States;
4. The vicissitudes of migration to the west; etc.

Nevertheless, after all allowances are made for the above factors, it is essential to stress the importance of the 'substitution effect' of immigration. 'Demand-for-labour' analysis indicates that a vast immigration is one method of adjusting the supply of population to demand for labour. *Other things being equal,* immigration and fertility will vary inversely.

In 'demand-for-labour' analysis, the situation favourable to population growth is one in which an increased demand for labour is accompanied by a reduction in the average quality (cost) of labour-power demanded.[1] A consideration of quantitative and qualitative changes in demand for labour consequent upon industrialization shows not only that demand for labour increased at an increasing rate but, also, that there was a reduction in the average quality (cost) of labour demanded.

Industrialization lowered (cheapened) the average value of labour-power in two ways:

1. Machinery spread the value of a man's labour-power over his whole family so that it was no longer necessary to pay him a wage sufficient for the maintenance of the whole family; and
2. The substitution of unskilled for skilled labour shortened the average period of production of labour-power.

The cheapening of labour-power consequent upon industrialization suggests that the customary explanation of population growth in 'backward' areas is inadequate. That is to say, it is generally held that the increase in population in colonial areas is due entirely to the mortality decline resulting from the introduction of Western techniques, e.g. an improved transport system which eliminates local famines, better sanitation, vaccines, etc. Certainly these operate to reduce mortality. However, unless in the long-run there are concomitant changes in demand for labour, a continued increase in population is inconceivable. Thus 'demand-for-labour' analysis suggests that more attention must be paid to factors which increase the demand for labour and reduce the average value of labour-power in colonial areas. Significant here are such things as the destruction of handicraft production, the introduction of a

---

[1] The significance that Ricardo attached to historical changes in the cost of labour-power is evident in his criticism of Adam Smith's formulation of the labour theory of value. *Op. cit.,* pp. 8 ff.

plantation system which enhances the relative value of women and children, etc.

The condition least favourable to population growth is one in which demand for labour falls absolutely; however, even a decreasing rate of growth in demand for labour is unfavourable to population increase. Also, if simultaneously with the declining rate of growth there is a rise in the average quality (cost) of labour-power demanded, then population increase is further retarded. An historic review of changes in demand for labour showed a decline in the rate of economic progress among industrialised capitalist countries. Further, modern industry requires a more highly educated labour force. The time and expense required for the preliminary preparation of an individual for 'productive' labour have greatly increased.[1] Thus, the decreasing rate of growth in demand for labour and the rise in the average quality (cost) of labour-power demanded, explain the secular fertility decline among the poorer classes.

'Demand-for-labour' analysis also implies that even in the absence of any decline in the total demand for labour, a rise in the average quality (cost) of labour-power demanded would lead to a fertility decline. This follows from a recognition that the aggregate demand for labour can be analysed *ex post facto*, i.e. as representing a particular sum which might have been expended on the purchase of a larger number of less costly employees or a smaller number of more costly workers.

Nevertheless, although the proposition that, *other things being equal*, fertility will vary inversely with the average quality of labour demanded is correct, there is a difficulty. It is possible that the relation between quality of labour demanded and population growth may be asymmetrical. That is to say, in general it will be found that a lowering of the average quality of labour-power demanded is favourable to population growth, whereas a rise in the average quality of labour-power demanded may or may not induce a fertility decline. The difficulty here is that the productivity of a higher grade of labour might, in the absence of institutional checks on economic progress, so

[1] The analysis of qualitative changes in demand for labour has been general and related to the evolution of industry. But, of course, market imperfections also operate to raise the cost of labour-power, e.g. when a professional class, for reasons of status and income, establishes artificially high entrance requirements.

increase the total 'fund' or aggregate demand for labour that no fertility decline would be necessary. In other words, abstractly considered, social productivity of labour determines the 'fund' or aggregate demand for labour. But social productivity is in turn a function of a number of variables both natural and institutional, among which the type of social organization looms large.

Recognition that demand for labour governs its supply and that the historic rise in labour's standard of living is but a reflection of necessary cost elements in the production of a higher average quality of labour-power also throws light on inter-occupational differential fertility. For just as an exclusive pre-occupation with the historic rise in labour's standard of living and the concomitant secular fertility decline overlooks qualitative changes in demand for labour, thereby engendering the superficial conclusion that wealth *per se* limits fertility; so, also, too great an emphasis on the inverse relation between income and fertility promotes a kindred oversimplification. The significant variable for differential fertility is not income *per se* but the ratio of remuneration to cost of production of a given quality of labour-power or, stated otherwise, the ratio of remuneration to relative costs of producing different grades of labour-power. Once this is appreciated it is easy to resolve the apparent paradox that although fertility generally varies inversely with income, there is evidence that fertility varies directly with income when fertility is standardized for occupation. Besides the significance of the ratio of remuneration to relative cost of labour-power, socio-economic differences in mortality rates are significant for differential fertility. For other things being equal, the higher the mortality rate, the higher the fertility rate, i.e. the adjustment of a particular supply of labour to its demand is realized through both differential fertility and differential mortality.

The economic interpretation of demography does not imply an 'international convergence of birth rates'.[1] The fundamental determinant of fertility patterns is demand for labour and not the democratization of knowledge of effective means of contraception. Nor does the economic interpretation accept the thesis that 'while changing economic conditions may cause some

[1] *Supra,* Chapter VI, p. 144.

fluctuations in the birth-rate, they do not affect the general trend'.[1] On the contrary, both long- and short-run changes in fertility are a function of changes in demand for labour. The continued fertility rise in the United States since 1933 and, in particular, the great post World War II population upsurge, is a case in point.

With reference to population projections, 'demand-for-labour' analysis indicates that a continued fertility decline is a function of a slowing down in the rate of economic progress. Thus, population projections which assume a continuing secular fertility decline involve the tacit assumption of a continuing decline in the rate of economic progress. Hence, although there is a difficulty in attempting to predict with accuracy the future population of a country since economists differ widely in their views of the future; nevertheless, the economic interpretation of demography is of value since it isolates the significant variable for population growth.

Finally, the economic interpretation of demography emphasizes the relativity of population laws. Thus, although in this work it has been contended that demand for labour still governs supply, this does not mean that such will always continue to be the case. On the contrary, when man is emancipated from the exigencies arising from scarcity, then, undoubtedly, a new law of population will come into existence.

[1] *Ibid.*, p. 144.

INDEX

Abrams, Charles, 120, n. 1.
Accumulation, *see* Capital accumulation.
Adams, Brooks, 154, n. 1.
Age distribution, *see* Fertility and age distribution.
Agriculture, 48–9, 53, 118–19, 128–9.
Anderson, 102.
Ariès, Philippe, 79–80, 141.
Aristotle, 24, 44, 158.
Arithmetic progression, 25, 33, 39, 84.

Baines, Sir Athelstane, 41, n.
Beales, H. L., 83.
Beard, Mary R., 163, n. 3.
Beauvoir, Simone de, 157.
Bebel, August, 66, 71.
Bennett, H. S., 149, n. 1, 2, and 3.
Bernardino, St., 158.
Bernstein, Eduard, 71.
Biological theories, 15, 22–55, 137, 188.
Birth control, 85, n.; knowledge of, 143–4; motives for, 62–4; *see also* Bradlaugh-Besant trial; Fertility and income; Fertility and socioeconomic status; Family, economic function of.
Birth rate, *see* Fertility.
Bloch, J., 18.
Bonar, James, 88.
Bortkiewicz, Ladislaus Von, 67, 84.
Bourgeois-Pichat, J., 139, n. 3.
Boyarski, A. Ya., 102, 130, n. 2.
Bradlaugh-Besant trial, 18, 19.
Brentano, L., 67–9.
Briffault, Robert, 156, n. 3.
Burns, Robert K., 179, n. 1.
Business cycle, *see* Fertility.

Cannan, 97.
Cantillon, Richard, 88.
Capital accumulation, and Classical theory, 86–90; Marxian theory, 102–27; Neo-Classical theory, 91–2, 104, 106, 108, 112–13.

Capital, constant and variable, *see* Capital accumulation; Marxian theory.
Capital, marginal efficiency of, 99–100; and population growth, 8, 188.
Capitalist development, 66 n.; *see also* Capital accumulation; Fertility decline and evolution of capitalism; Morphology of economic growth.
Capitalist mentality, and fertility decline, 69–72.
Carey, H. C., 56, n. 2.
Carr-Saunders, A. M., 77, 144, n. 2, 171, n. 2.
Castro, 15, 46–52.
Centralization of capital, 176; distinct from accumulation and concentration, 124–7.
Chamberlin, Edward, 98.
Charles the Great, 130.
Charles, Enid, 5–6.
Child labour, 63, 76, 130, 150–1, 169.
Clark, Alice, 150, n. 3, 160, n. 3, 161, n. 1, 162, n. 1.
Clark, Colin, 119, n. 1, 151, 176–7, 179, 180, 182–3.
Classical economic theory, *see* Economists, Classical.
Competition, imperfect and monopolistic, 97–8, 100.
Consumption function, 99–100.
Coulton, G. G., 149, n. 2 and 3, 158, n. 4.
Crum, Dr. F. S., 78.
Cultural theories, 15–16, 57–82, 85, 137, 145, 188.
Cycles of population growth, 34–7, 41.

Dant, Joan, 161, n. 1.
Daric, Jean, 78, 186, n. 2.
Darwin, 42, 65.
Davis, Joseph S., 6–7.

Index

Demand for labour, 20, 88–91, 93–7, 104–14, 127, 128, 130–4, 137, 141, 142–3, 151, 153, 166–87, 190–5; must be analysed both quantitatively and qualitatively, 168–87, 188–9.
Demographic findings, summary of, 139–41.
Demographic revolution, 139.
Demosthenes, 152.
Density, ambiguity of term, 37, 40; principle, 22–42.
Depoid, Pierre, 140, n. 2.
Diet principle, 42–53, 54–5.
Differential fertility, see Fertility and income; Fertility, rural and urban; Fertility and socio-economic status.
Diminishing returns, 84, 85, 86–7, 90–1, 92, 93, 96, 119.
Disease, see protein deficiency.
Division of labour and population growth, 8, 84; between the sexes, 150, 155–7.
Dobb, Maurice, 127, n. 1.
Donaldson, James, 153, n. 1, 157, n. 3, 158, n. 1.
Doubleday, 15, 41, 42–6, 50, 65.
Douglas, J. W. B., 186, n. 2.
Dowry, 148, 190, n. 2.
Dumont, Arsène, 57–61, 65–7, 72, 76.
Dunbar, Janet, 162, n. 1.

East, E. M., 42, n.
Economic interpretation, discussed, 16–21, 138–9, 141, 152, n.; application of, 137.
Economists, Classical, 7–8, 20, 58, 83 ff., 92, 133, 137, 138, 166–8, 189; German national, 84; Marxian, 102–127, see also Marx; Neo-Classical, 20, 83 ff., 104–8, 112–14, 119, 137, 138, 166–7, 188–9.
Economy of high wages, 174–5.
Edgeworth, 97.
Education, 87; and unskilled labour, 176; and white-collar workers, 177–8; see also Fertility and education.
Emigration, see Fertility and emigration.
Engels, Frederick, 18, 71, 116, 131–2, 146–7, n. 1.
Evolution, 54–6.
Exploitation, 50; Marxian doctrine of, 105–20.

Family, economic function of, 62–3, 146–52, 189–90; limitation, 62, 95, 148, 153–4, 190; in Sweden, 139; see also Fertility decline; Fertility and socio-economic status.
Fascism, 157.

Fertility: and age distribution, 25–6, 69; and business cycle, 52, 140, 144, 166; and density, 28, 39–40; and diet, 46–7, 50–2; and education, 140–1; and emigration, 184; French, 59–60, 131, 139, 140, 141, 173–4; and immigration, 163, n. 4, 184–5, 192; and income, 9, 13–14, 30–2, 43–6, 60–9, 76, 96, 139–44, 145, 185–6, 194, see also Fertility and socio-economic status; Family, the economic function of; international differences, 29–30, 61, 139–42, 144, 194; marital, 75, 78, n., 79; and mortality, 29–30, 69–70, 139, 170–4, 183, 186; and private ownership, 130–1; rural and urban, 30, 60–1, 74, 78–82, 133, 140, 141; and socio-economic status, 9, 41, 43–5, 55–6, 61–4, 66, 67–9, 73–6, 130–3, 140; see also Fertility and income; Family, the economic function of; United States, 139–40, 191–2; see also Genesis; Individuation; Pleasure principle; Women, social status of, and fertility.
Fertility decline, 2, 18–19, 20, 67–73, 75–6, 93, 127–8, 130–4, 137, 139–40, 142–3, 153, 189; and evolution of capitalism, 174–84; in United States, 139–40, 163.
Fetter, Frank, 57, 61–4, 72.
Feudalism, estimated population, 129.
Field, James Alfred, 18–19, 83.
Food and Agricultural Organization, 48.
Food, reserve, world, 48; synthetic, 48–9.
Forecasts, see Population forecasts.
Freud, 47.
Fromm, Erich, 176.
Frumkin, Gregory, 6.

Garnier, Joseph, 58, 84–5.
Genesis, 53–4, 65.
Geometric progression, of population, 25, 33–4, 90; in science and production, 90, 132.
George, Henry, 56 n.
Glass, D. V., 78–9, 83, 84, 170, n. 1.
Goldenweiser, Alexander, 17.
Gould, see Pearl and Gould.
Grossman, Henryk, 111, 112, n. 1.
Groves, Ernst R., 160, n. 2, 163, n. 2.
Growth equation, see Logistic curve.
Guillard, 58, 66.

Habakkuk, H. H., 170, n. 2.
Hadley, Arthur Twinning, 64.

Index

Contents

*wishing to submit manuscripts for any series in
logue should send them to the Social Science Editor,
& Kegan Paul Ltd, 39 Store Street,
CIE 7DD*

*marked are available in paperback
in Metric Demy 8vo format (216 × 138mm approx.)*

Routledge Social Science Series

Routledge & Kegan Paul

Broadway Ho

International Library of Sociology

General Editor John Rex

GENERAL SOCIOLOGY

Barnsley, J. H. The Social Reality of Ethics. *464 pp.*
Belshaw, Cyril. The Conditions of Social Performance. *An Exploratory Theory. 144 pp.*
Brown, Robert. Explanation in Social Science. *208 pp.*
● Rules and Laws in Sociology. *192 pp.*
Bruford, W. H. Chekhov and His Russia. *A Sociological Study. 244 pp.*
Cain, Maureen E. Society and the Policeman's Role. *326 pp.*
●**Fletcher, Colin.** Beneath the Surface. *An Account of Three Styles of Sociological Research. 221 pp.*
Gibson, Quentin. The Logic of Social Enquiry. *240 pp.*
Glucksmann, M. Structuralist Analysis in Contemporary Social Thought. *212 pp.*
Gurvitch, Georges. Sociology of Law. *Preface by Roscoe Pound. 264 pp.*
Hodge, H. A. Wilhelm Dilthey. *An Introduction. 184 pp.*
Homans, George C. Sentiments and Activities. *336 pp.*
Johnson, Harry M. Sociology: *a Systematic Introduction. Foreword by · Robert K. Merton. 710 pp.*
●**Keat, Russell,** and **Urry, John.** Social Theory as Science. *278 pp.*
Mannheim, Karl. Essays on Sociology and Social Psychology. *Edited by Paul Keckskemeti. With Editorial Note by Adolph Lowe. 344 pp.*
Systematic Sociology: *An Introduction to the Study of Society. Edited by J. S. Erös and Professor W. A. C. Stewart. 220 pp.*
Martindale, Don. The Nature and Types of Sociological Theory. *292 pp.*
●**Maus, Heinz.** A Short History of Sociology. *234 pp.*
Mey, Harald. Field-Theory. *A Study of its Application in the Social Sciences. 352 pp.*
Myrdal, Gunnar. Value in Social Theory: *A Collection of Essays on Methodology. Edited by Paul Streeten. 332 pp.*
Ogburn, William F., and **Nimkoff, Meyer F.** A Handbook of Sociology. *Preface by Karl Mannheim. 656 pp. 46 figures. 35 tables.*
Parsons, Talcott, and **Smelser, Neil J.** Economy and Society: *A Study in the Integration of Economic and Social Theory. 362 pp.*
Podgórecki, Adam. Practical Social Sciences. *About 200 pp.*
●**Rex, John.** Key Problems of Sociological Theory. *220 pp.*
Sociology and the Demystification of the Modern World. *282 pp.*
●**Rex, John** (Ed.) Approaches to Sociology. *Contributions by Peter Abell, Frank Bechhofer, Basil Bernstein, Ronald Fletcher, David Frisby, Miriam Glucksmann, Peter Lassman, Herminio Martins, John Rex, Roland Robertson, John Westergaard and Jock Young. 302 pp.*
Rigby, A. Alternative Realities. *352 pp.*
Roche, M. Phenomenology, Language and the Social Sciences. *374 pp.*

Sahay, A. Sociological Analysis. *220 pp.*

Simirenko, Alex (Ed.) Soviet Sociology. *Historical Antecedents and Current Appraisals. Introduction by Alex Simirenko. 376 pp.*

Strasser, Hermann. The Normative Structure of Sociology. *Conservative and Emancipatory Themes in Social Thought. About 340 pp.*

Urry, John. Reference Groups and the Theory of Revolution. *244 pp.*

Weinberg, E. Development of Sociology in the Soviet Union. *173 pp.*

FOREIGN CLASSICS OF SOCIOLOGY

●**Durkheim, Emile.** Suicide. *A Study in Sociology. Edited and with an Introduction by George Simpson. 404 pp.*

●**Gerth, H. H.,** and **Mills, C. Wright.** From Max Weber: *Essays in Sociology. 502 pp.*

●**Tönnies, Ferdinand.** Community and Association. (*Gemeinschaft und Gesellschaft.*) *Translated and Supplemented by Charles P. Loomis. Foreword by Pitirim A. Sorokin. 334 pp.*

SOCIAL STRUCTURE

Andreski, Stanislav. Military Organization and Society. *Foreword by Professor A. R. Radcliffe-Brown. 226 pp. 1 folder.*

Carlton, Eric. Ideology and Social Order. *Preface by Professor Philip Abrahams. About 320 pp.*

Coontz, Sydney H. Population Theories and the Economic Interpretation. *202 pp.*

Coser, Lewis. The Functions of Social Conflict. *204 pp.*

Dickie-Clark, H. F. Marginal Situation: *A Sociological Study of a Coloured Group. 240 pp. 11 tables.*

Glaser, Barney, and **Strauss, Anselm L.** Status Passage. *A Formal Theory. 208 pp.*

Glass, D. V. (Ed.) Social Mobility in Britain. *Contributions by J. Berent, T. Bottomore, R. C. Chambers, J. Floud, D. V. Glass, J. R. Hall, H. T. Himmelweit, R. K. Kelsall, F. M. Martin, C. A. Moser, R. Mukherjee, and W. Ziegel. 420 pp.*

Johnstone, Frederick A. Class, Race and Gold. *A Study of Class Relations and Racial Discrimination in South Africa. 312 pp.*

Jones, Garth N. Planned Organizational Change: *An Exploratory Study Using an Empirical Approach. 268 pp.*

Kelsall, R. K. Higher Civil Servants in Britain: *From 1870 to the Present Day. 268 pp. 31 tables.*

König, René. The Community. *232 pp. Illustrated.*

●**Lawton, Denis.** Social Class, Language and Education. *192 pp.*

McLeish, John. The Theory of Social Change: *Four Views Considered. 128 pp.*

Marsh, David C. The Changing Social Structure of England and Wales, 1871-1961. *288 pp.*

Menzies, Ken. Talcott Parsons and the Social Image of Man. *About 208 pp.*

● **Mouzelis, Nicos.** Organization and Bureaucracy. *An Analysis of Modern Theories. 240 pp.*

Mulkay, M. J. Functionalism, Exchange and Theoretical Strategy. *272 pp.*

Ossowski, Stanislaw. Class Structure in the Social Consciousness. *210 pp.*

● **Podgórecki, Adam.** Law and Society. *302 pp.*

Renner, Karl. Institutions of Private Law and Their Social Functions. *Edited, with an Introduction and Notes, by O. Kahn-Freud. Translated by Agnes Schwarzschild. 316 pp.*

SOCIOLOGY AND POLITICS

Acton, T. A. Gypsy Politics and Social Change. *316 pp.*

Clegg, Stuart. Power, Rule and Domination. *A Critical and Empirical Understanding of Power in Sociological Theory and Organisational Life. About 300 pp.*

Hechter, Michael. Internal Colonialism. *The Celtic Fringe in British National Development, 1536–1966. 361 pp.*

Hertz, Frederick. Nationality in History and Politics: *A Psychology and Sociology of National Sentiment and Nationalism. 432 pp.*

Kornhauser, William. The Politics of Mass Society. *272 pp. 20 tables.*

● **Kroes, R.** Soldiers and Students. *A Study of Right- and Left-wing Students. 174 pp.*

Laidler, Harry W. History of Socialism. *Social-Economic Movements: An Historical and Comparative Survey of Socialism, Communism, Co-operation, Utopianism; and other Systems of Reform and Reconstruction. 992 pp.*

Lasswell, H. D. Analysis of Political Behaviour. *324 pp.*

Martin, David A. Pacifism: *an Historical and Sociological Study. 262 pp.*

Martin, Roderick. Sociology of Power. *About 272 pp.*

Myrdal, Gunnar. The Political Element in the Development of Economic Theory. *Translated from the German by Paul Streeten. 282 pp.*

Wilson, H. T. The American Ideology. *Science, Technology and Organization of Modes of Rationality. About 280 pp.*

Wootton, Graham. Workers, Unions and the State. *188 pp.*

CRIMINOLOGY

Ancel, Marc. Social Defence: *A Modern Approach to Criminal Problems. Foreword by Leon Radzinowicz. 240 pp.*

Cain, Maureen E. Society and the Policeman's Role. *326 pp.*

Cloward, Richard A., and **Ohlin, Lloyd E.** Delinquency and Opportunity: *A Theory of Delinquent Gangs. 248 pp.*

Downes, David M. The Delinquent Solution. *A Study in Subcultural Theory. 296 pp.*

Dunlop, A. B., and **McCabe, S.** Young Men in Detention Centres. *192 pp.*

Friedlander, Kate. The Psycho-Analytical Approach to Juvenile Delinquency: *Theory, Case Studies, Treatment. 320 pp.*

Glueck, Sheldon, and **Eleanor.** Family Environment and Delinquency. *With the statistical assistance of Rose W. Kneznek. 340 pp.*

Lopez-Rey, Manuel. Crime. *An Analytical Appraisal. 288 pp.*

Mannheim, Hermann. Comparative Criminology: *a Text Book. Two volumes. 442 pp. and 380 pp.*

Morris, Terence. The Criminal Area: *A Study in Social Ecology. Foreword by Hermann Mannheim. 232 pp. 25 tables. 4 maps.*

Rock, Paul. Making People Pay. *338 pp.*

●**Taylor, Ian, Walton, Paul,** and **Young, Jock.** The New Criminology. *For a Social Theory of Deviance. 325 pp.*

●**Taylor, Ian, Walton, Paul,** and **Young, Jock** (Eds). Critical Criminology. *268 pp.*

SOCIAL PSYCHOLOGY

Bagley, Christopher. The Social Psychology of the Epileptic Child. *320 pp.*

Barbu, Zevedei. Problems of Historical Psychology. *248 pp.*

Blackburn, Julian. Psychology and the Social Pattern. *184 pp.*

●**Brittan, Arthur.** Meanings and Situations. *224 pp.*

Carroll, J. Break-Out from the Crystal Palace. *200 pp.*

●**Fleming, C. M.** Adolescence: Its Social Psychology. *With an Introduction to recent findings from the fields of Anthropology, Physiology, Medicine, Psychometrics and Sociometry. 288 pp.*

● The Social Psychology of Education: *An Introduction and Guide to Its Study. 136 pp.*

●**Homans, George C.** The Human Group. *Foreword by Bernard DeVoto. Introduction by Robert K. Merton. 526 pp.*

● Social Behaviour: *its Elementary Forms. 416 pp.*

●**Klein, Josephine.** The Study of Groups. *226 pp. 31 figures. 5 tables.*

Linton, Ralph. The Cultural Background of Personality. *132 pp.*

●**Mayo, Elton.** The Social Problems of an Industrial Civilization. *With an appendix on the Political Problem. 180 pp.*

Ottaway, A. K. C. Learning Through Group Experience. *176 pp.*

Plummer, Ken. Sexual Stigma. *An Interactionist Account. 254 pp.*

●**Rose, Arnold M.** (Ed.) Human Behaviour and Social Processes: *an Interactionist Approach. Contributions by Arnold M. Rose, Ralph H. Turner, Anselm Strauss, Everett C. Hughes, E. Franklin Frazier, Howard S. Becker, et al. 696 pp.*

Smelser, Neil J. Theory of Collective Behaviour. *448 pp.*

Stephenson, Geoffrey M. The Development of Conscience. *128 pp.*

Young, Kimball. Handbook of Social Psychology. *658 pp. 16 figures. 10 tables.*

SOCIOLOGY OF THE FAMILY

Banks, J. A. Prosperity and Parenthood: *A Study of Family Planning among The Victorian Middle Classes. 262 pp.*

Bell, Colin R. Middle Class Families: *Social and Geographical Mobility. 224 pp.*

Burton, Lindy. Vulnerable Children. *272 pp.*
Gavron, Hannah. The Captive Wife: *Conflicts of Household Mothers.*
190 pp.
George, Victor, and **Wilding, Paul.** Motherless Families. *248 pp.*
Klein, Josephine. Samples from English Cultures.
1. Three Preliminary Studies and Aspects of Adult Life in England.
447 pp.
2. Child-Rearing Practices and Index. *247 pp.*
Klein, Viola. The Feminine Character. *History of an Ideology. 244 pp.*
McWhinnie, Alexina M. Adopted Children. *How They Grow Up. 304 pp.*
● **Morgan, D. H. J.** Social Theory and the Family. *About 320 pp.*
● **Myrdal, Alva,** and **Klein, Viola.** Women's Two Roles: *Home and Work.*
238 pp. 27 tables.
Parsons, Talcott, and **Bales, Robert F.** Family: Socialization and Inter-
action Process. *In collaboration with James Olds, Morris Zelditch and
Philip E. Slater. 456 pp. 50 figures and tables.*

SOCIAL SERVICES

Bastide, Roger. The Sociology of Mental Disorder. *Translated from the
French by Jean McNeil. 260 pp.*
Carlebach, Julius. Caring For Children in Trouble. *266 pp.*
George, Victor. Foster Care. *Theory and Practice. 234 pp.*
Social Security: *Beveridge and After. 258 pp.*
George, V., and **Wilding, P.** Motherless Families. *248 pp.*
● **Goetschius, George W.** Working with Community Groups. *256 pp.*
Goetschius, George W., and **Tash, Joan.** Working with Unattached Youth.
416 pp.
Hall, M. P., and **Howes, I. V.** The Church in Social Work. *A Study of
Moral Welfare Work undertaken by the Church of England. 320 pp.*
Heywood, Jean S. Children in Care: *the Development of the Service for the
Deprived Child. 264 pp.*
Hoenig, J., and **Hamilton, Marian W.** The De-Segregation of the Mentally
Ill. *284 pp.*
Jones, Kathleen. Mental Health and Social Policy, 1845-1959. *264 pp.*
King, Roy D., Raynes, Norma V., and **Tizard, Jack.** Patterns of Residential
Care. *356 pp.*
Leigh, John. Young People and Leisure. *256 pp.*
● **Mays, John.** (Ed.) Penelope Hall's Social Services of England and Wales.
About 324 pp.
Morris, Mary. Voluntary Work and the Welfare State. *300 pp.*
Nokes, P. L. The Professional Task in Welfare Practice. *152 pp.*
Timms, Noel. Psychiatric Social Work in Great Britain (1939-1962).
280 pp.
● Social Casework: *Principles and Practice. 256 pp.*
Young, A. F. Social Services in British Industry. *272 pp.*

SOCIOLOGY OF EDUCATION

Banks, Olive. Parity and Prestige in English Secondary Education: a Study in Educational Sociology. *272 pp.*

Bentwich, Joseph. Education in Israel. *224 pp. 8 pp. plates.*

●**Blyth, W. A. L.** English Primary Education. *A Sociological Description.*
1. Schools. *232 pp.*
2. Background. *168 pp.*

Collier, K. G. The Social Purposes of Education: *Personal and Social Values in Education. 268 pp.*

Dale, R. R., and **Griffith, S.** Down Stream: *Failure in the Grammar School. 108 pp.*

Evans, K. M. Sociometry and Education. *158 pp.*

●**Ford, Julienne.** Social Class and the Comprehensive School. *192 pp.*

Foster, P. J. Education and Social Change in Ghana. *336 pp. 3 maps.*

Fraser, W. R. Education and Society in Modern France. *150 pp.*

Grace, Gerald R. Role Conflict and the Teacher. *150 pp.*

Hans, Nicholas. New Trends in Education in the Eighteenth Century. *278 pp. 19 tables.*

● Comparative Education: *A Study of Educational Factors and Traditions. 360 pp.*

●**Hargreaves, David.** Interpersonal Relations and Education. *432 pp.*

● Social Relations in a Secondary School. *240 pp.*

Holmes, Brian. Problems in Education. *A Comparative Approach. 336 pp.*

King, Ronald. Values and Involvement in a Grammar School. *164 pp.*

School Organization and Pupil Involvement. *A Study of Secondary Schools.*

●**Mannheim, Karl,** and **Stewart, W. A. C.** An Introduction to the Sociology of Education. *206 pp.*

Morris, Raymond N. The Sixth Form and College Entrance. *231 pp.*

●**Musgrove, F.** Youth and the Social Order. *176 pp.*

●**Ottaway, A. K. C.** Education and Society: An Introduction to the Sociology of Education. *With an Introduction by W. O. Lester Smith. 212 pp.*

Peers, Robert. Adult Education: *A Comparative Study. 398 pp.*

Pritchard, D. G. Education and the Handicapped: *1760 to 1960. 258 pp.*

Stratta, Erica. The Education of Borstal Boys. *A Study of their Educational Experiences prior to, and during, Borstal Training. 256 pp.*

Taylor, P. H., Reid, W. A., and **Holley, B. J.** The English Sixth Form. *A Case Study in Curriculum Research. 200 pp.*

SOCIOLOGY OF CULTURE

Eppel, E. M., and **M.** Adolescents and Morality: *A Study of some Moral Values and Dilemmas of Working Adolescents in the Context of a changing Climate of Opinion. Foreword by W. J. H. Sprott. 268 pp. 39 tables.*

●**Fromm, Erich.** The Fear of Freedom. *286 pp.*

● The Sane Society. *400 pp.*

Mannheim, Karl. Essays on the Sociology of Culture. *Edited by Ernst Mannheim in co-operation with Paul Kecskemeti. Editorial Note by Adolph Lowe. 280 pp.*
Weber, Alfred, Farewell to European History: *or The Conquest of Nihilism. Translated from the German by R. F. C. Hull. 224 pp.*

SOCIOLOGY OF RELIGION

Argyle, Michael and **Beit-Hallahmi, Benjamin.** The Social Psychology of Religion. *About 256 pp.*
Glasner, Peter E. The Sociology of Secularisation. *A Critique of a Concept. About 180 pp.*
Nelson, G. K. Spiritualism and Society. *313 pp.*
Stark, Werner. The Sociology of Religion. *A Study of Christendom.*
  Volume I. *Established Religion. 248 pp.*
  Volume II. *Sectarian Religion. 368 pp.*
  Volume III. *The Universal Church. 464 pp.*
  Volume IV. *Types of Religious Man. 352 pp.*
  Volume V. *Types of Religious Culture. 464 pp.*
Turner, B. S. Weber and Islam. *216 pp.*
Watt, W. Montgomery. Islam and the Integration of Society. *320 pp.*

SOCIOLOGY OF ART AND LITERATURE

Jarvie, Ian C. Towards a Sociology of the Cinema. *A Comparative Essay on the Structure and Functioning of a Major Entertainment Industry. 405 pp.*
Rust, Frances S. Dance in Society. *An Analysis of the Relationships between the Social Dance and Society in England from the Middle Ages to the Present Day. 256 pp. 8 pp. of plates.*
Schücking, L. L. The Sociology of Literary Taste. *112 pp.*
Wolff, Janet. Hermeneutic Philosophy and the Sociology of Art. *150 pp.*

SOCIOLOGY OF KNOWLEDGE

Diesing, P. Patterns of Discovery in the Social Sciences. *262 pp.*
● **Douglas, J. D.** (Ed.) Understanding Everyday Life. *370 pp.*
● **Hamilton, P.** Knowledge and Social Structure. *174 pp.*
Jarvie, I. C. Concepts and Society. *232 pp.*
Mannheim, Karl. Essays on the Sociology of Knowledge. *Edited by Paul Kecskemeti. Editorial Note by Adolph Lowe. 353 pp.*
Remmling, Gunter W. The Sociology of Karl Mannheim. *With a Bibliographical Guide to the Sociology of Knowledge, Ideological Analysis, and Social Planning. 255 pp.*

Remmling, Gunter W. (Ed.) Towards the Sociology of Knowledge. *Origin and Development of a Sociological Thought Style. 463 pp.*

Stark, Werner. The Sociology of Knowledge: *An Essay in Aid of a Deeper Understanding of the History of Ideas. 384 pp.*

URBAN SOCIOLOGY

Ashworth, William. The Genesis of Modern British Town Planning: *A Study in Economic and Social History of the Nineteenth and Twentieth Centuries. 288 pp.*

Cullingworth, J. B. Housing Needs and Planning Policy: *A Restatement of the Problems of Housing Need and 'Overspill' in England and Wales. 232 pp. 44 tables. 8 maps.*

Dickinson, Robert E. City and Region: *A Geographical Interpretation 608 pp. 125 figures.*

The West European City: *A Geographical Interpretation. 600 pp. 129 maps. 29 plates.*

● The City Region in Western Europe. *320 pp. Maps.*

Humphreys, Alexander J. New Dubliners: *Urbanization and the Irish Family. Foreword by George C. Homans. 304 pp.*

Jackson, Brian. Working Class Community: *Some General Notions raised by a Series of Studies in Northern England. 192 pp.*

Jennings, Hilda. Societies in the Making: *a Study of Development and Redevelopment within a County Borough. Foreword by D. A. Clark. 286 pp.*

●**Mann, P. H.** An Approach to Urban Sociology. *240 pp.*

Morris, R. N., and **Mogey, J.** The Sociology of Housing. *Studies at Berinsfield. 232 pp. 4 pp. plates.*

Rosser, C., and **Harris, C.** The Family and Social Change. *A Study of Family and Kinship in a South Wales Town. 352 pp. 8 maps.*

●**Stacey, Margaret, Batsone, Eric, Bell, Colin,** and **Thurcott, Anne.** Power, Persistence and Change. *A Second Study of Banbury. 196 pp.*

RURAL SOCIOLOGY

Haswell, M. R. The Economics of Development in Village India. *120 pp.*

Littlejohn, James. Westrigg: *the Sociology of a Cheviot Parish. 172 pp. 5 figures.*

Mayer, Adrian C. Peasants in the Pacific. *A Study of Fiji Indian Rural Society. 248 pp. 20 plates.*

Williams, W. M. The Sociology of an English Village: *Gosforth. 272 pp. 12 figures. 13 tables.*

SOCIOLOGY OF INDUSTRY AND DISTRIBUTION

Anderson, Nels. Work and Leisure. *280 pp.*

●**Blau, Peter M.**, and **Scott, W. Richard.** Formal Organizations: *a Comparative approach. Introduction and Additional Bibliography by J. H. Smith. 326 pp.*

Dunkerley, David. The Foreman. *Aspects of Task and Structure. 192 pp.*

Eldridge, J. E. T. Industrial Disputes. *Essays in the Sociology of Industrial Relations. 288 pp.*

Hetzler, Stanley. Applied Measures for Promoting Technological Growth. *352 pp.*
Technological Growth and Social Change. *Achieving Modernization. 269 pp.*

Hollowell, Peter G. The Lorry Driver. *272 pp.*

●**Oxaal, I., Barnett, T.,** and **Booth, D.** (Eds). Beyond the Sociology of Development. *Economy and Society in Latin America and Africa. 295 pp.*

Smelser, Neil J. Social Change in the Industrial Revolution: *An Application of Theory to the Lancashire Cotton Industry, 1770–1840. 468 pp. 12 figures. 14 tables.*

ANTHROPOLOGY

Ammar, Hamed. Growing up in an Egyptian Village: *Silwa, Province of Aswan. 336 pp.*

Brandel-Syrier, Mia. Reeftown Elite. *A Study of Social Mobility in a Modern African Community on the Reef. 376 pp.*

Dickie-Clark, H. F. The Marginal Situation. *A Sociological Study of a Coloured Group. 236 pp.*

Dube, S. C. Indian Village. *Foreword by Morris Edward Opler. 276 pp. 4 plates.*
India's Changing Villages: *Human Factors in Community Development. 260 pp. 8 plates. 1 map.*

Firth, Raymond. Malay Fishermen. *Their Peasant Economy. 420 pp. 17 pp. plates.*

Gulliver, P. H. Social Control in an African Society: a Study of the Arusha, Agricultural Masai of Northern Tanganyika. *320 pp. 8 plates. 10 figures.*
Family Herds. *288 pp.*

Ishwaran, K. Tradition and Economy in Village India: *An Interactionist Approach.*
Foreword by Conrad Arensburg. 176 pp.

Jarvie, Ian C. The Revolution in Anthropology. *268 pp.*

Little, Kenneth L. Mende of Sierra Leone. *308 pp. and folder.*
Negroes in Britain. *With a New Introduction and Contemporary Study by Leonard Bloom. 320 pp.*

Lowie, Robert H. Social Organization. *494 pp.*

Mayer, A. C. Peasants in the Pacific. *A Study of Fiji Indian Rural Society. 248 pp.*

Meer, Fatima. Race and Suicide in South Africa. *325 pp.*

Smith, Raymond T. The Negro Family in British Guiana: *Family Structure and Social Status in the Villages. With a Foreword by Meyer Fortes. 314 pp. 8 plates. 1 figure. 4 maps.*

Smooha, Sammy. Israel: Pluralism and Conflict. *About 320 pp.*

SOCIOLOGY AND PHILOSOPHY

Barnsley, John H. The Social Reality of Ethics. *A Comparative Analysis of Moral Codes. 448 pp.*

Diesing, Paul. Patterns of Discovery in the Social Sciences. *362 pp.*

●**Douglas, Jack D.** (Ed.) Understanding Everyday Life. *Toward the Reconstruction of Sociological Knowledge. Contributions by Alan F. Blum. Aaron W. Cicourel, Norman K. Denzin, Jack D. Douglas, John Heeren, Peter McHugh, Peter K. Manning, Melvin Power, Matthew Speier, Roy Turner, D. Lawrence Wieder, Thomas P. Wilson and Don H. Zimmerman. 370 pp.*

Gorman, Robert A. The Dual Vision. *Alfred Schutz and the Myth of Phenomenological Social Science. About 300 pp.*

Jarvie, Ian C. Concepts and Society. *216 pp.*

●**Pelz, Werner.** The Scope of Understanding in Sociology. *Towards a more radical reorientation in the social humanistic sciences. 283 pp.*

Roche, Maurice. Phenomenology, Language and the Social Sciences. *371 pp.*

Sahay, Arun. Sociological Analysis. *212 pp.*

Sklair, Leslie. The Sociology of Progress. *320 pp.*

Slater, P. Origin and Significance of the Frankfurt School. *A Marxist Perspective. About 192 pp.*

Smart, Barry. Sociology, Phenomenology and Marxian Analysis. *A Critical Discussion of the Theory and Practice of a Science of Society. 220 pp.*

International Library of Anthropology

General Editor Adam Kuper

Ahmed, A. S. Millenium and Charisma Among Pathans. *A Critical Essay in Social Anthropology. 192 pp.*

Brown, Paula. The Chimbu. *A Study of Change in the New Guinea Highlands. 151 pp.*

Gudeman, Stephen. Relationships, Residence and the Individual. *A Rural Panamanian Community. 288 pp. 11 Plates, 5 Figures, 2 Maps, 10 Tables.*

Hamnett, Ian. Chieftainship and Legitimacy. *An Anthropological Study of Executive Law in Lesotho. 163 pp.*

Hanson, F. Allan. Meaning in Culture. *127 pp.*

Lloyd, P. C. Power and Independence. *Urban Africans' Perception of Social Inequality. 264 pp.*

Pettigrew, Joyce. Robber Noblemen. *A Study of the Political System of the Sikh Jats. 284 pp.*

Street, Brian V. The Savage in Literature. *Representations of 'Primitive' Society in English Fiction, 1858–1920. 207 pp.*

Van Den Berghe, Pierre L. Power and Privilege at an African University. *278 pp.*

International Library of Social Policy

General Editor Kathleen Jones

Bayley, M. Mental Handicap and Community Care. *426 pp.*

Bottoms, A. E., and **McClean, J. D.** Defendants in the Criminal Process. *284 pp.*

Butler, J. R. Family Doctors and Public Policy. *208 pp.*

Davies, Martin. Prisoners of Society. *Attitudes and Aftercare. 204 pp.*

Gittus, Elizabeth. Flats, Families and the Under-Fives. *285 pp.*

Holman, Robert. Trading in Children. *A Study of Private Fostering. 355 pp.*

Jones, Howard, and **Cornes, Paul.** Open Prisons. *About 248 pp.*

Jones, Kathleen. History of the Mental Health Service. *428 pp.*

Jones, Kathleen, with **Brown, John, Cunningham, W. J., Roberts, Julian,** and **Williams, Peter.** Opening the Door. *A Study of New Policies for the Mentally Handicapped. 278 pp.*

Karn, Valerie. Retiring to the Seaside. *About 280 pp. 2 maps. Numerous tables.*

Thomas, J. E. The English Prison Officer since 1850: *A Study in Conflict. 258 pp.*

Walton, R. G. Women in Social Work. *303 pp.*

Woodward, J. To Do the Sick No Harm. *A Study of the British Voluntary Hospital System to 1875. 221 pp.*

International Library of Welfare and Philosophy

General Editors Noel Timms and David Watson

● **Plant, Raymond.** Community and Ideology. *104 pp.*

● **McDermott, F. E.** (Ed.) Self-Determination in Social Work. *A Collection of Essays on Self-determination and Related Concepts by Philosophers and Social Work Theorists. Contributors: F. P. Biestek, S. Bernstein, A. Keith-Lucas, D. Sayer, H. H. Perelman, C. Whittington, R. F. Stalley, F. E. McDermott, I. Berlin, H. J. McCloskey, H. L. A. Hart, J. Wilson, A. I. Melden, S. I. Benn. 254 pp.*

Ragg, Nicholas M. People Not Cases. *A Philosophical Approach to Social Work. About 250 pp.*

● **Timms, Noel,** and **Watson, David** (Eds). Talking About Welfare. *Readings in Philosophy and Social Policy. Contributors: T. H. Marshall, R. B. Brandt, G. H. von Wright, K. Nielsen, M. Cranston, R. M. Titmuss, R. S. Downie, E. Telfer, D. Donnison, J. Benson, P. Leonard, A. Keith-Lucas, D. Walsh, I. T. Ramsey. 320 pp.*

Primary Socialization, Language and Education

General Editor Basil Bernstein

Adlam, Diana S., with the assistance of Geoffrey Turner and Lesley Lineker. Code in Context. *About 272 pp.*

Bernstein, Basil. Class, Codes and Control. *3 volumes.*
  1. *Theoretical Studies Towards a Sociology of Language. 254 pp.*
  2. *Applied Studies Towards a Sociology of Language. 377 pp.*
● 3. *Towards a Theory of Educatiomal Transmission. 167 pp.*

Brandis, W., and **Bernstein, B.** Selection and Control. *176 pp.*

Brandis, Walter, and **Henderson, Dorothy.** Social Class, Language and Communication. *288 pp.*

Cook-Gumperz, Jenny. Social Control and Socialization. *A Study of Class Differences in the Language of Maternal Control. 290 pp.*

●**Gahagan, D. M.,** and **G. A.** Talk Reform. *Exploration in Language for Infant School Children. 160 pp.*

Hawkins, P. R. Social Class, the Nominal Group and Verbal Strategies. *About 220 pp.*

Robinson, W. P., and **Rackstraw, Susan D. A.** A Question of Answers. *2 volumes. 192 pp. and 180 pp.*

Turner, Geoffrey J., and **Mohan, Bernard A.** A Linguistic Description and Computer Programme for Children's Speech. *208 pp.*

Reports of the Institute of Community Studies

●**Cartwright, Ann.** Parents and Family Planning Services. *306 pp.*
  Patients and their Doctors. *A Study of General Practice. 304 pp.*

Dench, Geoff. Maltese in London. *A Case-study in the Erosion of Ethnic Consciousness. 302 pp.*

●**Jackson, Brian.** Streaming: *an Education System in Miniature. 168 pp.*

Jackson, Brian, and **Marsden, Dennis.** Education and the Working Class: *Some General Themes raised by a Study of 88 Working-class Children in a Northern Industrial City. 268 pp. 2 folders.*

Marris, Peter. The Experience of Higher Education. *232 pp. 27 tables.*
  Loss and Change. *192 pp.*

Marris, Peter, and **Rein, Martin.** Dilemmas of Social Reform. *Poverty and Community Action in the United States. 256 pp.*

Marris, Peter, and Somerset, Anthony. African Businessmen. *A Study of Entrepreneurship and Development in Kenya. 256 pp.*

Mills, Richard. Young Outsiders: *a Study in Alternative Communities. 216 pp.*

Runciman, W. G. Relative Deprivation and Social Justice. *A Study of Attitudes to Social Inequality in Twentieth-Century England. 352 pp.*

Willmott, Peter. Adolescent Boys in East London. *230 pp.*

Willmott, Peter, and Young, Michael. Family and Class in a London Suburb. *202 pp. 47 tables.*

Young, Michael. Innovation and Research in Education. *192 pp.*

● Young, Michael, and McGeeney, Patrick. Learning Begins at Home. *A Study of a Junior School and its Parents. 128 pp.*

Young, Michael, and Willmott, Peter. Family and Kinship in East London. *Foreword by Richard M. Titmuss. 252 pp. 39 tables.*
The Symmetrical Family. *410 pp.*

Reports of the Institute for Social Studies in Medical Care

Cartwright, Ann, Hockey, Lisbeth, and Anderson, John L. Life Before Death. *310 pp.*

Dunnell, Karen, and Cartwright, Ann. Medicine Takers, Prescribers and Hoarders. *190 pp.*

Medicine, Illness and Society

General Editor W. M. Williams

Robinson, David. The Process of Becoming Ill. *142 pp.*

Stacey, Margaret, *et al.* Hospitals, Children and Their Families. *The Report of a Pilot Study. 202 pp.*

Stimson, G. V., and Webb, B. Going to See the Doctor. *The Consultation Process in General Practice. 155 pp.*

Monographs in Social Theory

General Editor Arthur Brittan

● Barnes, B. Scientific Knowledge and Sociological Theory. *192 pp.*

Bauman, Zygmunt. Culture as Praxis. *204 pp.*

● Dixon, Keith. Sociological Theory. *Pretence and Possibility. 142 pp.*

Meltzer, B. N., Petras, J. W., and Reynolds, L. T. Symbolic Interactionism. *Genesis, Varieties and Criticisms. 144 pp.*

● Smith, Anthony D. The Concept of Social Change. *A Critique of the Functionalist Theory of Social Change. 208 pp.*

Routledge Social Science Journals

The British Journal of Sociology. *Editor – Angus Stewart; Associate Editor – Leslie Sklair. Vol. 1, No. 1 – March 1950 and Quarterly. Roy. 8vo. All back issues available. An international journal publishing original papers in the field of sociology and related areas.*
Community Work. *Edited by David Jones and Marjorie Mayo. 1973. Published annually.*
Economy and Society. *Vol. 1, No. 1. February 1972 and Quarterly. Metric Roy. 8vo. A journal for all social scientists covering sociology, philosophy, anthropology, economics and history. All back numbers available.*
Religion. Journal of Religion and Religions. *Chairman of Editorial Board, Ninian Smart. Vol. 1, No. 1, Spring 1971. A journal with an interdisciplinary approach to the study of the phenomena of religion. All back numbers available.*
Year Book of Social Policy in Britain, The. *Edited by Kathleen Jones. 1971. Published annually.*

Social and Psychological Aspects of Medical Practice

Editor Trevor Silverstone

Lader, Malcolm. Psychophysiology of Mental Illness. *280 pp.*
● **Silverstone, Trevor,** and **Turner, Paul.** Drug Treatment in Psychiatry. *232 pp.*

Printed in Great Britain by
Lowe & Brydone Printers Limited, Thetford, Norfolk
1177